LEAVING CERTIFICATE

LESS STRESS MORE SUCCESS

History Revision

Dermot Lucey

D1428301

Gill & Macmillan

Gill & Macmillan
Hume Avenue
Park West
Dublin 12
www.gillmacmillan.ie

© Dermot Lucey 2014

978 07171 5959 8

Design by Liz White Designs
Artwork by Keith Barrett
Print origination in Ireland by Carole Lynch

For permission to reproduce photographs, the author and publisher gratefully
acknowledge the following:
© Alamy: 64, 203, 210, 263, 266, 267, 268, 269, 270, 271, 272; © Corbis: 57, 125, 132,
134, 135, 201, 262; © Getty Images: 53, 56, 127, 128, 129, 131, 199, 206, 207, 212,
273, 298, 300, 302; © Hilda van Stockum / National Gallery of Ireland: 137; ©
National Museums & Galleries of Northern Ireland, Ulster Museum: 66; © Sheehy-
Skeffington Collection, National Library of Ireland: 67; © TopFoto: 59, 60, 62, 63, 197,
205, 301; Courtesy of MultiText Project, UCC: 138.

The author and publisher have made every effort to trace all copyright holders, but if
any has been inadvertently overlooked we would be pleased to make the necessary
arrangement at the first opportunity.

CONTENTS

Go to www.moresuccess.ie for extra online resources:

- Topic: Division and Realignment in Europe, 1945–92
- Topic: European Retreat from Empire and the Aftermath, 1945–91
- Additional material for the Topic: Further Notes on The United States and the World, 1945–89
- Past Leaving Cert Exam Questions by Topic

Introduction

 Note: Material that is to be studied only by those taking Higher level is indicated in the text.

Revising for the exam

There are five topics in History Revision Notes for Leaving Cert:

Three topics from Modern Ireland

1. Movements for Political and Social Reform, 1870–1914
2. The Pursuit of Sovereignty and the Impact of Partition, 1912–49
3. Politics and Society in Northern Ireland, 1949–93

Two topics from Modern Europe and the Wider World

1. Dictatorship and Democracy in Europe, 1920–45
2. The United States and the Wider World, 1945–1989

But you must select only **two topics** from Irish history and **two topics** from European and world history for study.

One of these topics is a **prescribed topic** for the **document-based question** in the examination.

Prescribed topic for the Leaving Cert examinations in 2014 and 2015
The Pursuit of Sovereignty and the Impact of Partition, 1912–1949

Prescribed topic for Leaving Cert examinations 2016 and 2017
Dictatorship and Democracy in Europe, 1920–1945
You should at all times check with your teachers which topics/case studies are the prescribed topics/case studies for the year in which you are sitting your Leaving Cert examination.

The **other topics** will be examined by short stimulus questions, paragraphs and long answers (for Ordinary level) and essays (for Higher level).

Revising for the exam

- Highlight the **heading of the topics** which you are studying (this is to ensure that you do not study the wrong topics).
- You should also **highlight the section of the contents** which concern the topics you are studying.

- Lay out a **revision plan** for each topic (or get the help of your teachers to do so).
- The notes are divided into **sub-headings** and **points** so that you can study them in short sections.

- After studying each short section, you should **test yourself** to ensure that you have learnt the information. (The eTests for *Modern Europe and the Wider World* and *Modern Ireland* on www.etest.ie can be used for most of the topics.)
- **Each topic** in History Revision Notes should be **revised** at **regular intervals**.
- Regular revision is important in the weeks and months before the Leaving Cert.
- The **Key personalities**, **Case studies** and **Key concepts** for each topic are in highlighted text boxes. This allows them to be studied both separately and as part of the topics.
  - The Key personalities and the Case studies should be linked to the **wider context** of the topics.
- After studying a **chapter or a few chapters**, use the Ordinary level questions and the Higher level questions from your textbooks or from the State Examinations Commission papers (available online at www.examinations.ie) and **plan** paragraphs, long answers (for Ordinary level) and essays (for Higher level).
- You must pay close attention to the **wording** of the question. *What is the question asking?*
  - Know a **brief definition** of the **Key concepts** in case they are used in the **wording** of the questions.
  - Have some understanding of the **headings** used in the syllabus, which are also **used through these notes**, because they too are used in the **wording** of the questions. (e.g. *pursuit of sovereignty*, *consolidation of democracy*, *impact of welfare state*, *cultural identity*, *changing patterns of religious observance*, *domestic factors in US foreign policy*. See past Leaving Cert exam papers.)
- Your **essay plan** should be a **list of paragraph headings**. Each paragraph heading will form the **main theme of the paragraph**, which will be supported or backed up by **historical information** learnt from your notes.
  - The **essay plan** should include an introduction, at least five to seven paragraph headings and a conclusion. The introduction, the paragraphs and the conclusion are **each** marked out of a total of **12 marks**.

Note: Ordinary level students
- Paragraph answers should be about twenty lines.
- 'Write on' or long answers should be about two pages.

Organise for less exam stress

There is still plenty of time to revise for exams. But the key to good revision is good organisation. Good organisation helps to relieve the stress of exams. It puts you in control.

What is good organisation?

You must work to a **revision plan**, and that plan must be written out. It will take you about half an hour for each subject to lay out the plan.

You will begin with an **overall study plan** for each subject. In this you break down the subject into separate topics to be studied. (Maybe your teacher has done this for you already.) You will break down the overall plan into a number of topics for each week. (If there are eight weeks left to the Leaving Cert, you should use seven for the plan and one week for overall revision.)

After this you will work on a **daily timetable for studying**. Your revision plan for the subjects gives you the topics you want to cover that week. The daily timetable breaks down your study time for each subject.

Your daily timetable will differ depending on whether it is a school day or a weekend.

> Overall study plans for each subject
>
> ↓
>
> Broken down into weeks
>
> ↓
>
> Refer to your overall study plan when following your Daily Timetable

What do you do when you are studying?

- Keep your study as **active** as possible – you don't want to fall asleep.
- You should vary your study between subjects where you have 'learning' to do and those where there is written work.
- Give a **focus** to your study. Begin with 'What am I learning for this study period?'
- Use your notes or your textbook – follow the *Less Stress More Success* revision books.
- Underline or highlight key information.
- **Test yourself** as you go along by covering what you have learnt and put it into your own words.
- Use past exam papers – how will you answer questions on the topic you are studying?
- Spend no more than 30–40 minutes on each subject.
- **Repetition** plays a very important part in learning.
- Tick off each topic in your Study Plan after you have studied it.

> No radios or TVs – they are a distraction – instead tune in when you are taking a break

More 'DO's' than 'DON'Ts'	
DO's	**DON'Ts**
● Organise	● No late nights – but, if you must, have all your goals or targets met for the week so that you can take the next morning off
● Keep to a routine	
● Stay healthy	
● Have regular meals	● No cramming – sometimes students think that if they revise too soon they will have it all forgotten. Rather, if they don't revise, they will have nothing learnt to forget
● Get exercise	

Answering Ordinary level questions

The marking scheme

In Ordinary level questions, paragraph and long-answer questions are preceded by a **stimulus-driven unit** (extract, cartoon or photograph) with four or five short questions to be attempted *(maximum: 30 marks)*.

Paragraphs and long answers (also called longer paragraphs) are marked according to **Core Statements**. A **Core Statement** may be defined as one of the following:

- A **significant factual statement** which is relevant to the question asked
- An **explanation, opinion or comment** which is relevant to the question asked
- A **significant introductory or concluding statement** which is relevant to the question asked.

Each **completed Core Statement** is awarded **5 marks**.

An **incomplete Core Statement** at the end of an answer may merit **1–4 marks**.

- In **short paragraph answers**, a maximum Cumulative Mark (CM) of 20 will be allowed for Core Statements and a maximum of 10 marks will be allowed for the examiner's Overall Evaluation (OE) of the answer.
  - **Maximum of 20 marks for CM and maximum of 10 marks for OE.**
- In **longer paragraph answers** (or long answers), a maximum Cumulative Mark of 30 will be allowed for Core Statements and a maximum of 10 marks will be allowed for the examiner's Overall Evaluation of the answer.
  - **Maximum of 30 marks for CM and maximum of 10 marks for OE.**

exam focus

When writing your answers, don't try to guess how many Core Statements you have written. Let the examiners work that out. Instead, you must write more than enough in the short paragraphs and long answers so that you get the maximum marks. You must balance this with the amount of time you can spend on each answer.

Short paragraphs = 10 minutes

Longer paragraphs (long answers) = 15 minutes

Basically, the CM gives you marks for the **content or historical information** you use, and the OE gives you marks for **how well you wrote it** (e.g. Did you stick to the question? Is your information in the correct order?).

Cumulative Mark (CM)

This is the total mark awarded for Core Statements, subject to a maximum of 20 marks in short paragraph answers and a maximum of 30 marks in long answers.

Excellent	9–10 marks
Very good	7–8 marks
Good	5–6 marks
Fair	3–4 marks
Poor	0–2 marks

Overall Evaluation (OE)

In awarding OE, the examiner will consider how well the answer responds to the heading or addresses the set question. The grading table shown here will apply.

Answering Higher level questions

Essay writing in the Research Study and the topics

The skills of essay writing are needed in the Extended Essay in the Research Study, and they form the basis of the remaining questions on the topics which will be examined in the final examination.

In the final examination in June:

- You will have a choice of **1 question** out of 4 in each of the 3 topics.
  - Each of the essays will be marked out of **100 marks**.

The marking scheme

You are asked to respond to a **historical question**. Your answers will be marked under two headings:

- **Cumulative Mark** (CM) for **historical content** which is **accurate** and **relevant** to the question as asked – maximum CM = 60 marks.
- **Overall Evaluation** (OE) for the **quality** of the answer as a whole in the context of the set question – maximum OE = 40 marks.

Your answer is marked in **paragraphs OR paragraph equivalents**:

A paragraph or paragraph equivalent is:

- a relevant introduction giving the background situation and/or defining the terms and explaining the approach;
- an episode, phase or stage in a sequence of events;
- an aspect of a topic/issue, with supporting factual references;
- a point in an argument or discussion, with supporting factual references;
- an explanation of a concept or term, with supporting factual references;

- a number of significant, relevant statements of fact, explanation or comment which, although not connected or related, can be taken together and assessed as a paragraph equivalent;
- a good concluding paragraph or summation, which is not mere repetition. (Summation which is mere repetition = max. 4 marks.)

The examiner will award marks to each paragraph or paragraph equivalent as follows (Brackets are used to designate a paragraph or paragraph equivalent when essays are marked.)

Cumulative Mark (CM)

Excellent	11–12 marks	Outstanding piece of analysis, exposition or commentary. Clearly expressed, accurate and substantial information.
Very good	8–10 marks	Very good material, accurately and clearly expressed.
Good	6–7 marks	Worthwhile information, reasonably well expressed.
Fair	3–5 marks	Limited information/barely stated.
Poor	0–2 marks	Trivial/irrelevant/grave errors.

Maximum = 60 marks

Note: Where individual questions have **two elements**, students are usually given a maximum CM = 50 if they refer to **only one** of those elements.

Example: The question 'How effective were the internal and external policies of Joseph Stalin?' (LC Higher level, 2010) has two elements to it – **internal policies** and **external policies**. If you answered this question and referred to internal policies only and did not mention external, then the maximum CM mark you could get is 50. However, you do not need to refer to both elements equally – an answer which deals mostly with Stalin's internal policies, and only a little with his external policies will be entitled to a maximum CM of 60 if it has enough historical content.

Overall Evaluation (OE)

Excellent	34–40 marks	Excellent in its treatment of the set question.
Very good	28–33 marks	Very good – but not excellent – in its treatment of the set question, i.e. accurate and substantial.
Good	22–27 marks	Good standard treatment of the set question.
Fair	16–21 marks	Fair attempt at the set question, but has identifiable defects, e.g. incomplete coverage, irrelevant data, factual inaccuracies.
Weak	10–15 marks	Poor, in that it fails to answer the question as set, but has some merit.
Very weak	0–9 marks	Very poor answer which, at best, offers only scraps of information.

Maximum = 40 marks

In awarding the OE, the examiner will evaluate the quality of the answer, taking into account the following, as appropriate:

- To what extent has the candidate shown the ability to analyse the issues involved in the question asked (i.e. provided more than mere narrative)?
- To what extent has the candidate marshalled the relevant evidence to support his/her analysis?
- To what extent has the candidate shown the ability to argue a case and to reach conclusions (i.e. to answer the question as asked)?

Questions on past Leaving Cert Higher level exams by year

These questions have been asked in past Leaving Cert Higher level exams. Sections of the course which have been examined directly are marked X, while those marked (X) have been included either specifically with other parts or in a general wording.

You can check the exact wording of questions under the additional resources for LSMS History Leaving Cert at www.gillmacmillan.ie or at www.examinations.ie under Examination Material Archive.

Movements for Political and Social Reform, 1870–1914

Politics and administration	2013	2012	2011	2010	2009	2008
The Home Rule Movement – Origins	X		X	(X)		
The Home Rule Movement – Development				(X)		
Leadership – Butt, Parnell, Redmond				X	X	X
The Suffragette movement		(X)				
The Sinn Féin party						
The Irish Volunteers						
Unionism and the Ulster Question		X	X	(X) (Carson)	X	(X)
Case Study: The elections of 1885 & 1886				(X)		

HL

Society and economy	2013	2012	2011	2010	2009	2008
Land agitation & land reform	X			(X)	(Davitt)	X
Unionisation of the working classes		(X)		X		X
The Co-operative movement	X					
Industrial development in Belfast: the shipyards	X			X	X	
Educational reforms: schools and universities						
Case Study: Dublin 1913 – strike & lockout	X	(X)		X	X	(X)

Culture and religion	2013	2012	2011	2010	2009	2008
The GAA		X		X		X
Cultural revivals: the Gaelic League, the Anglo-Irish literary revival		X		X		X
The consolidation of Catholic identity						
Case Study: The GAA to 1891		X		X		X

The Pursuit of Sovereignty and the Impact of Partition, 1912–49

Politics and administration	2013	2012	2011	2010	2009	2008
The Home Rule Bill, 1912–14		(X)		(X)		
The impact of World War I		(X)		(X)		
The 1916 Rising		(X)		(X)		
The rise of the second Sinn Féin Party	X			(X)		
The 1918 election		(X)		(X)		
The War of Independence		(X)		(X)		
Partition				X		
Treaty & Civil War		(X)			X	X
State Building & consolidate democracy – Cumann na nGaedheal – 1920s				X	(X)	X
State Building & consolidate democracy – Fianna Fáil – 1930s	(X)			(X)	(X)	X
Northern Ireland – the Unionist Party in power				X	X	X
The impact of World War II – North & South	X	X (NI)	(X)			
Anglo-Irish relations	X	X	(X)	X	(X)	
Case Study: The Treaty Negotiations			(X)		X	X

HL

Society and economy	2013	2012	2011	2010	2009	2008
Impact of partition on economy & society	(X)					
Impact of world economic crisis	(X)	X (NI)				
From free trade to protectionism	X				(X) (De Valera) (N Ireland)	
Impact of World War II		X (NI)	X			
Case Study: Belfast during World War II	(X)	(X)	X		(X)	

Culture and religion	2013	2012	2011	2010	2009	2008
State and culture, North & South				(X)		
Language, religion and education				X	(X)	
Promotion of cultural identity				X	X	
Case Study: The Eucharistic Congress		X	(X)	X	(X)	X

Politics and Society in Northern Ireland, 1949–93

Politics and administration	2013	2012	2011	2010	2009	2008
From Brookeborough to O'Neill						
The Civil Rights movement						X
Emergence of the Provisional IRA						
The Fall of Stormont						
Direct Rule						
Republican and Loyalist terrorism	X					
Sunningdale and power-sharing		(X)			X	X
The Anglo-Irish Agreement, 1985		(X)			X	X
The Republic – responses to the 'Troubles'		(X)				
The Downing Street Declaration, 1993		(X)			X	X
Case Study: The Sunningdale Agreement and the power-sharing executive, 1973–1974		(X)		Doc. Study	X	(X)

HL

Society and economy	2013	2012	2011	2010	2009	2008
Impact of the Welfare State: Education, health, housing	X					
Social & economic developments prior to 1969						X
Impact of the Troubles – (a) economy					X	
Impact of the Troubles – (b) society – education, health, housing	X				X	
Case Study: The Coleraine University controversy		X			X	X

Culture and religion	2013	2012	2011	2010	2009	2008
Religious affiliation & cultural identity	X					
Ecumenism						
Cultural responses to the Troubles	(X)					
Case Study: The Apprentice Boys of Derry	X	X	Doc. Study		X	

Dictatorship and Democracy in Europe, 1920–45

Politics and administration	2013	2012	2011	2010	2009	2008
Origins and growth of fascist regimes	X				(X)	
Nazi state in peace	X		X		(X)	
Nazi state in war		(X) Causes				
Communism in Russia: regime of Lenin			X			X
Regime of Stalin	X	X	X	X	(X)	X
Communist state in peace			(X)	(X)	(X)	(X)
Communist state in war				(X)		
France: The Third Republic, 1920–40		X			X	
The Vichy state					(X)	
Wartime alliances, 1939–1945	(X)				X	
Case Study: Stalin's show trials	X	(X)		(X)	(X)	(X)

Society and economy	2013	2012	2011	2010	2009	2008
Economic and social problems in inter-war years in Britain	X				X	X
Economic and social problems in inter-war years in Germany	(X)			X		X
The Soviet alternative	X	(X)		(X)		
Society during World War II: the Home Front; Rationing/evacuees	(X)					X
Refugees						X
Collaboration/resistance					X	X
Anti-Semitism and the Holocaust	(X)	X				(X)
Case Study: The Jarrow March, October 1936	(X)		X		(X)	

Culture, religion and science	2013	2012	2011	2010	2009	2008
Nazi propaganda – State control and the use of the mass media	(X)		(X)		X	X
Church-state relations under Mussolini and Hitler	(X)		(X)	X		
Anglo-American popular culture in peace and war: radio and cinema	(X)			X		
The technology of war					X	
Case Study: The Nuremberg Rallies	(X)		(X)		(X)	(X)

The United States and the Wider World, 1945–1989

Politics and administration	2013	2012	2011	2010	2009	2008
US politics: structures and tensions						
The Presidency			X	(X) (Johnson)		
Domestic factors in US foreign policy						
US foreign policy 1945–72: Berlin, Korea, Cuba, Vietnam	X				X	X Doc. Study
Case Study: Johnson & Vietnam	(X)					
Decline of Cold War certainties		X				

HL

Society and economy	2013	2012	2011	2010	2009	2008
Sources of the US economic boom		X		X		
Development of US industrial structure	X	X				
Vietnam War; federal deficit; domestic recession; international competition	X	X				
Demographic growth; Affluence, role of work, women, family						
Troubled Affluence, racial conflict, urban poverty, drugs and crime	X		X	(X)		(X)
Case Study: Montgomery Bus Boycott	(X)					Doc. Study

Culture and religion	2013	2012	2011	2010	2009	2008
Consensus 1945–68; Hollywood, American Dream, 'Red Scare'		X				
Collapse of consensus, 1968–89; youth culture, counter-culture, multiculturalism						
Religion; mass media; mass higher education	X	X				
Advances in military, space and information technology		X	X			
Case Study: Moon Landing						

For past questions under sub-headings for each of the above Topics,
see online at www.moresuccess.ie

PART ONE

Modern Ireland

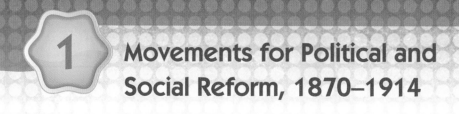

1 Movements for Political and Social Reform, 1870–1914

1. Home Rule – the Irish Question

aims In this section, you should understand:

- The origins and development of the Home Rule movement
- The leadership of Butt and Parnell (Key personality, p. 53)
- Case study: The Elections of 1885 and 1886 – Issues and Outcomes

The Government of Ireland

After the Act of Union (1800), Ireland was **ruled directly** from Westminster.

> **exam Q** Who was the more effective leader of the Home Rule movement, Butt or Parnell? Argue your case, referring to both.

- Irish Members of Parliament (MPs) sat in the House of Commons in London; Irish lords sat in the House of Lords.
- In Ireland, the Viceroy (or Lord Lieutenant) represented the British king or queen. The Chief Secretary represented the British government.

The Home Rule movement in 1870

1. **Origins: Isaac Butt** put forward the idea of **Home Rule** for Ireland. He was the son of a Church of Ireland clergyman, a barrister and MP for Youghal, Co. Cork.

2. **Home Rule** meant:
   - a **parliament in Dublin** to control domestic/internal affairs, e.g. education, police, roads;
   - a **parliament in London** (Westminster) dealing with external affairs, e.g. war and peace, customs, trade;
   - the **king/queen** would be king/queen of Britain and Ireland.

> **key point**
>
> **HOME RULE:**
> The belief that Ireland should have a parliament in Dublin to rule internal Irish affairs, and a parliament in Westminster to rule external affairs.

This was Butt's **federal solution** to the Irish Question.

3. In 1870, Butt founded the **Home Government Association** in Dublin. The Home Government Association was made up of **different groups**.

- Some **Protestants** believed the British parliament did not understand Irish affairs because the government had **disestablished the Church of Ireland** (1869), which took away government support from the Church; the government also passed the **1870 Land Act**, which weakened landlords.

POLITICAL AGITATION: Stirring up the interest of the people in a political cause or belief.

- **Tenants** were not happy with the 1870 Land Act.
- **Fenians** were using the Home Government Association to promote their own aims.

4. Over the next few years, the Home Government Association became **more Catholic and tenant-dominated**.
   - The Home Government Association contested by-elections; the Association was successful when candidates supported **land reform** and **denominational (church-controlled) education**; as more Catholics joined, Protestants, conservatives and landlords left.
   - The **1872 Secret Ballot Act** (secret voting at elections) reduced landlord influence over elections; now landlords would not be able to control a parliament in Dublin.

5. **Home Rule League:** The Home Government Association was mainly **Dublin-based**, so in 1873 Butt set up the Home Rule League. This began to organise **branches** around the country; membership was open to anyone who paid **£1**.
   - Butt also set up the **Home Rule Confederation of Great Britain** to promote Home Rule among the Irish in Britain.

6. **1874 general election:** Home Rulers won 59 seats out of 105 seats in Ireland.
   - The Home Rule League formed a **new, separate party** in Westminster: **the Home Rule Party** had **a policy of independent opposition** to the two main British parties, Liberals and Conservatives; they would support whichever party would grant them Home Rule.

7. **Problems for the Party:**
   - It had no central organisation – each constituency was separate.
   - It had only **20 to 30 committed** Home Rule MPs out of the 59 elected; there were only two Home Rulers in Ulster.
   - There were over **600 MPs** in the House of Commons, and they were not interested in Irish affairs; **Disraeli**, the prime minister and leader of the Conservative Party, was interested only in imperial and European affairs.
   - **Butt was a weak leader**; he did not want to impose discipline on the MPs – instead he wanted to use **persuasion** in Parliament. He behaved in a **gentlemanly fashion** in Parliament. He brought in **proposals** every year, but they were easily defeated.

- Butt was **often absent from Parliament** owing to work; he had to pay off debts of over £10,000 by working as a **barrister**.

8. **Obstructionism:** Extreme members (Fenians) of the Home Rule Party were **impatient** with Butt's tactics – they brought in **a policy of obstructionism**. **Joseph Biggar** (a Fenian from Belfast) was the leader and he was joined by **Charles Stewart Parnell** (MP for Meath).

9. **Obstructionism** meant holding up the business of parliament; the Obstructionists made boring speeches that went on for hours and read aloud long passages from government reports.

10. **Butt's attitude to obstructionism:** Butt **disapproved** of obstructionism; he said it upset the British MPs whose support was needed to pass laws for Ireland.

11. **Why Parnell joined the Obstructionists:** Parnell was the son of a **Protestant landlord**. He developed an **anti-English attitude** from his mother and while he was at university in Cambridge. Obstructionism earned Parnell a great deal of **popularity** in Ireland; he won Fenian support.
    - Parnell said the **Manchester Martyrs** (Fenians) were not murderers.
    - Parnell was elected **leader** of the **Home Rule Confederation of Great Britain**, which was Fenian-dominated.

12. **Split in Home Rule Party:** By the end of the 1870s there was a split in the Home Rule Party between those who supported Parnell and those who supported Butt. When Butt died suddenly in 1879, he was succeeded by **William Shaw** – Parnell did not yet have enough support.

13. **Butt's contribution:**
    - He put forward the **idea of Home Rule**, which was popular for the next forty years.
    - He founded the **Home Rule Party**.
    - He developed the **policy of independent opposition**.
    - He laid the **foundation** which Parnell built on.

Parnell and Home Rule

1. The question of **Home Rule** died down, because the **Land Question** became more important for the next few years. Parnell gained further popularity through his leadership of the **Land League**. Over the next year he built up his popularity and became leader in 1880.
    - Parnell was committed to the **New Departure**.
    - He joined the Land campaign as **president of the Land League**.
    - He had **natural leadership qualities**; he was ambitious.
    - Parnell gained the support of **Clan na nGael (Fenians) in America** when he visited there.
    - He also gained the support of the Catholic Church, especially **Archbishop Croke** of Cashel; Parnell supported state aid for Catholic schools.

- In the **general election** of March 1880, an increased number of **Parnellites** (Parnell's supporters) were elected. After the general election, Parnell was elected **leader of the Home Rule Party** (1880).

2. **Parnell concentrates on Home Rule**

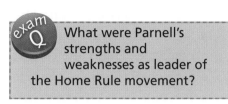

- In 1880 and 1881, Parnell worked on the Land Question. After **Gladstone**, the British prime minister, had passed the **1881 Land Act** and Parnell had agreed the **Kilmainham Treaty** with him (1882), Parnell felt the Land Question had been **solved**.

   What were Parnell's strengths and weaknesses as leader of the Home Rule movement?

- Parnell now began to **concentrate on Home Rule**.

3. **The Phoenix Park Murders** gave him his chance.
   - **Cavendish**, the Chief Secretary, **and Burke**, the Under-Secretary (head of the civil service), were **murdered** by the **Invincibles** in Phoenix Park.
   - Parnell first wanted to resign as leader of the Home Rule Party, but he was persuaded not to. Now nobody wanted to be associated with the extremists and the Fenians. This gave Parnell an excuse to **change his aims from Land to Home Rule**.

4. Parnell set up the **Irish National League** (1882). The **aims** of the Irish National League were:
   - to establish Home Rule
   - to work for land purchase.

5. **Differences** between the Land League and the Irish National League:
   - The **aims** were **reversed**.
   - The Land League was a **mass movement**; the Irish National League was a **political party**.
   - In the Land League, Parnell had to share power with the **Fenians**; in the Irish National League he was in **complete control**.

6. **The Great Lull, 1882–85**
   - During this time Parnell built up the **Irish Parliamentary Party** (the Irish Parliamentary Party was also called the Irish Party or the Home Rule Party). These were the **elected representatives** of the Irish National League.

7. **Parnell's control:** The Irish National League was built into a **highly disciplined political party**.
   - Parnell was helped in this work by his 'lieutenants', **Timothy Harrington** (Secretary), **William O'Brien** and **Timothy Healy**.
   - The strength of the party lay in the **branch network** of 1,200 branches.
   - It was supported by the **Catholic Church**.

8. **The functions of branches were:**
- **To collect money** – £30,000 was left over from the Land War, but American funds dried up. £60,000 was collected between 1882 and 1885 and the money was used for election expenses and to support MPs.
- **Selection conventions:** Conventions were organised to select Home Rule candidates. Priests often acted as chairmen.
- **Organised elections:** The branches got voters out to vote on election day.
- **Party pledge:** Candidates had to take a pledge of loyalty to the Party – **'sit, act and vote'** with the Irish Party; Parnell now had a **highly disciplined party** to back him at Westminster.

9. **Parnell, Chamberlain and the Central Board Scheme:**
- **Joseph Chamberlain** (an important Liberal leader) proposed a **Central Board Scheme** for Ireland instead of Home Rule. This was like county council powers for the country.
- Chamberlain used **Captain O'Shea** as an **intermediary** with Parnell.
- Parnell thought the Central Board Scheme was **a lead up to Home Rule**, not a replacement for it – but Chamberlain meant it as a **replacement**.
- When Parnell eventually **rejected** it, Chamberlain was **bitterly disappointed**; this led to conflict between them later.

Case study: The elections of 1885 and 1886: Issues and outcomes

1. **The Conservative Party in power in 1885:**
   The Conservatives were in power **temporarily** until an election could be organised.

   - They got **support** from Parnell and the Home Rule Party.
   - They dropped **coercion** in Ireland.
   - They passed the **Ashbourne Land Act**.

   > Information from Case studies should be used in questions even though the name of the Case study may not be used in the question.

2. **The 1885 general election:** Parnell wanted to force the Conservatives or the Liberals to grant Home Rule to Ireland. This depended on the result of the 1885 general election.

3. **Why did Parnell support the Conservatives in the general election?**
   - He wanted to make sure the Liberal Party majority was small.
   - Then he would force either party to agree to Home Rule, because they would need his support to get into government (**the balance of power**).

4. **Irish Unionists:** As Home Rule became more likely, **Irish Unionists became more and more disturbed.** They were opposed to Home Rule for **economic,**

religious and political reasons. (See *Unionism and the Ulster Question, 1870–1914, pp. 45–48*)

- The **Irish Loyal and Patriotic Union** was set up in 1885 by Southern Unionists to fight Home Rule.
- In Ulster the **Orange Order** was revived and the **Ulster Loyalist Anti-Repeal Union** was founded in January 1886.
- In the 1885 election, **2 Unionist MPs** were elected for the Trinity College, Dublin constituency, while **16 other Unionist MPs** were elected in Ulster.

5. In the **election in Britain**, the Liberals won 335 seats and the Conservatives 249 seats (historians said 25 of these came from Irish support in Britain).

6. The **Home Rule Party** won 86 seats – 85 in Ireland and 1 in Liverpool. The overall result of the election meant that **Parnell could put only the Liberals into power.**

7. **The Hawarden Kite:** Gladstone's son said his father intended to bring in Home Rule.
   - Parnell now supported Gladstone (January 1886), who became prime minister.

8. **Terms of the First Home Rule Bill, 1886:**
   - There would be a parliament in Dublin to deal with internal Irish affairs.
   - Parliament in Westminster would deal with external affairs, e.g. defence, war and peace, trade.
   - No Irish MPs were to sit in Westminster.
   - Ireland would pay 1/15 of the Imperial budget.
   - A separate **Land Purchase Bill** was introduced.

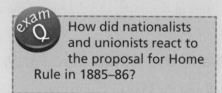

exam Q

How did nationalists and unionists react to the proposal for Home Rule in 1885–86?

9. **Opposition to the First Home Rule Bill:**
   - **The Conservatives opposed** the First Home Rule Bill. **Lord Randolph Churchill** proposed to play **'the Orange Card'**, that is, to support the Irish Unionists to block Home Rule.
   - Churchill went to Belfast to encourage resistance among unionists. He used the slogan, **'Ulster will fight and Ulster will be right'**.
   - **The Liberal Unionists:** These were members of Gladstone's Liberal Party opposed to Home Rule, who were led by **Joseph Chamberlain**. They believed that Home Rule would undermine the **British Empire**. Chamberlain was also **annoyed** by Parnell's rejection of his Central Board Scheme.

10. **Defeat of the First Home Rule Bill:**
    - Both sides **debated** Home Rule for Ireland:

- **Those in favour** said the majority of Irish people voted for Home Rule; an Irish parliament was needed to run Irish affairs; relations between Britain and Ireland would improve.

- **Those against Home Rule** (in favour of the Union) said the majority of British people voted for Union; a Home Rule parliament would be Catholic-controlled; Home Rule would lead to the break-up of the British Empire; Irish people were not able to govern themselves.

- The Conservatives and the Liberal Unionists **combined** to defeat the First Home Rule Bill in the House of Commons by 341 votes to 311 votes. Gladstone had to resign as prime minister.

11. **The 1886 general election**: The Conservatives won the **1886 general election**; this showed the majority in Britain were in favour of maintaining the Union with Ireland. In Ireland, the results were similar to the previous election.

12. **Overall results**:

- The **Conservative Party** was in government for most of the next 20 years. This lessened the possibility of Home Rule.

- Parnell was now tied to the **Liberal Alliance**; this was the only way to get Home Rule.

- The Irish Unionists were better organised; they founded the **Irish Unionist Party**.

- The election results showed clear **divisions** between a Unionist-dominated area in the north and the rest of the country, which favoured Home Rule.

Parnell and the Home Rule Party, 1886–90

1. **Parnell and the Plan of Campaign**

- Parnell did not favour the **Plan of Campaign**. He feared that a new land war would upset English Liberals. (See *Land Agitation and Land Reform, p. 22–32.*)

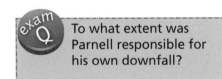

To what extent was Parnell responsible for his own downfall?

2. **Parnellism and crime**

- The London *Times* published articles on '**Parnellism and Crime**', which claimed that Parnell knew about and supported the Phoenix Park murders. These articles **endangered** the Liberal Alliance. Parnell denied the articles; the House of Commons set up a **commission** to investigate.

3. **The Piggott forgeries**: Richard Piggott, an Irish journalist, confessed to forging the letters. Piggott fled and killed himself in Madrid.

4. This was a **triumph** for Parnell.

- He **met Gladstone** at Hawarden to discuss Home Rule.

- Parnell was called the '**Uncrowned King of Ireland**'.

The O'Shea divorce case and the downfall of Parnell

1. In December 1889 **Captain William O'Shea** filed for divorce against his wife, **Katherine**. He named Parnell as co-respondent. Parnell's affair with Katherine O'Shea had lasted since 1880.

2. **Irish reaction:** Irish MPs at first supported Parnell; they believed it was another plot against him.
   - Parnell assured them he would escape **without a stain** on his character.

3. **The court case:** Parnell did **not contest** the court case, which made him look like a heartless adulterer. The **divorce** was granted in November 1890.

4. **Irish reaction:** Very few Irish people questioned Parnell. The only opposition was from **Davitt** – he suggested a temporary retirement for Parnell.

5. **British reaction:** The **Liberals** would lose votes if they kept the alliance with the Irish Party led by Parnell.
   - Gladstone warned **Justin McCarthy**, chairman of the Irish Party, that the Liberals could not support Home Rule if Parnell stayed as leader.

6. Parnell was **re-elected** leader by the Irish Party.

7. Gladstone **published the letter** which he had sent to Justin McCarthy. It gave Irish MPs **two choices:** (1) abandon Parnell, or (2) remain loyal to Parnell and risk destroying the Liberal Alliance.

8. Parnell agreed to **another party meeting**.

9. He issued a proclamation, **'To the People of Ireland'**; he attacked Gladstone for trying to dictate to the Irish Party. Parnell got support from the extremists, but destroyed the alliance with the Liberals.

10. **Committee Room 15:** 73 Irish MPs met. There were six days of debate, which became very bitter. Opponents asked Parnell to resign temporarily; Parnell refused.
    - There was no vote on the leadership. Instead, 45 MPs led by McCarthy walked out; 27 MPs continued to support Parnell.

11. **Catholic bishops:** The Catholic bishops condemned Parnell.

12. **By-elections**
    - There were contests between **Parnellite and Anti-Parnellite candidates** in by-elections.
    - Parnell appealed to the old **Fenian tradition**, but the **Anti-Parnellites** won with big majorities.

13. **The death of Parnell**
    - Parnell was in poor health. He caught **pneumonia** during the by-election campaigns and died in England. His **funeral** in Dublin was attended by 200,000 people. **GAA members** provided a guard of honour with hurleys.

14. **The Parnellites** elected **John Redmond** as leader. They won only **nine seats** in the 1892 general election.

15. **The Anti-Parnellites** were led by Justin McCarthy, who was a weak leader. They were split amongst themselves.

16. **The Parnell myth:**
    - This was the **romanticising** or **glorifying** of Parnell as a **republican figure**. Republicans believed he supported violence as a means of achieving independence, but Parnell did not favour violence.

17. **The achievements of Parnell:**
    - He became **leader** of the Home Rule Party.
    - He **united** extremists and moderates in the Land League to achieve its aims (the 3Fs).
    - He created **a united and modern political party** – the Home Rule Party.
    - He persuaded a **major British political party** – the Liberals – to support Home Rule.

2. Land agitation and land reform

 In this section, you should understand:
- The progress of land agitation and land reform
- The role of Michael Davitt (Key personality, p. 57)

The Land Question

1. **What was the Land Question?**
   - The Land Question was the **relationship between landlord and tenants**; the

- How significant was Michael Davitt's contribution to land agitation and land reform in Ireland?
- To what extent did the land agitation of the period, 1870–1914, lead to land reform?

land was owned by the landlords and rented by the farmers. The Land Question was about the **ownership** and control of land, and not the use of the land (farming). Tenant leaders demanded the **3Fs – fair rent, fixity of tenure and free sale.**

2. **Political power of tenants:** The influence of the tenant farmers grew in the late nineteenth century because they had more votes than any other group, farming was the biggest industry, and other businesses (such as shopkeepers) depended on farmers for a living.

3. **1870 Land Act: Gladstone**, the Liberal Prime Minister, said '**My mission is to pacify Ireland.**' One of the **problems** he had to solve was the Land Question. But if he satisfied tenants, he would offend the landlords.
   - Gladstone brought in the **1870 Land Act.**

4. **The aims of the Act** were:
   - to give some security to the tenant but also maintain the landlord's rights;
   - to reduce the number of evictions.

5. **The terms of the 1870 Act:**
  - **Ulster Custom** was legalised – when tenants left farms they were **compensated for any improvements** they had made.
  - Farmers got **compensation for disturbance** (eviction), except when they were evicted for non-payment of rent.
  - Under the **'Bright clause'**, tenants could get 2/3 of the purchase price as a loan to buy the farm; it was to be paid back over 35 years (this was called **land purchase**).

6. **The results of the 1870 Act:**
  - The Act **failed:** most tenants were evicted for non-payment of rent, so compensation for disturbance did not apply.
  - **Ulster Custom** was difficult to define, so tenants had to prove it applied to them in the courts.
  - Landlords were not given any incentive to sell; loans were too small – fewer than a thousand tenants bought land under the 'Bright clause'.
  - **Importance of the 1870 Act:** It was a **step** in solving the Irish Land Question. It set an important **precedent** for the future; the government had interfered in an economic area and begun to limit the power of the landlords.

The Land War, 1879–82

1. The **Beginning of the Land War:** The Land War was a conflict between landlords and tenants (and their organisation, the Land League). In the early 1870s harvests were good and farmers obtained decent prices for their products in Britain. But all this changed from **1877 onwards**.
  - The **Irish economy** almost collapsed towards the end of the 1870s, due mainly to a general British and European depression.
  - There was a **drop in the price of grain**.
  - There were **fewer seasonal jobs** in Britain for migratory workers from Ireland.
  - **Harvests** in the West of Ireland were **bad**; the potato crop failed; many people starved.
  - Because of poor prices and bad harvests, tenants fell into **arrears**. There were **increased evictions** – 1,238 of them in 1879. Evictions often led to **agrarian outrages** (attacks) against landlords and their agents.

These conditions led to the **founding of the Land League**.

The Land League and the Land War

1. **Michael Davitt** was born in Straide, Co. Mayo. His family was evicted from their farm in 1852. They went to England, where Michael **lost his right arm in an accident** in a cotton factory. He was **self-educated**. He joined the **Fenians** and was **jailed** in 1870. He was released on a **ticket-of-leave** in 1877. He visited Mayo in 1878 and was horrified by the conditions among the tenants.

2. **The New Departure:** Davitt went to **America** and met **John Devoy**, leader of **Clan na nGael** (the American Fenians). This led to the **New Departure** with Parnell. The New Departure was the coming together of the **revolutionary movement** (some Irish Fenians) and the **constitutional/parliamentary movement** (Home Rulers led by Parnell), backed by the **Irish in America** (Clan na nGael and John Devoy) and supported by the **tenants.**

- They came together to agitate for a **solution to the land problem** in Ireland.

3. A meeting was held at **Irishtown**, Co. Mayo, in April 1879 to protest about unfair rents.

- It was organised by **James Daly**, editor of the *Connaught Telegraph*. Over 10,000 people attended – Davitt and Parnell did not attend. It forced the local landlord, Canon Bourke, to **reduce rents by 25 per cent.**

4. Davitt called another meeting at **Westport** in June 1879. **Parnell** addressed the meeting – he said, 'Demand a fair rent' and 'Keep a firm grip on your homesteads.' Davitt founded the **Land League of Mayo.**

5. **The Irish National Land League** was founded in Dublin in October 1879. Parnell was **president** and Davitt was **secretary** of the Land League.

6. **The aims of the Land League:**

- **Short-term:** to get fair rents for tenants and to prevent evictions.
- **Long-term:** to abolish the landlord system – to bring about **tenant ownership** of the land of Ireland, or **peasant proprietorship**.

Progress of the Land League, 1879–81

1. **Parnell** had to satisfy both **moderates** and **extremists** of the 'New Departure'.

- He **spoke** like a revolutionary while **behaving** like a constitutionalist; he made a number of **fiery speeches** against landlords.

2. **Parnell visited America** in 1879–80; he made similar extreme speeches; Irish-Americans approved and Parnell's popularity increased.

3. **Parnell's** tour collected almost £80,000 to relieve distress in Ireland and to help the Land League.

4. **The Catholic clergy** were **suspicious** of the Land League, but the League grew so fast that many clergy came to support it.

5. **Gladstone** and the Liberals won the general election in 1880; Gladstone appointed the **Bessborough Commission** to see how the 1870 Land Act operated. But there were more **agrarian outrages** (attacks on landlords, agents and other tenants) in Ireland (863 in 1879; 2,585 in 1880); and there was **increased pressure** from the Land League.

6. **Land League methods:**

- The Land League **united all classes** in the countryside, i.e. big and small farmers, labourers, townspeople.

- They supported the **slogan: 'The land of Ireland for the people of Ireland'**.
- The League made good use of **propaganda** – the landlords were seen as **cruel absentees** who lived in England; all tenants were believed to be **poor**.
- The League used **demonstrations** to show the strength of the movement and to ensure the tenants did not use violence.
- There were Land League **branches** in many places.
- **Parnell** became **leader of the Home Rule Party in 1880**; to keep control of the violence, he proposed **boycotting** (use of moral force) – it was effective in reducing the number of evictions. It was first used against a land agent in Co. Mayo, **Captain Boycott**. He brought in Orangemen to harvest his crops. He later left for England. This was a **victory** for the League.

7. The Liberal government took **action against the Land League**:
   - The government **prosecuted Parnell, Davitt and other leaders** on a charge of conspiracy to prevent payment of rent; the prosecution failed.
   - The government passed a **Coercion Act (Protection of Persons & Property Act) in 1881**, which gave special powers of arrest.

8. Before the Act became law, **Davitt was arrested**. There was uproar in Parliament:
   - Parnell and 35 MPs were expelled.
   - Some Irish leaders urged Parnell to **withdraw** from Parliament and lead a 'no-rent' campaign in Ireland.
   - Others proposed that he **should stay** in Westminster.

9. **Parnell decided to remain in Parliament**, because there he could influence the new land bill (Gladstone's 1881 Land Act).
   - Parnell's decision to stay at Westminster was **a turning point in his career** – it showed his commitment to **parliamentary politics**.

The 1881 Land Act

1. **Gladstone** and the Liberal government introduced the 1881 Land Act.
   - **Terms:** The 1881 Act gave the League its main demand – the **3Fs**:
     - **Fair rent:** Land courts were set up to decide a fair rent; landlords or tenants could apply to the court to have rent fixed; the rents were fixed for 15 years.
     - **Fixity of tenure:** Tenants could not be evicted while they paid the fair rent.
     - **Free sale:** When a tenant left a holding he could get **compensation for improvements** from the incoming tenant.
   - **Land Purchase:** Tenants could also get 35-year loans for three-quarters of the purchase price to buy the land.
   - The Act's strengths and weaknesses:
     - **Strength:** There was **dual ownership** of the land – both landlords and tenants shared control of the land.

- **Weakness:** The Act did not apply to **leaseholders** and **those in arrears** (behind in their payments) – about one-third of Irish tenants.

2. **Reaction to the 1881 Act**
   - Only a **few hundred tenants** took advantage of the land purchase section; they could not raise the quarter of the purchase price needed.
   - In **Ulster**, tenants welcomed the Act and began to use the land courts.
   - The more **extreme section** of the League was against the Act; they wanted to drive out the landlords; they wanted full land purchase. Leaseholders and tenants in arrears were also angry.
   - **Moderates** (Catholic bishops and priests, most MPs, better-off farmers) wanted to keep the gains they had won; they wanted to settle the Land Question peacefully.

3. **Parnell's attitude: Parnell**, the president of the League, was in a **dilemma**. If he supported one side, he would lose the support of the other side. **Parnell** tried to keep both sides happy.
   - **In Parliament** he pointed out the weaknesses of the Act; when he was certain that the Act would become law, he got himself suspended from the House of Commons.
   - **Outside Parliament**, he made fiery speeches denouncing the Act – this again appealed to the extremists.
   - Parnell said tenants should bring **test cases** to the Land Courts.
   - Parnell made **extreme speeches** so that he would be arrested.

4. **Parnell's imprisonment in Kilmainham Jail:** The government imprisoned Parnell in **Kilmainham Jail** (October 1881) under the Coercion Act.
   - Parnell wrote to Katherine O'Shea, 'Politically it is a fortunate thing for me . . . as the movement is breaking fast . . .' Parnell was now a martyr; this would help him maintain his support.
   - Parnell claimed **Captain Moonlight** (i.e. agrarian violence) would take his place; agrarian outrages increased – more attacks, burnings, maiming of cattle.
   - The Land League leaders issued the **No Rent Manifesto**, calling for a general rent strike.

5. The Land League was declared **illegal**; the No Rent campaign was condemned by churchmen and moderates in Ireland and it got little support from the tenants, who wanted to go to the land courts.

6. Parnell's sister, Anna, set up the **Ladies' Land League** to replace the Land League.
   - They set up **300 branches** and collected money to help evicted tenants. They also organised protests.
   - They were supported by **Davitt** but opposed by the Catholic Archbishop of Dublin, **Dr McCabe**. They were **persecuted** by the government.
   - Parnell did not approve of the Ladies' Land League; after his release he closed it down.

7. **The Kilmainham Treaty:**
- The Liberal government realised the coercion policy was **not working**.
- Parnell wanted to get out of jail (**Why?** Katherine O'Shea had given birth to his child, who had died; and there was a danger the extremists would take over the movement.)
- **Negotiations** between Parnell and the British government were conducted by **Captain William O'Shea** and **Joseph Chamberlain**.
- The negotiations led to the **Kilmainham Treaty** in April 1882.

8. The **government promised** to:
- release Parnell and the other imprisoned leaders
- relax its coercion policy
- amend the Land Act so as to permit leaseholders to use the land courts
- help those tenants who had fallen into arrears (Arrears Act).

9. **Parnell promised** to:
- try to end agrarian outrages
- try to have the amended Land Act accepted
- co-operate in future Liberal Party reforms.

10. **The results of the Kilmainham Treaty:**
- **Extremists and Irish-Americans** regarded the Kilmainham Treaty as a **sell-out** of the Land League – they felt the politicians had betrayed them.
- Davitt (who was also released from prison), Dillon and others **did not criticise** the Treaty because of **loyalty**.
- Parnell favoured the **moderates**; he **switched** from a concentration on land reform to a concentration on winning some form of Home Rule. He realised that the 1881 Land Act and the Arrears Act had gone a long way towards solving the land question. **This was another turning point in Parnell's career.**

11. **The Phoenix Park Murders (1882)**
- On 6 May **Cavendish**, a new Chief Secretary, and **Burke**, the Under-Secretary (head of the civil service), were murdered in the Phoenix Park by the **Invincibles**, an extreme breakaway group from the Fenians.
- **Parnell denounced the killings**. He offered to **resign** as leader of the Home Rule Party, but was persuaded to change his mind; the murders shocked moderate opinion in Ireland and in England.

The Conservatives and land reform

1. **The Land Question, 1882–85**
- The Land League was banned in 1881 and Parnell made no effort to revive it; **instead he concentrated on Home Rule.**

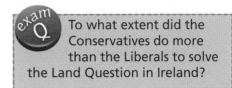

To what extent did the Conservatives do more than the Liberals to solve the Land Question in Ireland?

- Parnell set up the **Irish National League** in place of the Land League, and he controlled it.

2. **Conservatives in government, 1885**
   - In 1885, Parnell supported the Conservatives and helped to bring down Gladstone's government.
   - In return for Parnell's support, the new Conservative government dropped coercion and introduced a new land act.

3. **The Ashbourne Land Act (1885)**
   - Tenants were given **full loans** to buy out the farms; a fund of £5 million was provided.

4. **The results of the Ashbourne Act**
   - The Act was popular; annual repayments were now lower than rents. £5 million was used within three years; £5 million more was advanced (in the 1888 Balfour Land Act).
   - 25,000 tenants bought farms under this Act.

5. The Conservatives developed **a policy for Ireland**. This was called '**Killing Home Rule with Kindness**', or **Constructive Unionism**.
   - The Conservatives were **against Home Rule**, because they thought it would lead to the break-up of the British Empire.
   - They also believed that if they solved the social and economic problems of Ireland, then the demand for Home Rule would disappear. This policy was based on Joseph Chamberlain's pamphlet, '**A Unionist Policy for Ireland**' (1888).

6. **How did the Conservative policy operate?**
   - The Conservatives used **coercion** to put down lawlessness, mainly during the Plan of Campaign.
   - They also used **conciliation** by bringing in reforms to solve problems, including land reform, which would create tenant ownership of the land and relieve poverty.

The Plan of Campaign

1. **Causes**
   - A very bad harvest in 1886 led to demands for a reduction in rents; these were fixed for 15 years by the land courts.
   - Many landlords were unwilling to reduce rents; tenants fell into arrears and there were evictions.
   - These conditions led to the **Plan of Campaign**.

2. **The Plan of Campaign** was first proposed in **William O'Brien's newspaper *United Ireland***, in October 1886. Some members of the Home Rule Party, including **John Dillon and William O'Brien**, supported the Plan.

3. **The Plan:** According to the Plan, the tenants in an estate would offer the landlord a reduced rent where they thought rents were too high.

- If the landlord was not prepared to accept, tenants would pay the reduced rent into an 'estate fund'. This was used to help evicted tenants.

Progress of the Plan of Campaign

1. **Parnell's attitude**; Parnell did not approve of the Plan; he thought it might endanger the **Liberal alliance**. Parnell prevented the Plan spreading to more estates.

2. **Government reaction:** The **Conservative government** appointed **Arthur Balfour as Chief Secretary**.
   - He passed the **1888 Balfour Land Act** to help tenants whose rents were too high. Rents were reduced by 15 per cent, but the conflict continued.
   - Government tried to restore order with the **Perpetual Crimes Act**; leaders of the Plan were jailed.
   - In the '**Mitchelstown Massacre**', two people were killed when police (the Royal Irish Constabulary or RIC) fired into a crowd; Balfour defended the police and he was given the nickname '**Bloody**' **Balfour**.
   - Government tried to get the **papacy** to condemn the Plan of Campaign; the Plan and boycotting were both **condemned** by Pope Leo XIII in 1888. Catholic MPs met in Dublin and declared they would **not tolerate any interference from Rome** in political affairs.
   - Balfour encouraged a **landlord syndicate** to help some landlords fight the Plan.
   - Despite government action the Plan continued to be operated, mainly on estates in **Munster** and **Connacht,** until about 1891. The Plan was confined to **116 estates**; tenants were successful in having rents reduced in almost 3/4 of the estates.

The Balfour Land Act (1891)

1. The Conservative government also tried reform; in **1891 Balfour's Land Act** was passed.

2. **Terms:** £33 million was provided for **full loans** for tenants to buy the land. **Balfour** believed tenant purchase was the best way to solve the Irish Land Question.
   - Landlords were to be paid in **land stock** rather than in cash.

3. Tenants and landlords were **not happy** with the terms and the method of payment – for example, the value of land stock fluctuated and legal costs were high.
   - But **47,000 tenants** purchased farms under the Act.

4. The 1891 Balfour Land Act also set up the **Congested Districts Board (CDB)**.

5. **The Congested Districts Board, 1891:** Balfour realised that tenant purchase would not solve the problems of tenants who had very small farms with poor land.

6. **The aim** of the Board was to help those living in '**congested districts**' – poorer areas in counties mainly along the west coast of the country.

7. The main **methods** used by the CDB to improve conditions were to:
   - introduce **better agricultural methods**
   - encourage **home and local industries** (cottage industries), so as to provide another source of income
   - develop **piers** in small ports for fishing
   - increase the **size of farms** by land purchase and land redistribution
   - encourage **resettlement** in other places in Ireland where land was available.

8. **The results of the Congested Districts Board:**
   - There was **success** in promoting cottage industries, especially knitting and weaving.
   - The CDB was **responsible** for constructing roads and developing light railways to improve transport for trade and tourism.
   - The CDB promoted the **Irish fishing industry**.
   - The CDB spent £9 million in **land purchase** between 1891 and 1923 (when it ended); it redistributed 2 million acres among farmers, but the Board never had enough money for all its schemes.

The Wyndham Land Act, 1903

1. In 1898 **William O'Brien** founded the **United Irish League** to promote more land reform, especially in the West of Ireland. It grew rapidly within a few years. The League wanted the compulsory buying out of landlords, so that tenants would own the land.

2. Some **landlords** felt the time had arrived to solve the land question.

3. **Why did the landlords want to settle?**
   - Landlords would sell their estates if they got **good terms**.
   - The **Secret Ballot Act of 1872** reduced landlord influence in parliamentary elections.
   - The **Local Government Act in 1898** brought in elected county councils, which meant that the landlords lost control of local government.
   - The landlords had had enough of land agitation, boycotting and intimidation.

4. **Why did tenants want to settle?**
   - Tenants were prepared to buy if they got **full loans** and if repayments were **small**.

5. **A Land Conference** was held in Dublin between **landlord and tenant representatives** in December 1902 under the chairmanship of **Lord Dunraven**, a Southern unionist. The Land Conference proposed a solution to the land question that was supported by the **Chief Secretary, George Wyndham**.
   - This formed the basis of the **Wyndham Land Act of 1903**, passed by the **Conservative government**.

6. **Terms of Wyndham Land Act, 1903:**
   - **£100 million** was made available for land purchase.
   - Tenants had **68 years to repay** the purchase price, so the repayments were lower than the rent.
   - **Legal costs** were paid by the government rather than by tenants.
   - Landlords were encouraged to sell their entire estates with a **bonus scheme** (an extra 12½ per cent).

7. The **results of the Wyndham Land Act:** The Act was an **immediate success**.
   - Landlords obtained good prices for their estates.
   - 200,000 tenants purchased land under the Act.
   - The Act was amended in 1909 (**Birrell Act**) and this introduced compulsory purchase.
   - **The conflict between landlords and tenants was over; the tenants or farmers had won**.

The Co-operative movement

1. The Co-operative movement was founded by **Horace Plunkett**. He spent ten years farming in America and returned in 1889.

2. He said the **solutions to Ireland's farming problems** were improved agricultural methods and increased cooperation among farmers. He said there was too much emphasis on land ownership, rather than on production, distribution and marketing.

3. The first co-operative shop was established in **Doneraile, Co. Cork** in 1889. In 1894 Plunkett founded the **Irish Agricultural Organisation Society (IAOS)** to co-ordinate the work of local co-operative societies.
   - By 1914, there were over **1,000 co-ops**. These were mainly co-operative creameries, which processed the farmers' milk, and **co-operative societies**, which bought farming supplies (equipment and fertilisers) and sold them to the farmers.
   - These were mainly in the **dairying industry**; the Co-operative movement had little effect on other aspects of Irish farming.

4. In 1895 Plunkett founded a journal, the *Irish Homestead*, to promote his ideas on co-operatives.

5. Plunkett persuaded the government in 1899 to set up a **Department of Agriculture and Technical Instruction**, owing to the success of the Co-operative movement. Instructors were sent around the country to promote better methods of agriculture.

The results of the campaign for land reform

- The **landlords** lost their power.
- Both the **Liberal and Conservative governments** played important parts in solving the Land Question.
- The **Conservative policy** failed in its **main aim** of killing Home Rule; the demand for Home Rule (and for other forms of independence) continued.

- The victory of the tenants created a **socially conservative** farming class (did not want to see changes in society), but it was **politically radical** (wanted some form of independence). This class **dominated** the new Irish state after 1922.

3. Cultural revival

In this section, you should understand:

- The role of the GAA, the Gaelic League and the Anglo-Irish literary movement in cultural revival
- The role of Douglas Hyde (Key personality, p. 59)
- The role of W.B. Yeats (Key personality, p. 60)
- Case study: The Gaelic Athletic Association, 1884–91

What was cultural nationalism?

1. **Gaelic culture** had **declined** over the previous few hundred years, owing to the influence of the Plantations; the defeat of the Gaelic chiefs; the spread of industry; the growth of towns; education and newspapers; and the impact of the Great Famine. Instead there was a **spread of English culture** – language and customs.

ANGLICISATION:
The process whereby Ireland became more and more like England in adopting the English language and customs.

2. There was a **cultural revival** in the last decades of the nineteenth century and the early years of the twentieth century. This saw the growth of **cultural nationalism**.
   - Cultural nationalism was a **revolt against anglicisation** (the spread of English language and culture).
   - Cultural nationalism stressed **the importance of Irish identity and Irish culture**.

ANGLO-IRISH:
People of English descent who lived in Ireland.

3. The cultural revival mainly influenced:
   - sport (the GAA)
   - the Irish language (the Gaelic League)
   - Anglo-Irish literature.

Case study: The Gaelic Athletic Association, 1884–91

1. **Origins:** In the nineteenth century, sports were played without proper rules. The spread of organised sports began in England in the middle of the nineteenth century. Football (soccer), cricket, rugby and athletics were organised with **rules** and **competitions**.

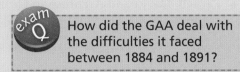

exam Q — How did the GAA deal with the difficulties it faced between 1884 and 1891?

2. These spread to Ireland. Some games, especially soccer and cricket, became **more popular**.
   - They were **organised**.
   - They were spreading both **in the towns and in the cities**.

3. But sports were mainly confined to **'gentlemen'** (upper and middle classes), and excluded the poorer classes. Games were **not played on Sundays**.

4. **Michael Cusack** was a sportsman and Gaelic supporter; he wanted to 'preserve the physical strength of the Irish race'. **Cusack** said that working men were **excluded** from cricket and rugby clubs.
   - He was supported by **Maurice Davin**, one of Ireland's top athletes. **Davin** wanted Irish control of athletics.

5. **Foundation:** Cusack and Davin called a meeting in November 1884 at **Hayes's Hotel in Thurles,** and the GAA was set up. Davin became **president** of the GAA; Cusack became **secretary**.
   - A second meeting was held in **Cork** in 1885 and drew up the first set of **rules**.

6. **The aims of the GAA were to:**
   - **stop the decline** of native sports
   - open sports to **all social classes**
   - achieve **Irish control** of sport.

7. **Progress of the GAA**
   - According to Cusack, 'The association swept the country like a prairie fire.'
   - Clubs and competitions were organised – Cusack encouraged the setting up of clubs, but he was dropped as secretary because of **inefficiency**. Soon there were **600 clubs**. The first All-Ireland championships in hurling and football were begun in 1887.
   - Games were played on **Sundays**. Clubs were based on **parishes** and they were supported by the **Catholic clergy; parish rivalry** was important in the spread of the GAA.
   - But the GAA **was not so popular** in the cities, especially **Cork** and **Dublin**, where soccer was popular in the working-class areas.

8. **Nationalist politics and the GAA**
   - **Parnell, Davitt and Archbishop Croke of Cashel** became the patrons of the GAA; **Archbishop Croke** was opposed to 'foreign and fantastical sports'.
   - Games were played only on Sundays, but **Protestants/Unionists** treated Sunday as a day of 'rest'.
   - **The influence of the Fenians** – some of the men who attended the first meeting in Hayes's Hotel were Fenians. The Fenian (Irish Republican Brotherhood (IRB)) influence grew; members of the Central Council were mainly IRB; Davin was replaced as president by a member of the IRB.
   - There was a **'ban'** on GAA players playing 'foreign games'; the **RIC** (the police) and the **British Army** were banned from membership of the GAA.
   - The **IRB** used the GAA as a **recruiting ground** for members.
   - The GAA was weakened by the **Parnellite split**; the IRB-led GAA supported Parnell.
   - GAA members provided a guard of honour for Parnell's funeral; but many **anti-Parnellites** left the GAA and it declined in the 1890s.

The GAA after 1891

1. There were some changes to the GAA, which led to success again after 1900:
   - There were **improved rules** for hurling and football.
   - **Inter-county teams** (rather than club teams) played in the All-Ireland championships.
   - The **provincial councils** of Munster, Leinster, Connacht and Ulster were set up.
   - In 1913 the Jones's Road Ground, Dublin, was bought by the GAA and renamed **Croke Park**.
2. **The GAA and cultural nationalism**
   - The GAA was linked to cultural nationalism by using the **Irish language**.
3. **The impact of the GAA**
   - Hurling and Gaelic football were **organised** and **revived**.
   - The GAA was **a mass movement**. It developed the **organisational skills** of its members.
   - It provided a **training in democracy** (like the Land League and the Home Rule Party); it helped to prepare the country for **self-government**.
   - A spirit **of local patriotism** and pride was encouraged.
   - The GAA played an important part in creating a **national identity** – Ireland was Gaelic and Catholic.
   - It encouraged the growth of the **separatist (independence) movement**.

key point

DEMOCRACY:
A type of government in which the people have the final say either directly or via representatives selected through elections.

The Gaelic League: Origins and background

1. **The decline of the Irish language**
   - In 1851 about a **quarter** of the people spoke Irish; by 1901 only a **seventh** spoke it.
   - **Causes: Irish declined because** the worst-hit areas during the Great Famine were Irish-speaking areas; Irish was associated with poverty and ignorance; parents wanted their children to speak English in case they emigrated; politics, trade and industry and education were conducted through the medium of English.

2. **Interest by scholars in Irish**
   - In the middle of the nineteenth century, **European scholars** began to study Irish, which had one of the oldest written literatures in Europe.
   - **Irish scholars** published books on Irish literature, e.g. Standish O'Grady, *The Bardic Literature of Ireland* – a collection of myths and legends. These books **inspired interest** in Gaelic traditions and folklore.

3. **The Society for the Preservation of the Irish Language** was set up in 1877. It got Irish onto the **Intermediate Examinations** syllabus. It also encouraged **some schools** to teach Irish.

The foundation of the Gaelic League

1. The Gaelic League was **founded** in 1893 by **Douglas Hyde and Eoin MacNeill.**
   - Hyde gave a lecture on **'The Necessity for De-Anglicising Ireland'**, in which he said Ireland had lost the 'notes of nationalism', that is, language and culture.
   - MacNeill admired Hyde's ideas, so both came together to form the Gaelic League.

2. The **aims** of the organisation were to:
   - revive Irish as **the national language**
   - promote the study and publication of **Irish literature**
   - develop **a new literature in Irish**
   - **de-anglicise** Ireland (by getting rid of other aspects of English culture).

key point

DE-ANGLICISATION:
In Ireland, reversing the trend of Anglicisation and reviving and restoring the Gaelic language and customs.

3. **The progress of the Gaelic League**
   - **Timirí** (teachers/organisers) travelled from place to place teaching Irish classes.
   - **Branches were set up**, slowly at first; there were only 43 clubs by 1897. After 1900 the Gaelic League **expanded rapidly**; by 1904 it had 600 league clubs with 50,000 members. Many joined for **social reasons** (to meet other people).
   - The League published **a newspaper**, *An Claidheamh Soluis* (edited by Pádraig Pearse), to promote the Irish language.
   - **Competitions** were organised in dancing and singing; these were feiseanna and céilí.
   - **An t-Oireachtas**, a national competition, was held.

- **A teacher-training college** was founded to train people to teach Irish; it was compulsory to have Irish for admission to the new national university.
- By 1906 the League had **branches** in Belfast and Ulster.

4. **Nationalist politics and the Gaelic League**
   - **Hyde** wanted the League to be **non-political**; he hoped that it would be a link between Catholics and Protestants, nationalists and unionists.

5. But **IRB (Fenian) influence** grew.
   - At the League Congress in 1915, **Hyde resigned as president** when the League agreed to promote **Irish independence**.

6. **The impact of the Gaelic League**
   - **It did not succeed in stopping the decline in the number of Irish speakers**. There was a decline of over 100,000 Irish speakers between 1891 and 1926.
   - The League contributed to the growth of **nationalism** before 1916; the Gaelic League encouraged independence; it became **a school for latter-day revolutionaries**.
     - Many of the **leaders of the 1916 Rising** were members of the Gaelic League, e.g. Pearse and de Valera.
     - The League contributed to the formation of **Irish identity – Gaelic and Catholic**. Pearse said Ireland should be 'not free merely, but Gaelic as well; not Gaelic merely, but free as well'.
   - The League influenced the **educational policy** of the Irish Free State after 1922.
     - The quality and quantity of **books** available in Irish increased.
     - Irish became a recognised subject in schools and universities.
   - **Women** became involved in **nationalist politics** through the League.
   - The League influenced social life – people met at Gaelic League classes.
   - The Gaelic League was mainly **town-based**; it did not grow in Irish-speaking areas.
   - **The League created greater divisions between North and South, unionist and nationalist**.
     - Some **nationalists** believed that an independent Ireland was needed to preserve the Irish language and culture; they changed the League's constitution in favour of an **independent republic**.
     - **Unionists** opposed the League because they said it **emphasised differences** with Britain.

exam Q

What did one or more of the following contribute to the cultural revivals of the period 1870–1914: the GAA; the Gaelic League; W.B. Yeats?

exam focus

When you are asked **'one or more'**, you will not lose marks if you refer to only one. But it is usually better to use more than one, because you have more information to draw on for an answer.

The Anglo-Irish literary revival

1. This was a **revival of Irish literature** using the English language and based on Irish folktales, legends and history. Many of those involved came from the **Anglo-Irish tradition**.

2. **Origins:** The poet **William Butler Yeats** was influenced by Irish folktales and legends.
   - Along with others, he formed the **Irish Literary Society** in London in 1891 and the **National Literary Society** in Dublin in 1892.

3. Yeats met **Lady Gregory** and **Edward Martyn**, Co. Galway landlords. They had an interest in Irish folk tales and Celtic sagas.

4. They founded the **Irish Literary Theatre** in 1898 to stage plays by Irish playwrights.

5. The first play was Yeats' *The Countess Cathleen*. Yeats wrote a play for Maud Gonne – *Cathleen Ni Houlihan* – about Ireland, which is represented by an old woman made young again when her men take up arms for her. Yeats later asked:

   > Did that play of mine send out
   > Certain men the English shot?

6. Yeats and Lady Gregory were supported by a rich Englishwoman, **Annie Hornimann**. In 1904 she donated money to buy and equip the **Abbey Theatre** in Dublin.

The literary revival and nationalist Ireland

1. **Synge and the Abbey**
   - Yeats supported the work of **John Millington Synge**. Synge was influenced by the speech patterns of the people of the **Aran Islands**.

2. In 1903 Synge's play *The Shadow of the Glen* was put on at the Abbey. It was about a young woman who leaves her older husband and runs away with a tramp. The audience was angered by the suggestion that Irishwomen could commit adultery.

3. In 1907 Synge's most famous play, *The Playboy of the Western World*, caused riots. Here the idea that an Irishman might have killed his father was seen as an insult to decent Irish people. Yeats defended the play, but nationalists were upset. Yeats thought people were becoming too narrow-minded.

4. **Nationalism versus literature**
   - Nationalists believed that literature should be judged on its **political merits**; that literature should present a favourable image of Ireland.
   - Yeats said this was **propaganda**; he said **literary merit** should be the main factor in judging literature.

5. **The influence of the Anglo-Irish literary revival:**
   - It produced a rich body of **modern Irish literature in English**.

> **key point**
>
> IRISH-IRELAND MOVEMENT:
> A movement to restore or revive all things Irish or Gaelic.

- It was part of the **Irish-Ireland movement**, like the GAA and the Gaelic League.
- But the **movement declined** in the first decade of the twentieth century because of problems about premises and actors; the conflict between the nationalists' view of Ireland and the writers' view of Ireland; the death of Synge in 1909; and Yeats' dislike of the narrow-mindedness of the Irish people.

The overall influence of Cultural Nationalism

- It shaped the view of **Irish identity** – Gaelic and Catholic.
- It influenced **political nationalism** by supporting the idea of an independent Ireland.
- It was **influenced by** the IRB; it produced many of the **leaders of the 1916 Rising**.
- It showed up the **differences** between Unionists and nationalists.
- It influenced **social life** through sport, dancing, singing and theatre.

4. Educational reforms: Schools and universities

 In this section, you should understand:
- The development of educational reforms in schools and universities

Schools

1. **National schools:** By 1900, there were 8,700 national or primary schools in Ireland, with 1.25 million pupils.

> **exam Q**
> What changes were introduced into Irish schools and universities in the late 19th and early 20th centuries and how successful were they?

2. Most national schools in Ireland were controlled by either the Catholic Church or the Protestant churches. This was **denominational education**.
3. The **curriculum** was laid down by the **National Board of Education** in Dublin. It was based on the **3Rs** – reading, writing and arithmetic.
4. Most children left school at the end of national school. By that time the majority of them could **read and write**.
5. Many **teachers** in Catholic-run national schools were untrained, because of a dispute between the Catholic Church and the government over who should control the training. This was settled when the government provided money for Catholic-controlled **training colleges**.
6. **Secondary schools:** Very few young people attended secondary school. They were mostly from the **better-off families** who could afford to pay school fees and who wanted their sons to become lawyers or doctors, or get jobs in the government service.
7. The government refused to give money to denominational secondary schools. But the Catholic Church campaigned for state aid.

8. A new system was brought in under the **Intermediate Education Act, 1878.**
   - Examinations were organised by the Intermediate Board.
   - There was payment by results to the schools.
   - This was an **indirect way** of supporting denominational secondary schools.
9. Most Catholic secondary schools were run by **priests, brothers or nuns**, such as the Christian Brothers or the Sisters of Mercy.
10. As a result of the Intermediate Education Act, **more girls** went to secondary school. But boys and girls were educated in **separate** schools.
11. Some people criticised the system of **payment by results**.
    - Pádraig Pearse called it the '**murder machine**', because it encouraged learning for exams and killed a spirit of enquiry.
    - But **others said** it provided **more money** for education for boys and girls.
    - It provided a **better system** of education in Ireland than existed before.

Universities

1. The numbers going to university were **very small**.
2. In 1870 the universities were **Trinity College, Dublin**, and the **Queen's University**, with colleges at **Cork, Galway** and **Belfast**. Maynooth College was used for training Catholic priests.
3. Since the Queen's colleges did not teach religion, the Catholic Church called them '**the godless colleges**'. Catholics were banned from attending them and this limited the numbers going to university.
4. The Catholic Church set up the **Catholic University**.
5. In 1878, the **Royal University Act** brought in **payment by results**.
   - This Act set up the Royal University, which was an **examining body**. It awarded **degrees** and also **scholarships** to students.
   - Students from any college, including the Catholic University, could sit their exams.
   - In this way the government provided money for the universities.
6. **Women:** Trinity College and the Catholic University did not allow men and women to sit in the same lecture. But university education for **women** expanded when:
   - The Queen's Colleges in **Cork, Galway** and **Belfast allowed women to attend**.
   - **University classes** were provided as an extension of secondary schools. Initially this was mainly done in Protestant girls' secondary schools.
   - Women could sit the exams for the Royal University.
7. Most of the women availing themselves of university education were Protestant. This forced Catholic schools to provide university classes for Catholic women, who could also sit the exams for the Royal University.
8. In the early twentieth century **Trinity College** and the **Catholic University** finally allowed women to attend.
9. **The Irish Universities Act** was passed in 1908.

- The universities were then Trinity College, the separate Queen's University in Belfast, and the National University of Ireland with colleges in Dublin, Cork and Galway.

10. The **reforms** at university level resulted in a small expansion in the number of men attending, but a large expansion in the number of women.

11. **Overall, the reforms in education resulted in:**
   - an increase in **literacy**
   - an increase in the numbers going to secondary schools and universities
   - a more **educated workforce**
   - an expansion of education for **girls and women**
   - a **largely denominational structure** of education from national school through to university.

5. The consolidation of Catholic identity

In this section, you should understand:
- How Catholic identity was consolidated between 1870 and 1914

1. In the second half of the nineteenth century the **influence** of the Catholic Church in Ireland grew significantly.
   - About **80 per cent** of the population was Catholic. In Munster and Connacht, the figure was over 90 per cent.
   - The Catholic Church was **reorganised** under **Cardinal Paul Cullen**; he strengthened the power and influence of the Pope and bishops over the Church.
   - The number of priests, brothers and nuns almost **trebled** between 1870 and 1900; the **ratio** of religious to people grew because the population declined. Their influence in their communities was greater – they provided leadership in politics (Home Rule) and sport (GAA).
   - There was a huge increase in the number of **churches** built – they were symbols of Catholic identity and power.
   - The **power of the Protestants** declined. The Church of Ireland was **disestablished** (it lost government support) in 1869. **Landlords**, who were mainly Protestant, lost their influence through the Land Acts, the Secret Ballot Act and the Local Government Act.
   - The **decline in the Irish language** meant that Irish people used the Catholic religion as a means to differentiate themselves from the British.
   - **Nationalists and Unionists:** In spite of some Protestant leaders such as Butt and Parnell, Home Rule became increasingly associated with Catholicism, and Unionism with Protestantism.
   - Catholics (as well as Protestants) controlled their own primary, secondary and university education.

- The Catholic Church issued the *Ne Temere* decree on marriages in 1908. It held that children raised in mixed marriages (Catholic and Protestant) had to be brought up as Catholics.
- The **cultural revival** became more associated with Catholics, as GAA matches were played on Sundays and the Gaelic League favoured an independent Ireland.

2. Many nationalist leaders stated that Irishness included Catholic and Protestant – that all people living in Ireland were Irish. This was **rejected** by others, who said that to be Irish was to be Catholic.

3. **D.P. Moran** put forward this idea in his weekly newspaper *The Leader*, and in his book *The Philosophy of Irish Ireland*.
   - He said that the **Irish language** and the **Catholic religion** were the signs of Irishness.
   - He said that the Irish language was the **protector** of Catholicism from the evils coming into Ireland through the English language. He looked on this as a **battle of two civilisations**.
   - Moran attacked the **literary revival**, because its best-known promoters were Protestant.

4. Moran's ideas appealed to **middle-class Catholics** who resented Protestant control of the best jobs in the country, whether in the professions or in government.

6. Industrial development in Belfast: The shipyards

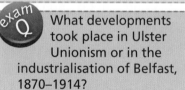
aims In this section, you should understand:
- How the shipyards contributed to the industrial development in Belfast

1. Industry in Ireland in the nineteenth century was confined largely to the **north-east** of the country, around Belfast. The rest of the country depended on agriculture or on industries processing agricultural produce.

exam Q What developments took place in Ulster Unionism or in the industrialisation of Belfast, 1870–1914?

2. Industrial development in **Belfast** was mainly concentrated on **textiles** and **shipbuilding**.
   - The linen industry was centred on Belfast, but shirt making was also carried on in Derry.

key point

3. Shipbuilding in Belfast was successful because of:
   - the **dredging** of Belfast Lough, which deepened the channel and created Queen's Island
   - the need for **local ships** for trade
   - British supplies of **coal and iron**

SOCIALISM:
The political belief that the ownership and control of factories, businesses and land should be in the hands of the government.

- the **British market** for ships
- the work of **Harland and Wolff**, which developed the latest ship-making technology.

4. Harland and Wolff
   - **Edward Harland** was an English-born engineer who took over a shipyard in Belfast in 1852. He was an outstanding engineer; he introduced a number of **improvements** by replacing the wooden upper decks with iron ones, which increased the strength of the ships; he also gave the hulls a flatter bottom and squarer section, which increased their capacity.
   - **Gustav Wolff** had links to the Liverpool shipping companies that bought Harland and Wolff ships.

5. Harland and Wolff built ships for the **White Star Line** and other big shipping companies. They included the *Oceanic*, the *Olympic* and the *Titanic*.
   - These were **large, ocean-going liners** that were faster and more luxurious than anything that had gone before them.
   - They benefited from, and contributed to, the huge growth in **migration** to the US in the second half of the nineteenth century.

6. Harland's work was carried on by **William Pirie**.

7. By 1914 Harland and Wolff employed 14,000 workers. Another 3,000 were employed at **Workman and Clark**, also shipbuilders.
   - The shipyard covered 300 acres of Queen's Island.
   - The workmen were **highly skilled and well paid**. They included welders, riveters, fitters, plumbers and carpenters.
   - Shipbuilding encouraged a number of **spin-off industries**, such as engineering and rope making. By the beginning of the twentieth century, Belfast had the world's largest shipbuilding yard, spinning mill, rope works and tobacco factory.

8. **Results:**
   - Owing to industrial development, **Belfast grew faster** than any other Irish city at the time; its population rose from 25,000 in 1808 to 350,000 in 1901.
   - The **workers** were housed in good-quality houses.
   - There was often **sectarian conflict** between Protestants and Catholics; Protestants dominated the shipyards and confined Catholics to the poorer-paid dockyard jobs.
   - This conflict between Protestants and Catholics became a conflict between **Unionists** and **Home Rulers** after 1885. The success of industry in Belfast and the fear that a Home Rule government would introduce tariffs was an important reason for Unionist support for union with Britain.

7. Unionisation of the working classes: The growth of trade unions

aims In this section, you should understand:
- How workers were unionised, especially in Belfast and Dublin
- The role of James Larkin (Key personality, p. 61)
- The role of James Connolly (Key personality, p. 63)
- Case study: Dublin 1913 – Strike and Lockout

1. **Working conditions** were difficult in Belfast, especially in the textile industry; it was very difficult to organise unskilled women workers. However, skilled workers had **craft unions** to protect them.

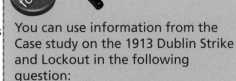

exam focus

You can use information from the Case study on the 1913 Dublin Strike and Lockout in the following question:

What were the problems facing Ireland's urban poor and what attempts were made to solve them in the period up to 1914?

2. The main growth in trade unions in Ireland occurred not in Belfast, but in Dublin.

3. There was a **large gap** between rich and poor in Dublin. Many Dublin workers depended on **casual labour** – they were unskilled, worked for low wages and were hired on a **daily basis**. Unskilled workers were not represented by trade unions.

exam Q

What contributions did James Larkin and James Connolly make to the unionisation of the working classes in Ireland up to 1914?

4. These workers lived in **poor conditions** – often in **tenements** three or four storeys high, with just one room per family.

5. **James Larkin** and **James Connolly** were very much involved in trying to unionise the unskilled workers.

6. **Larkin** was born in Liverpool. He became a union organiser in Belfast for the **National Union of Dock Labourers**. Here he organised strikes and used the **sympathetic strike** as a weapon – he brought out on strike other workers in sympathy with those initially on strike.

7. Larkin was transferred to Dublin. Here he set up his own union – the **Irish Transport and General Workers' Union** (ITGWU). This combined **skilled and unskilled workers**.
   - It had 10,000 members within a short time.
   - It also spread to Cork and Limerick.
   - It organised successful strikes for carters and railway workers.

8. **Connolly** was born in Scotland, but after working as a soldier and a carter, he was given the job of union organiser for the ITGWU in Belfast. He organised a dockers' strike in Belfast in 1911, and he improved working conditions for women workers in textile factories.

9. Larkin and Connolly founded the **Irish Labour Party** to represent workers when the new Home Rule Bill became law.

10. **Employers** were frightened by the success of Larkin's ITGWU. **The Dublin Employers' Federation** was led by **William Martin Murphy**. He was a very successful businessman and owned a newspaper, *The Irish Independent*. He was very much **opposed** to the growth of trade unions.

11. The employers **shut out** all workers when some went on strike during Horse Show Week in 1913. This became the **Dublin Strike and Lockout**. It led to the defeat of Larkin and the union, and weakened the ITGWU temporarily.

Case study: Dublin, 1913 – Strike and Lockout

 exam Q To what extent was the 1913 Dublin Strike and Lockout a success or a failure?

1. Many Dublin families lived in **slum conditions**; there was overcrowding and bad sanitation. Families rented single rooms in tenement blocks or in run-down houses.

2. Many workers found work only as **casual labourers** – they were taken on one day at a time in unskilled jobs. They were badly paid – less than £1 a week.

3. James Larkin founded the **Irish Transport and General Workers' Union** (ITGWU) to organise skilled and unskilled workers.

4. Larkin led a series of successful strikes. He depended on the **sympathetic strike** for some of his success – when workers who were not on strike refused to handle goods coming from a company which locked out workers or had workers on strike.

5. The success of Larkin's strikes led to the formation of the **Dublin Employers' Federation**, led by **William Martin Murphy**.
   - Murphy was the wealthy owner of *The Irish Independent* newspaper, a department store, hotels and the Dublin Tramway Company.

6. Larkin **organised** some Tramway workers in his union, the ITGWU. Murphy fired them and refused to allow union workers in his company.

7. Larkin organised a **strike** in the Tramway Company during **Horse Show Week** in August 1913.
   - Murphy was able to keep the trams running because only a third of the workers went on strike.

8. There were **street riots and clashes with the police** when Larkin was arrested after speaking from the **Imperial Hotel** window in Sackville Street (now O'Connell Street) in August 1913. There were riots in different parts of the city and the police often used excessive violence.

9. Employers **locked out** their workers. Employers demanded that workers sign a **pledge** to resign from the ITGWU and not to join the union. By September, 25,000 were out of work.

10. Help in the form of food, clothing and money came from Britain.

11. Larkin clashed with the **Catholic Church** over sending **children to England** to be looked after during the lockout.
   - The Catholic Church and the archbishop of Dublin, William Walsh, feared **socialism** and the **children's conversion to Protestantism**.
12. Larkin criticised the British Labour Party for not supporting the Irish workers with a sympathetic strike in England.
13. The government appointed the **Askwith Commission** to enquire into the Strike and Lockout.
14. Eventually the workers went back to work; the employers had won.
   - The intelligentsia and extreme nationalists backed the workers.
15. **Results:**
   - During the strike, the **Irish Citizen Army** was founded by James Connolly to protect the workers. Connolly then moved more towards nationalism, and eventually took part in the 1916 Rising.
   - The ITGWU declined in popularity; Larkin went to the US until 1923.
   - The employers quietly allowed workers to join the ITGWU later.

8. Unionism and the Ulster Question, 1870–1914

aims In this section, you should understand:
   - Developments in Unionism and the Ulster Question between 1870 and 1914
   - The role of Edward Carson (Key personality, p. 64)
   - Case study: The Elections of 1885 and 1886: Issues and Outcomes (see pp. 18–20)

Reasons for unionist opposition to Home Rule

1. **Economic**
   - Ulster, particularly **Belfast**, had prospered **industrially** under the Union much more than the rest of Ireland (shipping and linen – markets in Britain). The Union with Britain was seen as one of the **bases of this prosperity**.

exam Q How and why did unionists oppose Home Rule between 1885 and 1914?

2. **Religious**
   - Protestants feared that an Irish parliament would be **Catholic-dominated** and that their religious freedom would be in danger – that Home Rule would be 'Rome rule'. The Home Rule movement was mainly Catholic.
   - In Ulster there was an old tradition of sectarian rivalry between Catholics and Protestants.

3. **Political**
   - Protestants, particularly in Ulster, had many links with Britain. They were **loyal** to the Queen and to the Crown.
4. The **Secret Ballot Act** of 1872 and the **1884 Reform Act** reduced the political power of the Protestants and they felt increasingly threatened. Protestants would be in a **minority** in a Home Rule Ireland.
   - **Unionists were divided into Ulster Unionists and Southern Unionists:** Ulster Unionists came from **all classes**, from working class to landlords and businessmen. They were a **majority** in some counties in Ulster. Southern Unionists were mainly landlords and businessmen. They were a **small minority**, but they had close links with the Conservative Party in England.

Approach to the First Home Rule Bill, 1885–86

1. As Home Rule became more of a possibility, **Protestants became more and more agitated**.
   - In 1885 the **Irish Loyal and Patriotic Union** was set up to fight Home Rule.
   - In the 1885 election **2 Unionist MPs** were elected, both for the Trinity College, Dublin constituency, while **16 other Unionist MPs** were elected in Ulster.
   - In Ulster the **Orange Order** was revived; the Order was used to **unite Protestants of all classes** in opposition to Home Rule.
   - The **Ulster Loyalist Anti-Repeal Union** was founded in January 1886.
2. The **Conservative Party in England** decided to take advantage of the situation in Ireland. The Party said Home Rule for Ireland was the first step in the destruction of the Empire; it decided that '**The Orange card would be the one to play**' (Lord Randolph Churchill).
   - **With the defeat of the Home Rule Bill in 1886, the danger of Home Rule lessened.**
   - The Unionist MPs formed the **Irish Unionist Party**, led by **Edward Saunderson** (MP for Armagh).
   - An **alliance** was formed between the **Unionists** and **the Conservative Party in England**.

Between the First and Second Home Rule Bills: 1886–93

1. Since the Conservatives were in power there was no immediate danger of Home Rule.
2. When Home Rule became a possibility after the success of the Liberals in the 1892 election, **Edward Saunderson** (MP for North Armagh) set up the **Ulster Defence Union**, which collected money and made preparations to resist Home Rule.
   - **The Second Home Rule Bill passed the House of Commons, but it was defeated in the House of Lords.**

The Conservatives in power, 1896–1906

1. Unionists had the **support of the House of Lords** and no Home Rule Bill would be passed without its consent.
2. In 1904–5 Unionists stopped the **Devolution plan** for Ireland, brought in by the Conservative government.
3. The **Ulster Unionist Council** was founded in 1905 to coordinate the efforts of various Unionist organisations.
4. In December 1905 the **Liberals** came back to power, and **Home Rule was a possibility again**.

Unionism and Home Rule, 1906–12

1. The **new Liberal government in 1906** had a large overall majority and did not need the support of the Home Rule Party. They did not consider Home Rule an urgent matter.
   - But **Augustine Birrell**, the chief secretary, brought in a **Council bill** which was similar to the devolution plan of the Conservative government.
   - **Redmond** opposed the bill and it was **dropped**.
2. The bill kept Unionist opposition to Home Rule active.
   - The **Ulster Unionist Council** and the southern **Irish Unionist Alliance** influenced **public opinion** in Ireland and Britain against Home Rule.
3. Before the 1910 election, **Asquith** (Liberal prime minister) stated that Home Rule was the only possible solution to the **Irish Question**. This was in return for **Home Rule support** for his party.
4. After the 1910 election Redmond and the Irish Party held the **balance of power** at Westminster. In 1911 the **Parliament Act** deprived the House of Lords of its **veto** to stop Home Rule.
5. **The Unionists were now worried**.

Unionist resistance

1. Unionist resistance was led by **Edward Carson** and **James Craig**.
   - **Carson** was a Southern Unionist; he was an able speaker.
   - **Craig** was an Ulster businessman; he was the main organiser.

> exam Q
> In the period up to 1914, who was the more effective leader, John Redmond or Edward Carson? Argue your case, referring to both leaders.

2. In September 1911 **Carson** told a meeting in Belfast that Unionists should **set up their own government** to take over when Home Rule became law. The Ulster Unionist Council drafted a **constitution** and prepared for self-government.
3. Orangemen began to **drill and arm**. This was **legal** because any two Justices of the Peace could **authorise drilling**, provided that it was for the defence of the constitution of the United Kingdom.

4. In 1912, 400,000 Unionist men signed the **Ulster Solemn League and Covenant**. This was a **pledge** to fight Home Rule **'by all means which may be found necessary'**.

5. The Unionists were supported by **Andrew Bonar Law**, the Conservative Party leader, who said, 'I can imagine no length of resistance to which Ulster will go which I shall not be ready to support.'

6. In 1913 the Ulster Unionist Council founded the **Ulster Volunteer Force**; Sir George Richardson, a retired general, was appointed commander; he created a well-trained army, but the UVF needed arms.

7. **Larne gunrunning**; Craig and Carson decided **to import arms**.
   - Arms were bought in Germany.
   - In April 1914, thousands of rifles and millions of rounds of ammunition were landed **at Larne, Bangor and Donaghadee**.
   - The arms were distributed all over the North.

8. **The Curragh Mutiny** helped Unionists.
   - The government wanted to enforce Home Rule in north-east Ulster.
   - **Officers in the British Army** in the Curragh were asked to serve.
   - The officers said that they would **resign** rather than go against the Unionists.
   - The government had to back down.

Attempts at compromise, 1912–14

1. Attempts were made to achieve a **compromise** between Unionists and Home Rulers.
   - The solutions which were proposed were based on excluding **all or part** of Ulster, **permanently or temporarily**, from Home Rule.

2. **Redmond and the Home Rule party** would not accept **partition** (a division in the country), because there were many nationalists in Ulster.
   - Redmond was prepared to accept **'Home Rule within Home Rule'** for Ulster, which could have its own parliament **under the control** of the Dublin parliament.
   - The Unionists would not agree to that.

3. **Edward Carson** did not favour partition.
   - **Craig and many Ulster Unionists** were prepared to accept partition because they were **not concerned** about Unionists in Southern Ireland.

4. **Buckingham Palace conference:** King George V called a **conference** of Unionists, Home Rulers and British government officials at **Buckingham Palace** in July 1914.
   - The conference broke up **without agreement**.

5. Ireland seemed to be on the **verge of civil war**. The crisis was postponed by the **First World War**, which began in August 1914.

6. On 18 September 1914 **the Home Rule Bill became law**. The Unionists agreed to it provided it did not operate until after the war was over and the **Ulster Question** would be decided then.

9. Redmond and Home Rule, 1891–1914

 In this section, you should understand:
- Developments in the Home Rule movement from 1891 to 1914
- The leadership of John Redmond (Key personality, p. 56)

1. After the Parnell split, the **Irish Parliamentary Party** was disunited and weak. The party was divided between **Parnellites and anti-Parnellites**.

 How successful was John Redmond as leader of the Home Rule party from 1891 to 1914?

- The **Parnellites** were led by **John Redmond**. They gained only 9 seats in the 1892 general election.
- The **anti-Parnellites** were led by **Justin McCarthy**. They won 72 seats in the general election. They were tied to the Liberal alliance.

 HOME RULE:
The belief that Ireland should have a parliament in Dublin to rule internal Irish affairs, and a parliament in Westminster to rule external affairs.

2. When McCarthy retired as leader there was a **leadership struggle** between **John Dillon** and **Timothy Healy**, which Dillon won. Healy led his own small breakaway group.

3. **Gladstone** introduced the **Second Home Rule Bill** in 1893. It passed the House of Commons but was defeated in the House of Lords.

 SEPARATISM:
The political belief that Ireland should have complete independence from Britain.

- The **Conservatives** returned to power after this.

4. William O'Brien set up the **United Irish League** in 1898. It began to take support from both Parnellites and anti-Parnellites.

5. In 1900 the Irish Party was **reunited** under **John Redmond**; but the party was still **weak**.

- Redmond was a good leader in the House of Commons, but he lacked popular appeal.
- The **Conservatives** were in power until 1906.
- The Liberals had a **large majority** after they won the **1906 general election**, so they did not need Irish Party support between 1906 and 1910.

6. The Liberals introduced the **Irish Council Bill** in 1907. It provided little more than local government powers for Ireland. Redmond rejected it.

7. **The Third Home Rule Bill and the Home Rule crisis, 1912–14**

- After the 1910 general election Irish Party support was needed by the Liberals to form a government.

- The Liberals passed the **Parliament Act,** 1911. This limited the power of the House of Lords – now the Lords could delay bills for two years only.
- The Liberal government introduced the **Third Home Rule Bill**, 1912. It would become law in two years. The Irish Party seemed to be near success.

8. But **Unionist resistance** weakened the British government, which attempted to find a **compromise**.

9. The rise of the Irish Volunteers in the South threatened the Irish Party. The Volunteers were taken over by the Irish party, but they **split** over the First World War.

- **Most Volunteers** (about 170,000) followed Redmond, who said Irishmen should go wherever the fighting was.
- A **minority** (10,000) said they would defend Ireland only at home.

10. The Irish Volunteers

aims In this section, you should understand:
- How and why the Irish Volunteers developed

key point

1. **Eoin McNeill** wrote an article, '**The North Began**', in *An Claideamh Soluis*. He said that Irish nationalists should follow the example of Ulster unionists and form their own organisation to defend Home Rule.

MILITARISM: Glorification of military methods.

2. The **Irish Republican Brotherhood (IRB)** encouraged McNeill to hold a meeting at the **Rotunda**, in Dublin in November 1913, to form the **Irish National Volunteers**. Very soon the Volunteers had over 75,000 members.

3. **Cumann na mBan** was later set up as a women's auxiliary force.

4. The popularity of the Irish Volunteers threatened the position of the **Irish (Home Rule) Party**. Redmond forced members of the Home Rule Party onto the Volunteers' Committee and took it over.

5. The success of the Ulster Volunteers in importing arms encouraged the Irish Volunteers to import arms aboard the sailing ship *Asgard* in **Howth** in 1914.

6. Now two armed forces faced each other. It looked as if there would be **civil war** in Ireland if the Home Rule Bill became law.

7. The crisis was stopped by the **beginning of the First World War**. It led to a **split** in the Irish Volunteers.

8. John Redmond said that the war was an **opportunity** for Home Rulers to show their loyalty to the British Empire. He said that they should join the British Army and fight wherever they were needed.

9. A **large majority** of the Volunteers supported Redmond. They became known as the **National Volunteers**. A **small minority** – about 10,000 – did not support his view.

They continued under the name of the Irish Volunteers. They were largely under the **control of the IRB**, who now made plans to use them for a **rebellion** against Britain during the First World War.

11. The first Sinn Féin party

 In this section, you should understand:

- The formation, policies and development of the first Sinn Féin party

1. **Arthur Griffith** founded and edited a weekly newspaper, *The United Irishman*. He wanted to promote the Irish language, literature and history.

2. He founded **Cumann na nGaedheal** in 1900, with representatives from various clubs and societies, to support the Irish cultural revival and to encourage Irish industry.

3. Griffith was a **republican** – but he did not think people would support a republic then or a rebellion to achieve it. He proposed an alternative idea.

4. Griffith published *The Resurrection of Hungary* in 1904, which referred to Hungary's experience of gaining a separate government within the Austrian Empire.

   - In it he proposed the idea of a **dual monarchy** for Ireland and Britain; Ireland and Britain would have separate parliaments but the same king or queen.
   - He said the dual monarchy would be achieved by **parliamentary abstention** – Irish MPs would not take their seats in Westminster, but would set up a separate parliament (**Council of Three Hundred**) in Dublin.
   - Griffith's policy is also called **passive resistance**.
   - He also advocated **protectionism** (tariffs on imports) to help the growth of Irish industry.

5. These became the **policies** of **Sinn Féin** (Ourselves Alone), which he founded in 1905.

6. Sinn Féin made **progress** over the next few years.

   - By 1908, Sinn Féin had **100 branches**.
   - It also allowed **women** as full members.
   - The party won seats in the **local elections**.
   - **C.J. Dolan**, a former Home Rule MP, stood for election as a Sinn Féin candidate in a by-election in **North Leitrim**. He failed to get elected but he received about one-third of the votes.

7. By 1910, though, Sinn Féin was in **decline**.

   - **Griffith** was not an easy man to get on with.
   - His newspaper, now called *Sinn Féin*, was in **financial trouble** and he was almost bankrupt.
   - The Home Rule Party achieved the balance of power in the House of Commons, so **Home Rule now seemed likely**.

8. But the Sinn Féin name was used to describe all forms of extreme nationalism. In 1916 the British government mistakenly named the Easter Rising the 'Sinn Féin

Rising'. This contributed to the formation of a revived, second Sinn Féin which was different from the first.

12. The suffrage movement

aims In this section, you should understand:

- How the suffragette movement developed
- The role of Isabella Tod (Key personality, p. 66)
- The role of Hanna Sheehy-Skeffington (Key personality, p. 67)

exam Q
- What contribution did Isabella Tod and Hanna Sheehy-Skeffington make to the suffragette movement in Ireland?
- What factors influenced the development of the suffragette movement in Ireland up to 1914?

1. Women **could not vote** in either parliamentary or local elections in Ireland in 1870. The demand for votes for women (the suffrage movement) became stronger in the late nineteenth and early twentieth centuries.

- Women were **better educated**.
- There were **more employment opportunities** for women.
- Some campaigners worked for women's rights in many areas, such as **property and education**.
- Women believed that the best way to achieve these rights was to first get the **right to vote**.
- The demand for votes for women (the **suffrage** or **franchise**) in **Britain** set an example for Ireland.

key point

SUFFRAGETTE:
A woman who campaigned for the vote (or franchise) for women.

key point

FEMINISM:
Advocates the equal treatment of women in all aspects of life.

2. The early campaigners for votes for women were **middle-class Protestants**. Two of the first were **Isabella Tod** and **Anna Haslam**.
   - Tod founded the **Northern Ireland Society for Women's Suffrage** in Belfast in 1871. Five years later, Haslam founded the **Dublin Women's Suffrage Association**.
   - They demanded votes for women in parliamentary elections and in local elections.
   - They campaigned largely through **pamphlets, meetings** and **petitions** to Parliament.

3. The **Local Government Act, 1898**, gave the right to vote for local councils to women ratepayers.

4. Haslam founded the **Irish Women's Suffrage and Local Government Association**. It campaigned to get women elected to local councils. About 35 women were elected.

5. Other women who campaigned for women's votes at this time were **Jennie Wyse Power** and **Hanna Sheehy-Skeffington**.

6. Sheehy-Skeffington (along with **Margaret Cousins**) set up the **Irish Women's Franchise League** in 1908. She was not happy with the work done by other associations.

- The IWFL was **more militant**, following the pattern of the **Pankhursts in Britain**; it smashed windows in government buildings.
- Some leaders were arrested and jailed; they went on **hunger strike**. They were **not force-fed**. Women called off the hunger strike when they gained **political status**.
- The IWFL also published a newspaper, *The Irish Citizen*.

7. Some women wanted the vote to be included in the **Home Rule Bill**. This was opposed by the leaders of the Home Rule Party – **Redmond and Dillon** – who feared it would lead to the failure of Home Rule.

- **Others believed** that women **should not get the vote** because they were too excitable, they had no interest in political matters and they should concentrate on caring for their families.

8. Home Rulers were angered when **Redmond** became the accidental target of an attack by **English suffragettes** on Asquith, the British prime minister, when he visited Dublin.

9. **Divisions** occurred in the suffrage movement:

- As tensions rose during the Home Rule Crisis, 1912–14, some women followed **nationalist and unionist politics** rather than the franchise (vote).
- Women were also divided by **support for and against the war** when the First World War began.

10. Women over 30 won the right to vote in parliamentary elections in 1918 after the war was over.

Key personalities

Charles Stewart Parnell

1. **Charles Stewart Parnell** was the son of a **Protestant landlord**. He developed an **anti-English attitude** from his mother and while he was at university in Cambridge.
2. He was elected **Home Rule MP for Meath**.
3. Parnell joined **the Obstructionists** in the House of Commons. Obstructionism earned him a great deal of **popularity** in Ireland; he won Fenian support.
4. Parnell said the **Manchester Martyrs** (Fenians) were not murderers.
5. Parnell was elected **leader** of the **Home Rule Confederation of Great Britain**, which was Fenian-dominated.

6. When the leader of the Home Rule Party, **Isaac Butt**, died suddenly in 1879, Parnell did not have enough support, so Butt was succeeded as leader by **William Shaw**.

7. Over the next year Parnell built up his popularity and became leader in 1880.

8. Parnell was committed to the **New Departure** on the Land Question with **Davitt** and **Devoy**.

9. He joined the Land campaign as **president of the Land League**.

10. He had **natural leadership qualities**; he was ambitious.
    - Parnell gained the support of **Clan na nGael (Fenians) in America** when he visited there.
    - He also gained the support of the Catholic Church, especially **Archbishop Croke** of Cashel; Parnell supported **state aid** for Catholic schools (denominational education).
    - In the **general election** of March 1880, an increased number of **Parnellites** (Parnell's supporters) were elected.

11. After the general election, Parnell was elected **leader of the Home Rule Party** (1880).

12. In 1880 and 1881, Parnell worked for the Land Question.

13. **Gladstone**, the British prime minister, passed the **1881 Land Act**. The Act posed **a dilemma** for Parnell – should he support it or not?

14. When Parnell criticised Gladstone he was jailed in **Kilmainham Jail**.

15. Parnell agreed the **Kilmainham Treaty** with Gladstone (1882); he felt the Land Question had been **solved**.
    - Parnell now began to concentrate on Home Rule.

16. **The Phoenix Park murders:** When he heard about the Phoenix Park murders, Parnell first wanted to resign as leader of the Home Rule Party – but he was persuaded not to do so. This gave Parnell an excuse to **change his aims from Land to Home Rule**.

17. Parnell set up the **Irish National League** (1882) in order to:
    - establish Home Rule
    - work for land purchase.

18. In the Irish National League, he was in **complete control**.

19. Over the next few years, Parnell built up the **Irish Party** (or the Home Rule Party) into a **highly disciplined political party**.

20. **Parnell, Chamberlain and the Central Board Scheme**
    - Parnell disagreed with Joseph Chamberlain over Chamberlain's Central Board Scheme for Ireland.
    - Parnell thought the Central Board Scheme was **a lead up to Home Rule**, not a replacement for it. But Chamberlain meant it as a **replacement**.

- When Parnell eventually **rejected** it, Chamberlain was **bitterly disappointed**; this led to later conflict between them.

21. **The 1885 general election**

    - Parnell wanted to force the Conservatives or the Liberals to grant Home Rule to Ireland. Parnell **supported the Conservatives** in the general election to achieve a **balance of power**.

    - After the election, **Gladstone and the Liberals** needed Parnell and his party to form a government.

22. **Gladstone** was converted to Home Rule and brought in the **First Home Rule Bill,** 1886, but it was defeated.

23. **Parnell and the Plan of Campaign:** Parnell did not favour the Plan of Campaign. He feared that a new land war would upset English Liberals.

24. **Parnellism and crime:** The London *Times* published articles on '**Parnellism and Crime**', which included letters showing that Parnell knew about and supported the Phoenix Park murders. These articles **endangered** the Liberal Alliance. Parnell denied the articles; Richard Piggott, an Irish journalist, confessed to forging the letters.

25. This was a **triumph** for Parnell. He was called the '**Uncrowned King of Ireland**'.

26. **O'Shea divorce case and the downfall of Parnell**

    - In December 1889 **Captain William O'Shea** filed for divorce against his wife, **Katherine**. He named Parnell as co-respondent.

    - Parnell's affair with Katherine O'Shea had lasted since 1880.

27. Parnell **refused** to stand down as leader of the Home Rule Party. This led to a **split**, where the majority were against Parnell.

28. In fighting by-elections in Ireland, Parnell caught **pneumonia** and died in England. His **funeral** in Dublin was attended by 200,000 people. **GAA members** provided a guard of honour with hurleys.

29. **The achievements of Parnell:**

    - He became **leader** of the Home Rule Party.

    - He **united** extremists and moderates in the Land League to achieve its aims (the 3Fs).

    - He created **a united and modern political party** – the Home Rule Party.

    - He persuaded a **major British political party** – the Liberals – to support Home Rule.

John Redmond

1. John Redmond was born in **Co. Wexford** in 1856. He was educated in Clongowes Wood and at Trinity College, Dublin. He became a **barrister**.

2. He was elected **Home Rule MP** for New Ross in 1880. He represented New Ross, later North Wexford, and finally he was MP for **Waterford City** from 1891 until his death in 1918.

3. When the Irish Parliamentary Party (Home Rule Party) split over the O'Shea divorce case, Redmond **sided** with Parnell. He led the **Parnellites** after Parnell's death in 1891. They gained only 9 seats in the 1892 general election and remained weak during the 1890s.

4. In 1900, the Irish Party was **reunited** under **John Redmond**, but the Party was still **weak**.

5. Redmond was a good leader in the House of Commons, but he lacked popular appeal.

6. Redmond opposed the **Irish Council Bill**, 1907, brought in by the Liberal government, because it gave very limited power to Ireland and did not give full Home Rule.

7. As a result of the 1910 general election, Redmond and the Irish Party held the **balance of power** in Westminster. With the passage of the **Parliament Act 1911**, Home Rule became likely. In 1912, the **Third Home Rule Bill** was introduced.

8. But **Unionist resistance** weakened the British government, which attempted to find a **compromise**.

9. **Redmond and the Home Rule Party** would not accept **partition** (the division of the island of Ireland), because there were many nationalists in Ulster.

10. Redmond was prepared to accept '**Home Rule within Home Rule**' for Ulster, which could have its own parliament **under the control** of the Dublin parliament.

11. The Unionists would not agree to that.

12. Redmond agreed to the **temporary exclusion** of Ulster from Home Rule, but this was rejected by the Unionists.

13. Redmond and John Dillon represented the Home Rulers at the **Buckingham Palace conference** called by King George V in July 1914.

14. The conference broke up **without agreement**.

15. Ireland seemed to be on **the verge of civil war**.

16. The crisis was stopped by the **beginning of the First World War**. The Home Rule Bill became law, but the Act was suspended until after the war.

17. At the same time, the rise of the **Irish Volunteers** in the South threatened the popularity of the Irish Party. Redmond forced members of the Home Rule Party onto the Volunteers' Committee and took it over.

18. The issue of the First World War led to a **split** in the Irish Volunteers.

19. In a speech at **Woodenbridge, Co. Wicklow**, Redmond said that the war was an **opportunity** for Home Rulers to show their loyalty to the British Empire. He said that they should join the British Army and fight wherever they were needed. This would guarantee Home Rule after the war. Redmond believed that **Germany** threatened the freedom of peace-loving people in Europe and that it was Ireland's duty to defend the freedom of 'small nations'.

20. A **large majority** of the Volunteers supported Redmond. They became known as the **National Volunteers.**

21. But during the war Redmond disagreed with the way the **British War Office** treated Irish soldiers, that is, by **refusing** to allow a separate Irish brigade with its own officers.

22. Redmond died in 1918 as the Home Rule Party was in decline after the 1916 Rising.

Michael Davitt

1. **Michael Davitt** was born in Straide, Co. Mayo. His family were evicted from their farm in 1852. They went to England and Michael **lost his right arm in an accident** in a cotton factory. He was **self-educated**. He joined the **Fenians** and was **jailed** in 1870. He was released on **ticket-of-leave** in 1877. He visited Mayo in 1878 and was horrified by the conditions he saw amongst the tenants.

2. **The New Departure:** Davitt went to **America** and met **John Devoy**, leader of **Clan na nGael** (the American Fenians). This led to the **New Departure** with Parnell.

   • They came together to agitate for a **solution to the land problem** in Ireland.

3. When Davitt saw the success of a meeting held at **Irishtown**, Co. Mayo, he called another meeting for **Westport** in June 1879. He invited **Parnell** to address the meeting. After this, Davitt founded the **Land League of Mayo.**

4. Davitt and Parnell founded the **Irish National Land League** in Dublin in October 1879. Parnell was **president** and Davitt was one of the **secretaries** of the Land League. Their aims were to:
   - establish fair rents for tenants and prevent evictions
   - abolish the landlord system – to bring about **tenant ownership** of the land of Ireland, or **peasant proprietorship**.

5. **Land League methods:**
   - The Land League made good use of **propaganda, demonstrations** and **boycotting**.
   - There were Land League **branches** in many places.

6. **Davitt** got the agreement of the Land League to sanction the formation of a **Ladies' Land League**. He believed that if the men were arrested, the Land Campaign could be kept going by the women.

7. Davitt was **arrested and jailed** in early 1881 for criticising the government's Coercion Act. There was uproar in Parliament and Parnell and 35 MPs were expelled; but Parnell decided to remain in Parliament.
   - Davitt was in jail in England from early 1881 to the middle of 1882.

8. During this time **Gladstone** and the Liberal government introduced the **1881 Land Act.**
   - **Davitt was critical of the Act.**

9. When Parnell and the other Land League leaders were imprisoned, Davitt supported the **No Rent Manifesto**. But he did not support Parnell's agreement with Gladstone, **the Kilmainham Treaty**, even though he was released under its terms. However, Davitt **did not criticise** the treaty publicly because of **loyalty to Parnell**.

10. **Davitt was invited to become one of the patrons of the GAA.** Davitt later supported the **Plan of Campaign**.

11. Davitt's influence in Irish politics lessened. One reason for this was his commitment to **land nationalisation**. He believed that the government should take over the land of Ireland and lease it out to the farmers. This idea was not popular.

12. He also supported the **Liberal Alliance**. In the O'Shea divorce case, Davitt sided with the **anti-Parnellites**. He said Parnell should resign as leader, because the **Liberal Alliance** was needed if Ireland was to achieve Home Rule. He was later elected as anti-Parnellite MP for **Mayo**.

13. Davitt was very strongly opposed to **social injustice.**
   - He supported improvements in the **working and living conditions** of the British working class.
   - He supported **minority peoples**, such as the Aborigines in Australia and the Boers in South Africa.
   - He supported **votes for women**.

14. Davitt wrote a number of books, including *The Fall of Feudalism in Ireland*, about the Land Campaign; and *Leaves from a Prison Diary*, about his own experiences in jail.

15. Davitt died in 1906 and was buried in his home place of Straide.

Douglas Hyde

1. Douglas Hyde was born in **Castlerea, Co. Roscommon**, where his father was the local Church of Ireland rector.

2. Hyde took a great interest in **listening** to older people in the locality speak the **Irish language**.

3. Hyde was educated in **Trinity College, Dublin**, where he qualified in law; but his main interests lay in the **Irish language, history and folklore**. Hyde also knew French, German, Latin, Greek and Hebrew.

   - Hyde became a noted **scholar** of Irish folklore.
   - He collected and translated older **Irish poems**, as well as writing his own.
   - His published books included *Beside the Fire, Love Songs of Connacht* and *A Literary History of Ireland*.

4. The **Gaelic League** was **founded** in 1893 by **Douglas Hyde and Eoin MacNeill**.

   - Hyde gave a lecture to the **National Literary Society** on 'The Necessity for De-Anglicising Ireland'. He said Ireland had lost the 'notes of nationalism': that is, its own language and culture. He said that Ireland should follow its own traditions in language, literature and even in dress.
   - MacNeill admired Hyde's ideas, so both came together to form the Gaelic League.
   - Hyde became **president** of the League.

5. They set up the Gaelic League to:

   - revive Irish as **the national language**
   - promote the study and publication of **Irish literature**
   - develop **a new literature in Irish**
   - **de-anglicise** Ireland (by getting rid of other aspects of English culture).

6. The League flourished.

   - It had **50,000 members** by 1904.
   - Hyde had a **very successful tour of America** in 1905–6, when he raised over $50,000 for the League.

- Hyde and the League made Irish a **compulsory subject** for entry into the National University.

7. Hyde was involved in other aspects of the **cultural revival:** he wrote a series of **plays in Irish**, beginning with *Casadh an tSúgain*, which were performed for the **Irish Literary Theatre**. *Casadh an tSúgain* was performed by members of the Keating Branch of the Gaelic League.

8. Hyde was appointed **professor of Modern Irish** at University College, Dublin.

9. Many of the new generation of Irish leaders, including **Patrick Pearse, Éamon de Valera** and **Michael Collins**, first became politicised about Irish independence through their involvement in the Gaelic League.

   - But **Hyde** wanted the League to be **non-political**; he hoped that it would be **a link** between Catholics and Protestants, nationalists and unionists.

10. But the **IRB (Fenian) influence** grew. At the League Congress in 1915, **Hyde resigned as president** when the League agreed to promote **Irish independence**.

W.B. Yeats

1. William Butler Yeats was born in **Dublin** to a middle-class Protestant family. His father was a portrait painter. The family moved between London, Dublin and Sligo, where Yeats lived for some of his early years and spent summer holidays with his grandparents.

2. Yeats was influenced by **Irish folklore and legends**. He was also influenced by Irish nationalists such as **John O'Leary**, an old Fenian. He also met **Standish O'Grady**, who had published *The Bardic Literature of Ireland* – a collection of myths and legends.

   - Yeats' early poetry, such as *The Wanderings of Oisin and Other Poems* (1889), shows the influences of Irish myth and folklore.

3. In 1889 Yeats met and fell in love with **Maud Gonne**; she influenced his poetry and his life. Yeats proposed to her a number of times, but she rejected him.

4. Along with others, Yeats formed the **Irish Literary Society** in London in 1891 and the **National Literary Society** in Dublin in 1892.

   - After the downfall and death of Charles Stewart Parnell in 1891, Yeats felt there was a vacuum in Irish political life that could be filled by art and literature.

5. Yeats was one of the **most important figures** of the **Anglo-Irish Literary Revival**.

6. In 1896 he met **Lady Gregory** and **Edward Martyn**; they too had an interest in Irish folktales and Celtic sagas. She encouraged Yeats' nationalism and his drama writing.

7. In 1899 Yeats, Lady Gregory and Martyn founded the **Irish Literary Theatre** to stage plays by Irish playwrights. This survived for about two years, but was not successful.

   - The first play was Yeats' *The Countess Cathleen*. Yeats wrote a play for Maud Gonne – *Cathleen Ni Houlihan* – about Ireland, which is represented by an old woman made young again when her men take up arms for her. Yeats later asked:

     Did that play of mine send out
     Certain men the English shot?

8. Yeats, Gregory and Martyn worked with the **Fay brothers**, William and Frank, and **Annie Horniman** (a wealthy Englishwoman) to establish a permanent home for the Literary Theatre. They achieved that when they bought and opened the **Abbey Theatre** in 1904. Two of Yeats' plays were featured on the opening night.

   - Yeats' plays which were staged in the Abbey Theatre included *On Baile's Strand, The Hour Glass, The King's Threshold* and *Deirdre*.

9. Yeats supported the work of **John Millington Synge**.

   - In 1907 Synge's most famous play, *The Playboy of the Western World*, led to riots. Yeats **defended** the play, but nationalists were upset. Yeats thought people were becoming **too narrow-minded**.

10. Nationalists believed that literature should be judged on its political merits; that literature should present a **favourable image** of Ireland.

    - Yeats said this was **propaganda**; he said **literary merit** should be the main factor in judging literature.

11. **D.P. Moran** criticised Yeats and the Literary Revival because of his **Protestant background**. This criticism and the conflict with nationalists over literature disappointed Yeats.

James Larkin

1. James Larkin was born in **Liverpool**. He became union organiser for the **National Union of Dock Labourers**.

2. He was sent to **Belfast** to organise the dockers there. He was then sent to Dublin, where he organised **successful strikes** among dockers, carters and labourers.

3. He founded the **Irish Transport and General Workers' Union** (ITGWU) in 1909 for unskilled and skilled workers.

   - Larkin was a tall man ('Big Jim'), who was a very able speaker and this contributed to his success.

4. Larkin was a **socialist.** He advocated:

- **nationalisation** (government ownership) of factories, mines and transport
- the land of Ireland for the people of Ireland.

5. He favoured **syndicalism – direct action** by the working class to overthrow capitalism and the state.
   - Because of this, he believed in **militant union tactics** and the use of **sympathetic strikes**.

6. Larkin, along with James Connolly, founded the **Irish Labour Party** in 1912 to represent workers when the new Home Rule Bill became law.

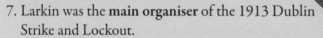

7. Larkin was the **main organiser** of the 1913 Dublin Strike and Lockout.
   - The success of his strikes in Dublin led to the formation of the Dublin Employers' Federation, led by **William Martin Murphy**.
   - Larkin and Murphy **hated** each other and the Strike and Lockout had a personal edge to it.
   - He organised his members to strike during Horse Show Week; employers locked out workers.
   - **Larkin** was arrested after speaking from the **Imperial Hotel** window in Sackville Street (now O'Connell Street) in August 1913. This caused **street riots and clashes with the police** in what became known as **Bloody Sunday**.
   - Larkin **criticised** the British Labour Party for not supporting sympathetic strikes in England.
   - He clashed with the **Catholic Church** over sending children to England to be looked after during the lockout.
   - Eventually Larkin advised the workers to go back.

8. After the Strike and Lockout, Larkin went to **America** until 1923.

9. He had laid the foundations of **union action and workers' solidarity** that others later built on.

James Connolly

1. James Connolly was born in **Edinburgh**. He served as a soldier in the British Army, and later worked as a carter and a trade union organiser.

2. He was **widely read and self-educated**, especially in politics, history and economics. He followed **Karl Marx's ideas** on how society and the economy should be organised. He became involved in **socialist politics** in Scotland.

3. He came to Dublin to work for the **Dublin Socialist Society**. There he founded the **Irish Socialist Republican Party** (IRSP).

4. He published a newspaper – *The Workers Republic* – in 1898. He promoted his ideas on socialism and nationalism. He linked the **Social Question** and the **National Question**.

   - 'The struggle for Irish freedom has two aspects: it is national and it is social.' He said Ireland must be 'a nation free and independent'. He said it did not matter which government was in power; so long as there was private property, then one class would rule another class.
   - Other publications which outlined his ideas included *Labour, Nationality and Religion* and *Labour in Irish History*.

5. Connolly advocated:
   - **public (government) ownership** of the means of production
   - **nationalisation** (government ownership) of railways and canals
   - state banks
   - the **abolition** of private property, and no classes
   - an **independent** Ireland.

6. He went to **America** from 1903 to 1910 to work.
   - When Connolly returned from America he was sent to **Belfast** to organise the **Irish Transport and General Workers' Union** (ITGWU). He was involved in a dockers' strike and in improving working conditions for women in the linen factories.

7. In 1912 Connolly founded the **Irish Labour Party** with James Larkin to represent workers when the new Home Rule Bill became law.

8. Connolly was very much involved in the **1913 Strike and Lockout in Dublin**.

9. He set up the **Irish Citizen Army** to protect the workers from attacks by the police. There were about 250 members; their aim was the establishment of an **independent and socialist Irish republic**.

10. Connolly became **general secretary** of the ITGWU when Larkin left for America in 1914.

11. He was **opposed** to the war in Europe. He did not want to see the workers of different countries fighting one another.

12. Connolly was persuaded to join the rebellion organised by the **Military Council** of the **Irish Republican Brotherhood (IRB)**. He was involved in planning the **military operations** of the Rising. He also influenced the **social thinking** of the 1916 Proclamation.

13. He was wounded in the fighting in the GPO and was later **executed**.

Edward Carson

1. Carson was born in **Dublin** to a wealthy Protestant family. He was educated at Portarlington School and Trinity College, Dublin. He became a **barrister**.

2. Carson represented **tenants** at the Land Courts to get a **fair rent** after Gladstone's 1881 Land Act.
   - But he opposed Gladstone's First Home Rule Bill in 1886.

3. He was **government prosecutor** during the **Plan of Campaign**, when he enforced the Coercion Act. He was called '**Coercion Carson**'.

4. He held the positions of Solicitor-General for Ireland and later Solicitor-General for England.

5. Carson was elected **MP for Trinity College, Dublin,** in the 1892 general election, a position he held until 1918.

6. **Wilde trial:** In 1895 he successfully defended the Marquess of Queensberry against Oscar Wilde's libel action.

7. **Ulster Unionism:** Carson became leader of the **Irish Unionist Party** in 1910.
   - After the passage of the Parliament Act in 1911, it became clear that the **Third Irish Home Rule Bill** would become law.

8. **Unionist leaders:** Carson and Craig complemented each other as leaders: Carson was an **able speaker**, while Craig preferred to **organise** in the background.
   - But Carson had no special connection with Ulster; he was a **Southern Unionist** who opposed Home Rule for **any part of Ireland**. He was using Ulster Unionist opposition to achieve this. He **did not favour partition**, which would leave Southern Unionists in a Home Rule southern Ireland.

9. Carson campaigned against Home Rule and supported both **constitutional and illegal means.**

   - He spoke against the Third Home Rule Bill in the House of Commons.
   - In September 1911, **Carson** told a meeting in Belfast that unionists should **set up their own government** to take over when Home Rule became law.
   - On 28 September 1912 he was the **first signatory** to the **Ulster Solemn League and Covenant**, which pledged its signatories to resist Home Rule by **all means necessary.**
   - In January 1913 he established the **Ulster Volunteer Force** (UVF).
   - **Larne gunrunning:** Craig and Carson decided to **import arms** for the UVF, which were distributed throughout Ulster.
   - Carson used his **links with the Conservative Party** in England to ensure their support for Ulster Unionism.

10. Carson was involved in attempts to achieve a **compromise** between Unionists and Home Rulers.

    - The solutions which were proposed were based on excluding **all or part** of Ulster, **permanently or temporarily**, from Home Rule.
    - Both **Carson and Craig** represented the Unionists at the **Buckingham Palace Conference**, which was called by King George V in July 1914. The conference broke up **without agreement.**

11. Ireland seemed to be on the **verge of civil war**. The crisis was postponed by the **First World War**, which began in August 1914.

12. In September 1914 **the Home Rule Bill became law**. Carson agreed to it provided that it did not operate until **after the war** was over; the **Ulster Question** would be decided then.

13. Carson pledged Unionist support for the war effort, including the enlistment of **Ulster Unionist volunteers** in the British Army. Carson later was a member of the British government during the war.

14. Carson was disappointed when the **Government of Ireland Act** was passed in 1920, which set up a **separate parliament for Northern Ireland**. But his leadership between 1910 and 1914 contributed to ensuring that Northern Ireland remained part of the Union with Britain.

15. Carson warned Ulster Unionist leaders **not to alienate** (isolate) northern Catholics, because he foresaw the trouble which would be caused.

Isabella Tod

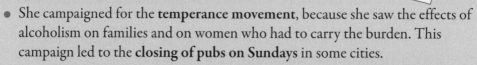

1. Isabella Tod was born in Edinburgh to a **middle-class Presbyterian family**. She moved to **Belfast** in the 1860s.

2. Tod was very much involved in **all aspects of women's rights**.

   - Tod campaigned for **better education** for women. She called for practical education similar to that provided in the Belfast Ladies' Institute, which she founded in 1867. She campaigned for the successful inclusion of girls in the **Intermediate Education Act** of 1878. She also demanded that women be allowed into **universities**.

   - She campaigned for the **temperance movement**, because she saw the effects of alcoholism on families and on women who had to carry the burden. This campaign led to the **closing of pubs on Sundays** in some cities.

   - Tod also wanted the repeal of the **Contagious Diseases Act**. This allowed the arrest of women suspected of being prostitutes. Women could be examined for sexually transmitted diseases, but men who used prostitutes were not examined. The law was repealed in 1887.

   - Tod also campaigned to improve **property rights for women**. Women's property became the man's on marriage. The **Married Women's Property Act, 1882**, gave women the right to own property separately from their husbands.

3. Women **could not vote** in either parliamentary or local elections in Ireland in 1870. Tod realised the importance of the **right to vote** for women. She believed that the best way to achieve women's rights was first to secure the right to vote.

4. Tod founded the **Northern Ireland Society for Women's Suffrage** in Belfast in 1871.

   - She demanded votes for women in parliamentary elections and in local elections.

   - Tod **toured Ireland** to get across her message. She also campaigned through **pamphlets, meetings** and **petitions** to Parliament.

5. Tod was **opposed** to Home Rule. As a **unionist** she distrusted the influence of the Catholic Church on a Home Rule Ireland. She also said the Home Rule Party was against women's rights. She campaigned against Gladstone's First Home Rule Bill (1886). She was the **only female member** of the executive committee of the **Ulster Liberal Unionist Association**.

6. Tod founded the **Ulster Women's Liberal Unionist Association** in 1888.

7. She died in 1896.

Hanna Sheehy-Skeffington

1. Hanna Sheehy was born in **Kanturk, Co. Cork**. She was the **daughter** of David Sheehy, a Home Rule MP.

2. Sheehy was educated at the **Dominican School** and **University College, Dublin**. She received a Master's Degree from the **Royal University**. While at college she met Frank Skeffington, and when they married in 1903 they combined their names.

3. Hanna Sheehy-Skeffington became interested in **women's rights** while in university.

   - She founded the **Women's Graduate Association**.
   - She **resigned** as registrar of the Royal University over a dispute concerning the non-recognition of women graduates.
   - She joined the **Irish Women's Suffrage and Local Government Association** (IWSLGA).

4. She was not satisfied with the quiet campaigns run by the IWSLGA. Instead she was impressed by the more militant actions of the **Pankhursts in Britain**.

5. Sheehy-Skeffington founded the **Irish Women's Franchise League** in 1908, along with Margaret Cousins and their husbands. Hanna was the **secretary**. By 1912 the IWFL had **1,000 members**.

6. She was also involved in the newspaper, *The Irish Citizen*, set up by the League.

7. Sheehy-Skeffington threw **stones** at the windows of government buildings in Dublin. Along with 34 others, she was **arrested** and **jailed**. While in jail she went on **hunger strike**.

8. Her actions caused a **rift** between herself and her father.

   - As a Home Ruler, he believed that the campaign for women's suffrage was endangering the campaign for Home Rule.
   - On the other hand, Sheehy-Skeffington was a **dedicated suffragette** who believed that the vote for women was more important than Home Rule.

9. Sheehy-Skeffington was also involved in **labour politics**.

   - She helped found the **Irish Women's Workers' Union** in 1912.
   - She was also involved in the **1913 Dublin Strike and Lockout**, when she helped with the soup kitchen in Liberty Hall.

10. She was **opposed** to the First World War and Irishmen fighting in the war.

11. After this Sheehy-Skeffington became more involved in **nationalist politics**.

    - Her husband, Frank, was **murdered** by a British officer during the 1916 Rising.
    - She **opposed** the Anglo-Irish Treaty and was active in Sinn Féin in later years.

Key concepts

Anglicisation: The process whereby Ireland became more and more like England in adopting the English language and customs.

Anglo-Irish: People of English descent who lived in Ireland.

De-Anglicisation: In Ireland, reversing the trend of Anglicisation and reviving and restoring the Gaelic language and customs.

Democracy: A type of government in which the people have the final say either directly or via representatives selected through elections.

Feminism: Advocates the equal treatment of women in all aspects of life.

Home Rule: The belief that Ireland should have a parliament in Dublin to rule internal Irish affairs and a parliament in Westminster to rule external affairs.

Irish-Ireland movement: The movement to restore or revive all things Irish or Gaelic.

Militarism: Glorification of military methods.

Political agitation: Stirring up the interest of the people in a political cause or belief.

Separatism: The political belief that Ireland should have complete independence from Britain.

Socialism: The political belief that the ownership and control of factories, businesses and land should be in the hands of the government.

Suffragette: A woman who campaigned for the vote (or franchise) for women.

2   The Pursuit of Sovereignty and the Impact of Partition, 1912–49

1. The Third Home Rule Bill, 1912–14

 In this section, you should understand:

- How and why unionists resisted Home Rule
- The role of James Craig (Key personality, p. 125)
- The nationalist's response

1. In the early twentieth century, Ireland was divided into **nationalists** and **unionists**.
   - Most of the nationalists were **Home Rulers**.
2. **Home Rulers** felt that the country would be better off with a parliament in Dublin running Irish affairs.
   - The Home Rule Party was led by **John Redmond**.
3. **Unionists** wanted to maintain the Union with Britain. They were **opposed** to Home Rule because of:

- How successful were unionist attempts to resist Home Rule from 1912 onwards?
- Why was Ireland on the verge of civil war in 1914?

ULSTER UNIONISM:
The belief of those in Ulster that Ulster should continue to be part of Britain in accordance with the Act of Union.

- **Economic reasons:** Ulster, especially **Belfast**, prospered under the Union, with shipbuilding and linen. Britain provided raw materials and markets. In addition, unionists believed that a Dublin government would be **more concerned with agriculture** than with industry.
- **Religious reasons:** Protestants feared that an Irish parliament would be **Catholic-dominated** and that '**Home Rule would be Rome Rule**'.
- **Political reasons:** Unionists had many links with Britain. They were **loyal** to the king and to the Crown.
4. The Unionists were **strongest** in Ulster, particularly Antrim and Down. Unionists were represented by the **Ulster Unionist Council**, which coordinated opposition to Home Rule, **the Irish Unionist Party** and **the Orange Order**. The Unionists were led by **Edward Carson** and **James Craig**.

- **Carson** was a Southern Unionist; he was an able **speaker** and wanted to prevent Home Rule for any part of Ireland.
- **Craig** was an Ulster businessman; he was prepared to allow Home Rule for the south of Ireland, provided Ulster remained part of Britain. He was the party's main organiser.

5. **Unionists were divided into Ulster Unionists and Southern Unionists:**
   - Ulster Unionists came from **all classes**, from working class to landlords and businessmen. They were a **majority** in some counties in Ulster.
   - Southern Unionists were mainly landlords and businessmen. They were a **small minority**, but they had **close links** with the Conservative Party in England.

6. The **Conservative Party** feared that Home Rule for Ireland would lead to the **breakup** of the British Empire.

7. Britain was ruled by a **Liberal government** led by **Herbert Asquith**. In 1912 the Liberal government introduced the **Third Home Rule Bill**.
   - The Home Rule Party held the **balance of power** after the 1910 general elections.
   - Asquith committed himself to Home Rule for Ireland in return for the support of the Home Rule Party.
   - The **Parliament Act of 1911** meant that the **House of Lords** could delay bills in Parliament only for 2 years, after which they had to become law.

8. The **terms** of the Third Home Rule Bill were:
   - There would be a parliament in Dublin to deal with **internal Irish affairs**.
   - Parliament in **Westminster** would control **external affairs**, such as peace and war and trade.
   - Ireland would send **40 MPs** to Westminster.
   - The king/queen would be king/queen of both Britain and Ireland.

9. It seemed likely that Home Rule would become law by 1914.

Unionist resistance

Up to this time Unionists could rely on the Conservative-dominated **House of Lords** to stop Home Rule, but now they had to find **other methods**.

1. In September 1911 **Carson** told a meeting in Belfast that Unionists should **set up their own government** to take over when Home Rule became law.
   - The Ulster Unionist Council drafted a **constitution** and prepared for self-government.

2. Orangemen began to **drill and arm**. This was **legal**, because any two Justices of the Peace could **authorise drilling**, provided that it was for the defence of the Constitution of the United Kingdom.

3. In 1912 over 400,000 Unionist men signed **the Ulster Solemn League and Covenant** in rallies all over Ulster. This was a **pledge** to fight Home Rule 'by all means which may be found necessary'.

4. The Unionists were supported by **Andrew Bonar Law**, the Conservative Party leader, who said, 'I can imagine no length of resistance to which Ulster will go which I shall not be ready to support.'

5. In 1913 the **Ulster Volunteer Force (UVF)** was organised. By 1914 there were 100,000 members.

6. **The Curragh Mutiny** (March 1914) helped Unionists.
   - The British government wanted to enforce Home Rule in north-east Ulster. But **officers in the British Army** in the Curragh said that they would **resign** rather than go against the Unionists. The government had to **back down**.

7. **Larne gunrunning:** Craig and Carson decided **to import arms**.
   - Arms were bought in Germany. In April 1914, 25,000 rifles and 3 million rounds of ammunition were landed at **Larne, Bangor and Donaghadee**. The arms were distributed all over the North.

8. Southern Unionists **published pamphlets** and **influenced public opinion**, especially in Britain, against Home Rule.

Nationalist response

1. In November 1913 **Eoin McNeill** wrote an article, '**The North Began**', in *An Claideamh Soluis*. He said that Irish nationalists should follow the example of Ulster Unionists and form their own organisation to defend Home Rule.

2. In November 1913, the **Irish National Volunteers** were formed in Dublin. Eoin McNeill was elected **commander** of the Volunteers, but the **Provisional Committee** of the Volunteers was dominated by the IRB (Irish Republican Brotherhood). By June 1914 there were about 180,000 members.

3. The success of the Ulster Volunteers in importing arms encouraged the Irish Volunteers to import arms on board the *Asgard* at **Howth** (1914).
   - British soldiers failed to stop the arms and fired on a crowd in Dublin, who jeered them, killing three people. This incident increased nationalist resistance.

4. Now **two armed forces** faced each other. It looked as though there would be **civil war** in Ireland if the Home Rule Bill became law.

Attempts at compromise, 1912–14

1. Liberal Party politicians wanted to prevent conflict in Ireland. They wanted a **compromise** between the Home Rulers and the Unionists.
   - Attempts at **compromise** proposed either the **permanent or temporary exclusion** of **all or part** of Ulster from a Home Rule Ireland. How much of Ulster should be excluded? Should it be temporary or permanent?

2. **Redmond and the Home Rule party** would not accept **partition** (dividing the country), particularly since all the Ulster counties had a nationalist population.
   - Redmond was prepared to accept '**Home Rule within Home Rule**' for Ulster – Ulster could have its own parliament, but it would be under the control of the Dublin parliament.

3. But the **Unionists rejected** these proposals.

4. King George V called a **conference** of Unionists, Home Rulers and the British government at **Buckingham Palace** in July 1914.

   - The Unionists were represented by Carson and Craig and the Home Rulers by Redmond and John Dillon, the deputy leader of the Home Rule Party. Asquith and Lloyd George represented the British government.
   - They debated whether Ulster, or part of the province, should be permanently excluded from Home Rule.
   - The conference broke up **without agreement**.

5. The Home Rule Bill was due to become law within a few weeks. The crisis in Ireland and the danger of civil war were postponed by the coming of the **First World War**, which began in August 1914.

   - In September 1914 the **Home Rule Bill became law**. Carson and the Unionists agreed to it on the understanding that it would not operate until the end of the war, and that the **Ulster Question** would be considered then.

2. The impact of the First World War on Ireland

 In this section, you should understand:

- How Ireland was influenced by World War I

1. Carson and the Unionists called on the **Ulster Volunteers** to join the British Army.

   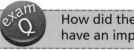 How did the First World War have an impact on Ireland?

   - They would show their **loyalty** to the British Empire.
   - They would guarantee consideration of the Ulster Question after the war.

2. About **30,000 Ulster Volunteers** joined the British Army. They formed the 36th Ulster Division, with their own officers and badges.

3. After the Home Rule Bill became law, **John Redmond** spoke at **Woodenbridge, Co. Wicklow**. He said that the Irish Volunteers should join the British Army and fight wherever they were needed.

   - This led to a split in the Irish Volunteers. A **large majority** of the Volunteers supported Redmond; they became known as the **National Volunteers**. A **small minority** – about 10,000 – did not support his view; they continued under the name of the Irish Volunteers. They were largely under the **control of the IRB**, who now made plans to use them for a **rebellion** against Britain during the First World War.

4. Estimates differ about the total number of Irishmen who **fought and died** in the war. Over 200,000 enlisted in the British Army and at least 30,000 were killed in the fighting.

- They wanted to ensure Home Rule would be granted after the war.
- Men joined for **other reasons**, such as to get a job, in a spirit of adventure, to protect Catholic Belgium against the 'mighty Hun', and out of loyalty to the British Empire.
- **Recruiting campaigns** were run during the war and Irish **Victoria Cross** winners, such as Michael O'Leary and Sergeant Cosgrove from Cork, spoke at these.
- The numbers enlisting declined during 1915. This also happened in Britain and the government introduced conscription (compulsory enlistment) there in 1915, but not in Ireland.

5. **Irish regiments** were involved in all the main battle areas. Famous regiments included the **Royal Munster Fusiliers**, the **Leinster Regiment**, the **Connaught Rangers** and the **Irish Guards**.
   - They were fighting in **France and Belgium** in the early months of the war.
   - Irish regiments fought at **Gallipoli** in 1915. Irish regiments from both north and south fought side by side in the **Battle of the Somme** in 1916.

6. Ireland was used as a **base for patrols** out in the Atlantic to protect convoys from U-boat attack. In 1915 the *Lusitania* was sunk by torpedo off the Old Head of Kinsale and over 1,000 people were drowned. The survivors were helped in Queenstown (Cobh) and Kinsale. In 1918, just before the war ended, the *Leinster*, an Irish passenger ferry, was torpedoed in the Irish Sea with the loss of over 500 lives.

7. **Industry:** The economy of Belfast and north-east Ulster benefited from the increased demand for ships and linen, but the rest of the country was not sufficiently developed industrially to benefit.

8. **Farming:** Farmers benefited from increased demand for food in Britain, owing to the U-boat campaign. Prices increased, but wages did not rise as fast.

9. Small farmers and labourers were not as well off as bigger farmers; this led to unrest in 1917 and 1918.

10. **Inflation:** Overall prices increased during the war, while wages did not improve as much. This affected workers and labourers, who went on strike.

11. **Opposition to the war:** Opposition to the war was centred on the **Irish Volunteers** and the **IRB**. There was also opposition amongst some of the **suffragette leaders**, but these groups were in a minority early in the war.

12. The IRB planned and carried out the **1916 Rising** because England was distracted by the war. (See *The 1916 Rising*, pp. 74–77)

13. The First World War contributed to the **decline of Redmond and the Home Rule Party**.
    - The war dragged on for longer than expected, so Home Rule seemed more distant.
    - Redmond's demands for a separate Irish Brigade were rejected.
    - Carson's influence in government increased when he became a member of it.

- The executions after the 1916 Rising lessened the popularity of the Home Rule Party.
  - Attempts to solve the Irish Question after the Rising, by Lloyd George in 1916 and the Irish Convention in 1917, failed.
  - The British government attempted to introduce conscription into Ireland in 1918.
14. **Conscription, 1918:** The British Army needed more soldiers in 1918, so the government introduced conscription in Ireland in that year.
    - **Sinn Féin** ran a very successful campaign against conscription. It united all nationalists and led to the decline of the Home Rule party. (See *The Rise of the Second Sinn Féin party and the 1918 General Election*, pp. 81–83)
15. At the end of the war Britain introduced **votes for women over 30**, because of the part that women had played in the war.

3. The 1916 Rising

In this section, you should understand:
- The origins, planning, progress and results of the 1916 Rising
- The role of Pádraig Pearse (Key personality, p. 127)

Origins and planning

Causes

> **exam Q**
> - What were the aims and achievements of Pádraig Pearse?
> - How successful was the Easter Rising, 1916?

> **key point**
> REPUBLIC:
> A completely independent Ireland.

1. **Cultural nationalism:** The Gaelic League and the GAA influenced many of the leaders of the 1916 Rising. Some people believed that an independent Ireland was needed to protect Irish culture. Cultural nationalism encouraged the growth of separatism – the idea that Ireland should be fully independent.
2. **Revived IRB:** The IRB (Irish Republican Brotherhood) was revived in the early twentieth century. It had a tradition of physical force – that a rebellion or rising was necessary to gain independence for Ireland.

> **key point**
> PHYSICAL FORCE:
> The use of violence (force of arms) to achieve political aims.

3. **Volunteer split:** The Irish Volunteers split over Ireland's participation in the First World War. The minority (about 10,000) said Irishmen should defend Ireland at home.
   - They were led by Eoin McNeill, but they were dominated by the IRB. They could provide the armed men who would be necessary for a rising.
4. **The First World War:** Britain's participation in the First World War provided the timing. The old slogan was 'England's difficulty is Ireland's opportunity', so that while England was involved in war a rising could be organised.

5. **Blood sacrifice:** Some leaders, particularly Patrick Pearse, believed military success was not needed; instead, their deaths would change people's attitudes and revive the spirit of the Irish nation.

key point

BLOOD SACRIFICE:

The conviction of Pádraig Pearse that he and others would be prepared to sacrifice their lives to rise up the spirit of Irish people for independence.

Planning

6. The Supreme Council of the IRB decided to stage a rising during the war. The Council set up a Military Council to plan it.

7. The Military Council was composed of Pearse, Plunkett, Ceannt, MacDonagh, Clarke and MacDermott. They continued the secret planning of the rising, unknown to the Supreme Council. They set the date as Easter Sunday, 1916.

8 The **Military Council** became aware that James Connolly was planning his own rising with the Citizen Army. Connolly set up the Irish Citizen Army during the 1913 Dublin Strike and Lockout to protect the workers from attacks by the police. There were about 250 members; their aim was the establishment of an independent and socialist Irish republic.

   • The Military Council persuaded him to join their rising.

9. **Secrecy**: The Military Council wanted to ensure the plans for the rising were kept secret, so they did not tell anybody else. They believed many previous attempts at rebellion in Ireland had been unsuccessful because of spies.

German help

1. The Military Council needed weapons. **Roger Casement** was sent to Germany.
   • Casement was a former British diplomat who had become a member of the IRB.

2. His mission was to:
   • form an Irish brigade from Irish prisoners of war held in Germany
   • acquire arms and ammunition for the rising.

3. He failed to raise an Irish brigade, because the men were supporters of Home Rule. He was given one shipload of arms for the rising.

4. In Ireland, there was growing disappointment with the progress of the First World War.
   • The war dragged on for longer than expected, so Home Rule seemed more distant.
   • Redmond's demands for a separate Irish Brigade were rejected.
   • Carson's influence in government increased when he became a member of it.

The plan

The Military Council planned to land the arms from Germany.
   • When the Volunteers were on manoeuvres, they would distribute the arms to them. This would create a countrywide rising.

The plan goes wrong

1. The Germans sent the *Aud* to Ireland with 20,000 rifles and 10 machine guns. It was captured off the Kerry coast by the British Navy.
   - There were now few or no arms for a countrywide rising.
2. Roger Casement landed from a submarine near Tralee and was captured. He wanted to stop the rising, because he thought it would not be successful.
3. **The Irish Volunteers**: The Irish Volunteers were the key to the success of the rising; but MacNeill, leader of the Volunteers, would rise only if the Volunteers were attacked.
4. The Military Council had a plan to deceive MacNeill; they published the **'Castle Document'** – this was supposed to be a document from Dublin Castle with a plan to arrest the leaders of the Volunteers.
   - As a result, MacNeill sanctioned manoeuvres for the Irish Volunteers for Easter Sunday.
5. Soon MacNeill learnt that the document was a forgery, and also that the *Aud* had been captured. So he cancelled the manoeuvres (with his countermanding orders).
6. Now the Military Council had neither arms nor men for a countrywide rising.
   - The plan for a rising on Easter Sunday was in ruins.
7. The Military Council decided on a rising for **Easter Monday.**
   - The rising would now be mainly a Dublin rising.

The Rising

1. On Easter Monday morning, about 1,600 Irish Volunteers and 200 Citizen Army members marched through the streets of Dublin from Liberty Hall.
2. Some captured the GPO in Sackville Street (now O'Connell Street), where they set up their headquarters.
3. Pearse read the **1916 Proclamation** outside the GPO. It was written mainly by Pearse, but it was influenced by some of Connolly's thinking.
4. Its main ideas were:
   - The Rising was linked to a revolutionary tradition in Ireland.
   - The leaders formed a provisional government.
   - It demanded a republican Ireland.
   - It promised social reform based on equality – 'cherishing all the children of the nation equally'.

The fighting

1. The insurgents (or rebels) took up defensive positions. Apart from the GPO, other groups captured the Four Courts, Jacob's Factory and Boland's Mills.
2. There were some incidents in Wexford, Galway and Ashbourne, Co. Meath, but the fighting was confined mainly to Dublin.

3. The British Army brought in reinforcements from the Curragh and from Britain.
   - They used artillery and a gunboat, the *Helga*, which was brought up the Liffey.
4. It was only a question of time before the Volunteers would surrender. The GPO went on fire and the Volunteers had to withdraw.
5. Pearse ordered the surrender on Saturday.

Reaction to the Rising

1. Unionists saw it as a disloyal attack during the World War.
2. Home Rulers saw it as an insult to Irishmen fighting for Home Rule in the war. Many were angry over the destruction of the city.
   - But John Dillon warned in the House of Commons that 'You are washing our whole life's work in a sea of blood.'
3. The British Army imposed martial (military) law.
   - Fifteen of the leaders were executed, including the seven signatories of the Proclamation.
   - The British arrested more than 2,000 suspects, who were interned in England; many were innocent people.
4. After the Rising, Lloyd George tried to negotiate a deal between Redmond and Carson, but he failed.

The results

1. Death and destruction – about 500 people, mostly civilians, were killed and 2,500 were injured. The centre of Dublin was destroyed.
2. The executions and the arrests had a huge influence:
   - They contributed to the rise of Sinn Féin and the decline of the Home Rule Party.
   - The idea of a 'republic' began to replace 'home rule' as a solution to the Irish Question.

4. The rise of the second Sinn Féin party and the 1918 general election

In this section, you should understand:
- Why Sinn Féin rose in popularity from 1916 to 1918

1. The **Home Rule Party declined** after the 1916 Rising.
   - Redmond was tricked by Lloyd George into agreeing to partition, because he thought it was temporary. But Lloyd George told Carson it would be permanent. Even though Redmond rejected Lloyd George's proposals, he lost support.

What were the factors that contributed to the success of Sinn Féin in the 1918 general election?

2. The rising became known as the **Sinn Féin Rising**, even though Sinn Féin had nothing to do with it. Sinn Féin became more popular as the rising became more acceptable to people.

3. **Lloyd George** became prime minister. He released Irish prisoners from jails to win over Irish-American opinion. In jail, the prisoners had become more republican and opposed to British rule in Ireland.

4. Griffith was not involved in any way in the 1916 Rising, but was jailed afterwards. When he was released, he began to rebuild Sinn Féin. He proposed:
   - an **abstentionist policy** (Sinn Féin MPs would not attend Westminster, but would form an alternative parliament and government in Dublin)
   - to appeal to the post-war Peace Conference to recognise Ireland's right to self-government.

5. Other nationalist bodies were reorganising, including the Irish Republican Brotherhood (IRB) and the Irish Volunteers.

6. Sinn Féin put forward **Count Plunkett** for a by-election in Roscommon in February 1917. He was the father of Joseph Plunkett, who was executed after the 1916 Rising.
   - Plunkett won and then refused to take his seat in Westminster.

7. Sinn Féin won the by-election in South Longford with Joseph McGuinness, who was in jail – **'Put Him in to Get Him Out'**.

8. De Valera won the by-election in East Clare. He was the last surviving senior commanding officer of the 1916 Rising.

9. Sinn Féin held an Árd Fheis in October 1917. They elected de Valera as **president** of Sinn Féin. The party also adopted the policies of:
   - abstentionism
   - setting up an Irish government in Dublin
   - appealing to the peace conference after the war.

10. The Irish Volunteers held a convention. They elected de Valera as president.
    - Sinn Féin and the Irish Volunteers were united under one president.

11. The British government organised the **Irish Convention**. This brought together Unionists and Home Rulers (Sinn Féin refused to attend) to work out a solution to Ireland's problems.
    - The Ulster Unionists wanted permanent exclusion from a Home Rule Ireland.
    - The Home Rule party rejected this and withdrew from the convention after John Redmond died.

12. For a time support for Sinn Féin declined, because they were associated with increased violence in the countryside.

13. **Conscription crisis**: The British government planned to introduce conscription to Ireland in 1918 to make up for a shortage of soldiers on the Western Front.
    - Sinn Féin led a successful campaign against conscription; it united all nationalists and had the support of the Catholic Church leaders.

- The campaign increased support for Sinn Féin.

14. **The German plot**: The British government arrested over 70 Sinn Féin leaders, including de Valera, because of a German plot to import arms into Ireland – but they had no evidence. This affair only increased the popularity of Sinn Féin.

15. **1918 general election**: After the war, a general election was held. Sinn Féin won 73 seats against 6 for the Home Rule Party (and the Unionists won 26 seats).

16. Sinn Féin had advantages:

- The members were younger and more active. The younger Home Rule Party members were fighting in the war.
- Sinn Féin were better organised; the Home Rule Party failed to contest some constituencies because of poor organisation.
- The Home Rule party failed to achieve Home Rule; people began to think that Sinn Féin deserved a chance with their new policies on abstentionism and the republic.

5. The War of Independence, 1919–21

 In this section, you should understand:
- The political and military aspects of the War of Independence
- The role of Michael Collins (Key personality, p. 129)

1. The War of Independence, also known as the Anglo-Irish War, was a war between

> **exam Q** How successful was the War of Independence?

Sinn Féin, together with the Irish Volunteers (IRA), and the British government.

2. There were two aspects to the war:
- The **political aspect** involved a policy of passive resistance pursued by Sinn Féin
- the **military side** involved a campaign of guerrilla warfare pursued by the Irish Volunteers (IRA).

Political – the Sinn Féin government

1. Sinn Féin, following Griffith's ideas, wanted to form an alternative government.

2. The **First Dáil** met on 21 January 1919 in the Mansion House, Dublin. Present were 27 Sinn Féin MPs – the rest were in jail. The First Dáil issued:
- the Declaration of Independence of the Irish Republic
- 'A Message to the Free Nations of the World' – to gain international recognition at the Paris Peace Conference. A delegation, led by Seán T. O'Kelly, was chosen to put the Sinn Féin case to the Peace Conference.
- the Democratic Programme – a programme of educational and social welfare reform.

3. The Dáil met again in April. It elected de Valera as president and appointed government ministers.

These included:

- Arthur Griffith as Minister for Home Affairs
- Cathal Brugha as Minister for Defence
- Michael Collins as Minister for Finance
- W.T. Cosgrave as Minister for Local Government.

They also took the name Teachta Dála (TD) instead of MP.

4. **Finance**: The Dáil loan was organised by Collins; he collected £358,000 from people in Ireland and abroad to finance the running of the government and to buy guns for the Volunteers. De Valera also raised money when he went to America.

   - The Sinn Féin courts were established, along with the Volunteers (IRA) acting as Republican police to maintain law and order.
   - After the local government elections in 1920, Sinn Féin controlled most of the county councils and corporations.
   - The Dáil organised propaganda at home and abroad, especially through the *Irish Bulletin*, to get across its message.

5. Sinn Féin faced a number of **problems** in setting up an alternative government:
   - They lacked experience of administration.
   - There was difficulty in establishing control over the Irish Volunteers (IRA).
   - The Dáil government had limited success, but it disrupted the workings of the British government in Ireland.

6. De Valera spent most of the War of Independence in America; he became involved in disputes among Irish-Americans and failed to get recognition for Ireland from the Democratic and Republican parties.

The military campaign

1. The military side of the conflict began at **Soloheadbeg**, Co. Tipperary, on the same day the First Dáil met, 21 January 1919. The local brigade of the Volunteers shot dead two RIC constables who were guarding gelignite on its way to a quarry.

> **key point**
>
> IRA:
> Irish Republican Army, the military wing of Sinn Féin, which grew out of the Irish Volunteers and which fought in the War of Independence to establish an independent Ireland.

2. The Irish Volunteers became known as the **Irish Republican Army** (IRA). The IRA was divided into brigades and battalions. It operated largely independently of the Dáil.

3. The IRA developed **guerrilla war tactics.**
   - The military side of the conflict developed in stages, but much of the IRA activity was confined to certain counties, especially parts of counties Cork, Tipperary and Kerry and Dublin city.

4. **January 1919 to early 1920**
- Mainly there were attacks on RIC (Royal Irish Constabulary) barracks and patrols for arms and ammunition.
- The IRA usually attacked small, isolated barracks with four to six men.
- In 1919, nineteen policemen were killed.

5. Effects of attacks and intimidation: Recruiting to the RIC stopped. The IRA controlled many country areas when smaller RIC barracks were closed down.

6. **The role of Michael Collins**
- Collins became the chief organiser of the conflict in Ireland. He held the key posts of Adjutant-General of the Volunteers, Director of Organisation and Director of Intelligence. Collins was also president of the IRB.
- The IRA looked to Collins rather than Brugha (Minister for Defence) for instructions.
- Collins was determined that spies and informers would not betray the IRA. He established his own spy network, with contacts among civil servants, typists, maids, railwaymen and hotel porters.
- Collins had his '**Squad**' of men, 'the twelve apostles' – they formed a group of specially selected gunmen. The Squad tracked down and murdered detectives, especially the G-men (members of 'G division' of the Dublin Metropolitan Police who were charged with subverting the republican movement) working in Dublin Castle.

key point

IRB:
Irish Republican Brotherhood or Fenians, a secret organisation aimed at establishing an Irish republic by force of arms.

Early 1920

1. **British government policy: Black and Tans and Auxiliaries**
- David Lloyd George, British prime minister, refused to recognise that the IRA was a national army.
- Lloyd George recruited extra police – these were ex-soldiers who had fought in the First World War. They became known as the **Black and Tans** because of their khaki army trousers and green RIC tunics; 7,000 men were taken into service.
- In August 1920 the **Auxiliaries**, who were ex-British Army officers, were sent to Ireland. There were over 2,000 of them.
- The Black and Tans and the Auxiliaries found it very difficult to cope with the guerrilla tactics of the IRA.

2. **Reprisals**: Violence in Ireland increased after March 1920.
- The Black and Tans and Auxiliaries were involved in shooting incidents, the destruction of property (including the burning of creameries) and the burning of

towns, such as Balbriggan in Co. Dublin, Mallow in Co. Cork and Tuam in Co. Galway. Ordinary people began to fear and hate the Black and Tans and the 'Auxies'.

- This increased the support of the people for the IRA.

3. The British army was given authority to arrest and imprison, without trial, anybody suspected of involvement in the IRA.
   - The IRA retaliated with shootings and the burning of unionist/Protestant homes.

4. **The Government of Ireland Act, 1920**
   - Lloyd George passed the Government of Ireland Act in 1920. This provided a parliament for Dublin and Belfast. The parliament in Belfast controlled the six counties and the country was **partitioned**.
   - The Unionists accepted the Government of Ireland Act but Sinn Féin rejected it.

Autumn/Winter, 1920: The bitterness continues

A series of incidents increased the bitterness.

- Terence MacSwiney, Lord Mayor of Cork and local IRA Commander, died in Brixton prison after 74 days of a hunger strike.
- Kevin Barry, a young medical student, was hanged in Dublin for his part in an ambush of British soldiers.
- **Bloody Sunday, 2 November**
  - Collins' Squad killed 14 people, including 11 British Intelligence officers.
  - In the afternoon the police surrounded Croke Park, because they thought the killers had come to Dublin with the football supporters; they fired on the players and crowd. Twelve people were killed and 60 wounded. That evening Conor Clune and two IRA prisoners, Clancy and McKee, were shot in Dublin Castle.

Late 1920–21: Flying Columns

1. Towards the end of 1920, the IRA formed new units called **Flying Columns**.
   - Their leaders included Tom Barry (West Cork), Sean MacEoin (Longford) and Liam Lynch (North Cork).
   - The flying columns staged hit-and-run ambushes against British forces. They were hidden and supported by local people.

2. **Ambushes**: Some of the major ambushes included Kilmichael and Crossbarry, Co. Cork.

3. In December 1920 a group of Auxiliaries burned the centre of Cork city.

4. The British government imposed martial (military) law in some counties; many arrests weakened the IRA.

5. De Valera and Brugha insisted on the IRA mounting a large-scale attack.
   - In May 1921 the IRA attacked and burned the **Customs House**, Dublin. But the Dublin IRA suffered heavy losses; five people were killed and 80 captured.

Towards a truce, 1921

1. Factors influencing a truce:
   - Public opinion in Britain and abroad favoured peace.
   - Lloyd George had to fully defeat the IRA or else negotiate.
   - In the general election of May 1921, Sinn Fein won 124 out of 128 seats in the south.
   - The IRA was hard pressed; Collins said they had ammunition for only a few more weeks.
   - Irish people were growing tired of the conflict.
2. **The truce**: King George made a speech at the opening of the Northern Ireland Parliament which began the process. De Valera accepted Lloyd George's invitation to talks in London after a truce was agreed.
   - Sinn Féin won the right to negotiate directly with the British government.
   - By agreeing to talk to Lloyd George, de Valera also agreed to work out a compromise.
3. The truce came into operation on 11 July 1921.

Assessment of the War of Independence

- **Deaths**: About 1,400 people were killed; the British police force and army suffered over 600 deaths and about 1,000 injured. Over 500 IRA and about 200 civilians were killed.
- **Use of guerrilla warfare**: Guerrilla warfare had been effective in combating much stronger forces. But the Sinn Féin government could not control the IRA, and that contributed to the origins of the Civil War later.
- **Politics**: The war achieved greater freedom than was achieved under the Home Rule bills; but it failed to achieve its aim of a republic, and it failed to stop partition.
- **Protestants**: Because of the attacks on isolated Protestant families, some Protestants left the South to settle in England.
- **Economy**: The economy was disrupted and there was destruction in Dublin, Cork and country towns.

6. Partition

 In this section, you should understand:

- The factors or conditions which contributed to partition in Ireland
- The factors or conditions which consolidated partition after 1920

What factors contributed to the partition of Ireland in 1920?

- Situation of Protestants in Northern Ireland
- Ulster unionist resistance to Home Rule (See pp. 70–71)
- 1916 Rising and the rise of Sinn Féin (See pp. 74–79)
- War of Independence (See pp. 79–82)

Using the headings here, develop your own notes on the factors which contributed to the partition of Ireland in 1920

What factors consolidated partition after 1920?

PARTITION:
The border dividing Northern Ireland and Southern Ireland based on the Government of Ireland Act (1920).

- Anglo-Irish Treaty and the Boundary Commission
- Development of a Catholic, Gaelic state in the South after independence (Eucharistic Congress, language and education policies)
- Dominance of the Ulster Unionist Party in the North
- Differing educational, economic and social policies; new Constitution in the South
- The experiences of World War II
- The Republic of Ireland Act (1948) and the Ireland Act (1949)
- Development of the Welfare State in Northern Ireland after World War II

7. The Anglo-Irish Treaty, 1921

In this section, you should understand:

- The issues, negotiations and personalities involved in the Anglo-Irish Treaty, 1921

Case study: The treaty negotiations, October–December, 1921

Preliminary negotiations, July–October 1921

1. Preliminary negotiations began between de Valera and Lloyd George. They met four times in London. After that they corresponded. In these negotiations, they outlined their demands:
   - De Valera wanted a 32-county republic.

- Lloyd George wanted Ireland to remain within the British Commonwealth as a dominion.
- He also wanted to maintain the government of Northern Ireland.
- He wanted naval bases for the British Navy.

The British proposals were rejected by the Cabinet in Dublin and the Dáil.

2. **Lloyd George** invited an Irish delegation to London 'with a view to ascertaining how the association of Ireland within the community of nations known as the British Commonwealth may best be reconciled with Irish national aspirations'.

The delegations

3. The **Irish delegation** consisted of Arthur **Griffith**, leader of the delegation; Michael **Collins**, who was reluctant to go but did so out of a sense of duty; Robert **Barton**, a republican; Eamon **Duggan** and Charles **Gavan Duffy**, both lawyers.
   - Erskine **Childers** was a non-voting secretary; de Valera wanted him to uphold the republican position, and this led to distrust between himself and Griffith and Collins.

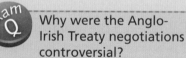

exam Q · Why were the Anglo-Irish Treaty negotiations controversial?

4. The **British delegation** was Prime Minister David **Lloyd George**, Winston **Churchill**, Minister for War, and Austen **Chamberlain** and Lord **Birkenhead**, Conservative Party leaders.

5. The Irish delegation were given **instructions** as 'envoy plenipotentiaries', i.e. envoys with full power to conclude a treaty. But de Valera also wanted the delegation to refer back any proposals to Dublin before they were agreed. These contradictions caused **controversy** later.

6. De Valera was not included in the delegation – **Why not?** He decided that he should not go. He said that he:
   - was head of state;
   - was needed in Dublin to keep more extreme or militant republicans in check;
   - would give the delegation an excuse to refer British proposals to Dublin and to resist British pressure.

This caused **controversy**. Later critics said he knew from his negotiations with Lloyd George that he would not achieve a republic and that he did not want to be blamed for this.

Negotiations by delegations, October–December 1921:

Weaknesses and strength of delegations

1. **De Valera's exclusion** – he was the only person who understood the idea of 'external association' of Ireland with the British Commonwealth, which the

delegation were to propose – Ireland would be independent in domestic affairs but would be externally associated with the Empire for defence and foreign policy; also de Valera had already negotiated with Lloyd George.

2. The **instructions** to the Irish delegates – there was a conflict between the role of envoy plenipotentiaries and having to refer agreements to Dublin; the regular return of the delegation to Dublin to report to the Cabinet was tiring.

3. **Location** – the negotiations were held in London, the centre of the British Empire, which gave a psychological advantage to the British; the British delegation had more back-up from their civil servants.

4. It was an **experienced** British delegation, including long-serving politicians; for example Lloyd George – 'the Welsh Wizard' – had been involved in the Paris Peace Conference.

The issues

The issues to be decided by the negotiations were:

- The constitutional status of Ireland – how much independence or sovereignty would Ireland get and how would it be linked to Britain?
- Partition and unification – would Ireland be 26 or 32 counties?
- British defence requirements in Ireland – there was a danger that an independent Ireland might join up with Britain's enemies.

The strategies

1. If the negotiations broke down:
   - The Irish delegation wanted to break on the question of Irish unity and the **Ulster Question** – whether the Six Counties would be united with the rest of the country.
   - The British delegation wanted to break on the **Imperial Question** – whether Ireland would be part of the Commonwealth or not.

2. Each side believed that they were more likely to receive support from their own people on these issues.

The negotiations

1. The negotiations began on **11 October, 1921**. The early discussions were conducted by **full delegations**; however, it proved difficult to make progress, so **sub-committees** were set up; most of the work on the Irish side was done by Griffith and Collins.

2. There was **early agreement** on British naval bases in Ireland, trade and the portion of the UK national debt that would be paid by Ireland (see Terms later).

Dominion status or External association?

1. The British delegation wanted Ireland to remain part of the Commonwealth – dominion status; whereas the Irish delegation wanted 'external association' – to be

outside the Commonwealth but to be associated with it through a treaty.

2. The British delegation rejected external association and the Irish delegation rejected dominion status.

- The British offered to write into the agreement that the dominion status would be the same as Canada's.

DOMINION STATUS:
Countries that were members of the British Commonwealth but had a degree of power over their own affairs.

ALLEGIANCE:
Loyalty to a person's own government or country.

Partition and the Ulster question

1. The British offered that the Six Counties would be put under an All-Ireland parliament if Ireland stayed in the British Empire.

- Griffith promised that if '**essential unity**' was guaranteed, he would recommend that Ireland stay in the British Empire/Commonwealth.

2. This proposal was rejected by Craig and the Northern Unionist leaders, so Britain proposed a **Boundary Commission** to redraw the border between North and South.

- The Irish delegation accepted this eventually; they assumed that three or four counties would be given to the South and the North would be too small to succeed on its own; the Cabinet in Dublin also accepted this.
- Now the Irish delegation was not able to 'break on the Ulster Question'.

Tensions

1. There were tensions in the Irish delegation:

- Griffith and Collins thought Childers was interfering too much in the proceedings of the delegation even though he was not a full member.
- When Pope Benedict wrote to King George V wishing the talks success, the King replied by referring to 'the Troubles' in Ireland and to 'my people'. De Valera was critical of the Pope's intervention and Griffith and Collins thought de Valera's interference would cause difficulties in the negotiations.
- The delegation were also upset about de Valera's interference in the negotiations when he wrote to them to make the British realise that war was the alternative.

2. The Irish delegation returned to Dublin early in December to meet with the Cabinet. There were bitter **divisions** between Brugha and Griffith and Collins. The delegation was instructed to propose External Association again.

Final days

1. De Valera's **External Association** was again proposed by the Irish delegation. This was rejected again by the British because it involved leaving the Empire and signing

a treaty of permanent alliance with it. Britain did not want to be seen to be weakening the Empire.

2. There was **eventual agreement** on the Oath of Allegiance that members of the Dáil and the Senate would take. The oath recognised dominion status for Ireland but it gave more importance to swearing 'true faith and allegiance' to the Irish constitution and less importance to being 'faithful' to the King.

Britain also made further concessions on trade and tax.

3. On 6 December 1921, Lloyd George used the threat of war – 'immediate and terrible' – within three days if there was no agreement.

- The Irish delegation signed the Treaty; Griffith agreed first, then Collins, Duggan and later Barton and Gavan Duffy. They felt it was a case of peace or war.

- Collins wrote; 'Will anyone be satisfied at the bargain? Will anyone? I tell you this – early this morning I signed my own death warrant. I thought at the time how odd, how ridiculous – a bullet may just as well have done the job five years ago... these signatures are the first real step for Ireland. If people will only remember that: the first real step.'

Effects

- The Anglo-Irish Treaty finally **ended the war** between the IRA and British forces in Ireland.

- It also brought about the end of British control of most of Ireland.

- It represented a compromise between the two countries but it provided a significant step to further independence for the south of Ireland.

- However, divisions over the negotiations and terms of the Treaty led to civil war.

The terms of the Anglo-Irish Treaty:

i.   It provided dominion status for Southern Ireland, giving it the same constitutional status as Canada and other dominion countries.

ii. Ireland would be known as the Irish Free State.

iii. The king's representative in Ireland would be the Governor-General.

iv. An Oath of Allegiance would be taken by members of the Dáil and the Senate.

v.   Three Treaty ports – Queenstown (Cobh), Berehaven, Lough Swilly – were to be kept by the British Navy for defence.

vi. A Boundary Commission would decide the boundary or border between Northern Ireland and the rest of Ireland.

8. The Treaty debates

 In this section, you should understand:
- The arguments for and against accepting the Anglo-Irish Treaty

1. The **Cabinet** debated the terms of the Anglo-Irish Treaty. Griffith, Collins, Barton and Cosgrave voted in favour, while de Valera, Brugha and Stack voted against.
   - The majority insisted that the Dáil should decide the issue.
2. Before the Dáil met, the newspapers, the clergy and public opinion came out in favour of the Treaty.
3. The **IRA** was divided – some did not want to return to everyday life; others said the settlement was a sell-out; some were influenced by Collins to favour the Treaty.
4. The **IRB** was in favour of the Treaty, largely because of the influence of Collins who was president of the Supreme Council.

The Dáil debate: 14 December 1921 to 7 January 1922

De Valera asked the Dáil to reject the Treaty.
- He proposed what became known as **Document No. 2** – the external association proposal.
- The extreme republicans rejected Document No. 2, so de Valera withdrew his proposal.

The anti-Treaty case

1. The main speakers against the Treaty were de Valera, Brugha and Austin Stack.
2. **Extreme republicans** rejected the treaty completely because it did not provide a republic. They said:
   - The republic had been declared in the 1916 Proclamation.
   - The delegates who negotiated had betrayed the republic.
   - They would fight if the only alternative was war.
   - They would not accept the Dáil's decision if it voted for the Treaty.
3. **Moderate republicans** rejected the Treaty because they thought a better deal could have been negotiated.
   - They objected to the king being head of state and TDs having to take an oath to him.
   - They said Britain would go on interfering in Irish affairs.
   - They believed that Ireland could not follow an independent foreign policy so long as Britain had the 'treaty ports'.

The pro-Treaty case

1. The main speakers in favour of the Treaty were Griffith, Collins, Mulcahy and Cosgrave.

2. Those in favour of the Treaty said:
   - The Treaty was the best deal that could be obtained.
   - A new war would fail because the leaders were recognisable, the IRA had lost the advantage of surprise and there would be less support from the people. Richard Mulcahy said; 'We have not yet been able to drive the enemy from anything but a fairly good-sized police barracks.'
   - They argued that the Treaty was the first step to a republic. Collins said the Treaty 'gives us freedom, not the ultimate freedom that all nations desire and develop to, but the freedom to achieve it'. He said that the dominions were gaining more and more independence.
   - They said dominion status was better than Home Rule.

The vote

1. All deputies had spoken by the time the vote was taken on 7 January 1922.
   - The six women TDs, including Countess Markievicz, spoke against the Treaty.
   - There was little reference to partition, because most TDs believed that the Boundary Commission would end it.

2. During the Christmas break many TDs were influenced by the opinions of the people who wanted peace – farming, business, legal, and church leaders along with the media favoured the treaty.

3. The vote in favour of the Treaty was carried by **64 votes** for and **57 votes** against.

9. The Irish Civil War

 In this section, you should understand:
- The causes, progress and results of the Irish Civil War

1. After the Treaty debates, de Valera resigned as president. He was succeeded by Arthur Griffith as president of the Dáil. Griffith headed a government of pro-Treaty ministers.

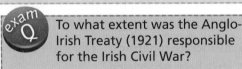
To what extent was the Anglo-Irish Treaty (1921) responsible for the Irish Civil War?

2. A separate provisional government was formed, which had to take over gradually from the British government and set up the institutions of the new Free State.

3. Collins became head of the provisional government and accepted power from the British government in Dublin Castle.

4. As the provisional government took power, the country drifted towards civil war.

Causes

1. Some of the IRA were attached to the **ideal of a republic** and the Treaty did not grant a republic.
   - The republic was declared in the 1916 Proclamation.
   - They swore an oath to the republic.
   - They had fought for a republic, and some had died for a republic.
2. The IRA had operated **independently** of the Sinn Féin government and Dáil during the War of Independence.
   - The commanders of the flying columns fought the war independently.
   - They claimed success in the War of Independence.
3. **Drift to war**
   - As the British Army evacuated their barracks, pro- and anti-Treaty IRA took over the barracks.
   - The anti-Treaty IRA set up their own Executive Committee. Then Rory O'Connor and others seized the Four Courts in the centre of Dublin; this was a snub to the provisional government.
4. De Valera campaigned against the Treaty; some of his speeches were extreme.
5. Collins and de Valera made an **election pact** to fight the election together and form a coalition government afterwards. Collins called off the pact just before the election.
   - The pro-Treaty candidates won the election easily. This showed that the people supported the Treaty.
   - The election results gave Collins the go-ahead to attack the Four Courts garrison.

Pro-Treaty	Anti-Treaty
58 government TDs	35 TDs
35 other TDs	

6. The British government put pressure on the Irish government to capture the Four Courts. They were afraid that the anti-Treaty forces would become too powerful and overthrow the Treaty.
7. The anti-Treaty forces in the Four Courts kidnapped General O'Connell of the Free State Army. This gave Collins an excuse to attack the Four Courts. The Civil War had begun.
   - The pro-Treaty government forces were also called the National Army or Regulars.
   - The anti-Treaty forces were called the Irregulars or Republicans.

Progress of the Civil War

1. The fighting in Dublin lasted about a week. The government forces, with artillery borrowed from the British Army, were much too strong.
2. They captured the **Four Courts** and the leader, Rory O'Connor. Cathal Brugha was killed in O'Connell Street. The centre of the city was destroyed for the second time in six years.
3. The anti-Treaty forces retreated to the **Munster Republic**, behind a line from Limerick to Waterford.

4. Recruitment increased the size of the Regulars or pro-Treaty forces to 60,000.
5. They successfully attacked Limerick and Waterford.
   - They attacked and captured Cork from the sea.
6. Griffith died of a brain haemorrhage; a week later Collins was killed in an ambush in Beal na mBláth, Co. Cork.
   - W.T. Cosgrave and Kevin O'Higgins took over the government.
7. The Civil War became very **bitter** as the Irregulars used guerrilla warfare. The Irregulars began a campaign of assassinating pro-Treaty TDs and Senators. Sean Hales, TD, was shot in Bandon. They also attacked Protestants.
8. The government passed the **Emergency Powers Act**, which set up military tribunals.
   - They used the death penalty – Erskine Childers was executed for having a gun. In revenge for the death of Hales, four Irregular prisoners were executed without trial.
9. The government used internment to hold 12,000 anti-Treaty prisoners.
10. The war dragged on until Liam Lynch, chief of staff of the IRA, was shot in North Cork. Frank Aiken succeeded him and he called a ceasefire.

The impact of the Civil War

- **Deaths**: About 4,000 people, soldiers as well as civilians, were killed.
- Some of the ablest leaders of the rise of Sinn Féin and War of Independence died: Griffith, Collins, Brugha and O'Connor.
- **Destruction**: The centre of Dublin was destroyed and other cities and towns suffered much destruction, as well as the roads and railways.
- **Politics**: The pro-Treaty side had won, so the Treaty would now be put into practice.
  - The two main political parties in the south had their origins in the Treaty and Civil War – Cumann na nGaedheal (later Fine Gael) were pro-Treaty, while Sinn Féin (later Fianna Fáil) were anti-Treaty.
  - **Partition** was reinforced by the Civil War, as the Unionist government was able to strengthen its position.
- **Bitterness**: The bitterness caused by the Civil War continued long after the war.
- **Economy**: The economy was disrupted again, as it had been by the 1916 Rising and the War of Independence.

10. State building and the consolidation of democracy: Cumann na nGaedheal in power, 1922–32

In this section, you should understand:
- How Cumann na nGaedheal built up the new state, consolidated democracy and pursued sovereignty (independence)
- The role of William T. Cosgrave (Key personality, p. 132)

1. The new state called the Irish Free State was established in December 1922.

- Between 1922 and 1932, what steps did the Cosgrave governments take to establish the Irish Free State on firm foundations?
- What steps did Irish governments take to consolidate democracy, 1923–45?

2. The pro-Treaty party, Cumann na nGaedheal, was in government; its leader, W.T. Cosgrave, became president of the Executive Council; another minister, Kevin O'Higgins, Minister for Home Affairs, was very influential.

3. Cumann na nGaedheal did not have an overall majority in the Dáil, but Sinn Féin followed an abstentionist policy (they would not take their seats in the Dáil because of the Oath of Allegiance); the Labour Party was the main opposition.

Summary: Consolidation of democracy

1. Under Cumann na nGaedheal
- Constitution
- Administration
- Law and order
- Army mutiny
- Transfer of power to Fianna Fáil

2. Under Fianna Fáil
- Managing the IRA and the Blueshirts
- New Constitution

Founding the State

1. **Constitution**: The Constitution was a liberal democratic one like others in Western Europe, but modelled on the British. It was based on the Anglo-Irish Treaty.
   - The head of state was the British king. An **oath of allegiance** was taken by the TDs to the king; the **governor-general** represented the British Crown; the first governor-general was Tim Healy.
   - The Free State government insisted on the governor-general being Irish and a commoner, which was different from other Commonwealth countries.
   - The Oireachtas (or Parliament) was composed of the Dáil and Senate; the Dáil elected the president (now called Taoiseach) who appointed the Executive Council (cabinet).
   - Proportional representation: PR was the system of voting used in parliamentary elections, to give representation to minorities.

2. **Administration**: Most of the 20,000 civil servants from the British administration stayed on; they provided stable, fair and efficient administration.

3. **Law and order**: The Civil War was still in progress in early 1923 and there was lawlessness

exam focus

State building can include building the economy as well as political structures such as the constitution, law and order, etc.

afterwards – there were 800 cases of arson and armed robbery between August 1923 and February 1924.

- The **Public Safety Act** (1923) was passed to stamp out armed resistance.
- There was **internment** of suspects; about 12,000 people were interned during the Civil War, including de Valera and other leaders of Sinn Féin and the anti-Treaty IRA.
- The **Garda Síochana** was set up by Kevin O'Higgins in 1924; it was unarmed and respected. It dealt with poteen making, drunkenness, land disputes and intimidation of shopkeepers. It restored order.
- The **1924 Courts of Justice Act** set up new courts; District Courts, Circuit Courts, a High Court, a Court of Criminal Appeal and a Supreme Court were provided for. English common law was used; this gave stability and continuity.
- The Free State government gradually succeeded in establishing the **rule of law**.

The 1924 army mutiny

1. **Causes**: after the Civil War the government planned to demobilise 2,000 army officers and 35,000 soldiers. These soldiers faced unemployment.
   - There was a reduction in the army budget from £14.7 million to £4m by 1925.
   - Some said the government was not moving fast enough towards a republic.
   - Others were unhappy with the dominance of the Army Council by IRB men.
   - There was tension between the 'Old IRA' and ex-British Army soldiers who had joined the Free State Army.

2. **Progress**: In March, Cosgrave received an ultimatum from army officers demanding:
   - an end to demobilisation
   - removal of the Army Council
   - some steps leading closer to a republic.

3. The government reacted decisively:
   - **O'Duffy**, Commissioner of the Garda, was put in charge of the army.
   - The signatories of the ultimatum were arrested; this led to the resignation of other officers from the army.
   - Officers who deserted were deemed to have resigned.
   - Richard **Mulcahy** resigned as Minister of Defence – there was conflict between Mulcahy and O'Higgins about the handling of the crisis.
   - J. McGrath, Minister of Industry and Commerce, also resigned because he objected to government policy on the 'Mutiny'.

4. **Kevin O'Higgins** also tried to solve the complaints of the men.
   - An enquiry was promised into army administration.
   - Pro-IRB men on the Army Council were replaced by neutrals.
   - A pension scheme for soldiers was guaranteed.

5. **Results – consolidating democracy**
   - The government established that the army of the Free State was under the control of the Dáil and the government. O'Higgins said, 'Those who take the pay and

wear the uniform of the State, be they soldiers or police, must be non-political servants of the State.'

Economic policy of Cumann na nGaedheal, 1922–32

1. The Free State government of Cumann na nGaedheal was confronted with a contracting economy; the prosperity of the First World War was over.

2. **Budgetary policy**: the government followed a policy of **balancing the budget** and avoiding borrowing.

> **FREE TRADE:**
> The elimination of tariffs (taxes) on imports to encourage trade between countries.

- Income tax was reduced.
- Government expenditure was reduced from £42 million in 1924 to £24 million in 1926.
- There was a cut of 1 shilling from the old-age pension (1924).
- Little was spent on housing, and social welfare benefits were limited and means-tested.

J.J. McElligott

J.J. McElligott became Secretary of the Department of Finance in 1927 and was very influential in deciding government policy. He believed in keeping taxes low and avoiding borrowing; he served on the Banking Commission; he was opposed to protectionism and believed in free trade. He became chairman of the Tariff Commission, and he supported the Shannon Scheme to harness the river for electricity. (See Key personality: *J.J. McElligott*, p. 138)

---

3. **Agriculture**
   - Agriculture was regarded as the main industry – it provided over 50 per cent of the jobs in the country and 84 per cent of exports.
4. But farming was **backward** and **inefficient** – many farms were small; farmers could not afford technology, e.g. tractors, and older farmers held onto their land for too long.
5. The Cumann na nGaedheal government saw the development of agriculture as its main economic objective.
   - It passed the (Hogan) Land Act (1923) to complete land purchase.
   - In 1924 it passed an act for the regulation of livestock breeding.
   - Minimum standards were laid down for dairy products, meat and eggs.
   - The Agricultural Credit Corporation (ACC) was set up to provide loans to farmers to develop their farms – but few farmers took loans.

Results: Agricultural exports increased up until 1929.

Summary: Economic progress

Under Cumann na nGaedheal
- Budgetary policy
- Agriculture
- Industry
- Shannon Scheme
- Role of J.J. McElligott
- Wall Street Crash and the Great Depression

Under Fianna Fáil (See pp. 101–103)
- Economic War with Britain
- Industry – Free trade to protectionism
- Agriculture
- Economy during World War II

6. **Industry: Free Trade or protectionism?**

Industry earned two-thirds of national income.

- The government had to decide whether to introduce **protectionism** (tariffs on imports) or not.
- A **Fiscal Inquiry Commission** was set up (1923) to decide the matter.
- The bigger, exporting industries (e.g. Guinness, Jacob's) were against protectionism; they wanted free trade.
- The smaller, home-based industries favoured protectionism to stop British competition.

> **key point**
>
> PROTECTIONISM:
> Using tariffs (taxes) to protect home industry against competition from foreign industries.

- The Commission was against the use of tariffs. But the Minister of Finance was forced to bring in some tariffs – on boots, shoes, soap, clothing, furniture.

7. **The currency**: The Currency Act of 1927 held the Irish pound at the same level as sterling. Since the Irish pound was overvalued, Irish exports were dearer.

8. **The provision of electricity**: The **Shannon Scheme** was built at a cost of £5 million. A German company built the hydroelectricity station between 1925 and 1929.

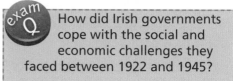

> **exam Q**
>
> How did Irish governments cope with the social and economic challenges they faced between 1922 and 1945?

- 4,000 labouring jobs were provided in building the station.
- The Electricity Supply Board (ESB) was set up in 1927 to manage the production and sale of electricity. It set up the first national grid in Europe to carry electricity to towns and later to rural areas.

9. The European economies improved in the mid-1920s and that helped the Irish economy. Industrial employment increased from 102,000 in 1926 to 110,000 in 1929.

10. **The Wall Street Crash of 1929 and the Great Depression**

- Ireland was not affected by these events until 1931 – trade collapsed, agricultural exports fell and there was a rise in unemployment. The government introduced more tariffs. Using the balanced-budget approach, it cut the salaries of civil servants, teachers and gardaí.

11. **Other problems:**
   - Emigration continued during the 1920s – 25,000 to 30,000 left each year.
   - Taxes were low, so the government did not have money to tackle the housing and healthcare problems affecting the people.

Foreign policy: Anglo-Irish affairs

Irish foreign affairs were dominated by the relationship with England.

1. Ireland, the '**Restless Dominion**', was always trying to extend its independence; it used the Treaty as a 'stepping stone' to independence.

2. Ireland was different from other dominion countries.
   - Other dominions (e.g. Canada) were settled by people from the mother country (Britain). Irish nationalist leaders looked on membership of the Commonwealth as a '**second-best**' status.
   - The Anglo-Irish Treaty had a less royalist oath than the other dominions; and the governor-general was an Irishman and a commoner.

3. The Free State government followed an **independent foreign policy**:
   - It joined the League of Nations in 1923.
   - In 1924 the government registered the Treaty with the League of Nations; this meant it was a treaty between two sovereign governments.
   - The Free State sent its own representative to the United States.

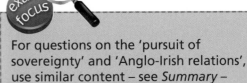

exam focus

For questions on the 'pursuit of sovereignty' and 'Anglo-Irish relations', use similar content – see *Summary – Anglo-Irish relations, 1922–49,* p. 117

key point

SOVEREIGNTY:
The authority of a state to control itself, and to be free of outside control.

key point

DOMINION STATUS:
Countries that were members of the British Commonwealth but had a degree of power over their own affairs.

The Boundary Commission

1. The Boundary Commission was set out in the Treaty – to determine the exact boundary between North and South. In October 1924 Cosgrave and Baldwin, the British prime minister, set up the Commission.

2. **Commissioners:** Chief Justice Feetham (South Africa) was the chairman; the Northern representative was J.R. Fisher, an Ulster Unionist; the Free State representative was Eoin MacNeill, Minister for Education – he was also Professor of History at UCD.

3. The Free State government believed that large areas of the North would be transferred to the South.

4. Craig, the prime minister of Northern Ireland, ignored the Commission.

5. **Terms and progress**: The Commission had to adjust the border 'in accordance with the wishes of the inhabitants so far as may be compatible with economic and geographic conditions'.

6. The Commission heard legal arguments about the terms; it had private discussions and visited border areas.

7. Feetham believed that geography and economics were more important than the wishes of the people.

8. MacNeill did not inform Cosgrave of the progress of the Commission, but Fisher kept Craig informed.

9. In November 1926 information leaked to the *Morning Post* newspaper. It published an article stating that the Commission would leave the border as it was except for small changes. The Free State would get small parts of Armagh and Fermanagh, and lose part of Donegal.

10. There was **uproar** in the South.
    - Eoin MacNeill resigned from the government and from the Commission.
    - Cosgrave, O'Higgins and McGilligan went to London to stop the report of the Boundary Commission being made public.
    - There was agreement with the British government – the report would not be published and the Free State did not have to contribute to British public debt.

11. **Results**: Partition was made permanent. 'Partition' became an issue in Southern politics again.
    - Damage was done to the Cumann na nGaedheal government because of its handling of the affair.

12. **Relationship with the Commonwealth – expanding sovereignty**: After the failure of the Boundary Commission, the Free State representatives used the **Imperial Conferences** of the Commonwealth to expand the power of each of the countries of the Commonwealth.

13. This led to the **Balfour Declaration** in the 1926 Imperial Conference: the Commonwealth countries were 'autonomous (self-governing) communities within the British Empire, equal in status, in no way subordinate to one another in any aspect of their domestic or external

Summary: Pursuit of sovereignty

Under Cumann na nGaedheal
- 'Restless Dominion'
- Independent foreign policy
- Boundary Commission – failure
- Balfour Declaration
- Statute of Westminster

Under Fianna Fáil
- Dismantling the Treaty
- New Constitution
- Economic War
- Neutrality in World War II

Under Inter-Party government
- Republic of Ireland Act 1949

affairs, though united by a common allegiance to the Crown and freely associated as members of the British Commonwealth of nations'.

14. This resulted in the **Statute of Westminster, 1931** – Britain could not make laws for the dominions and the dominions could repeal laws previously passed by Britain.

15. Now the Free State government could change the Anglo-Irish Treaty.
   - De Valera later used the freedom achieved by the Free State government within the Commonwealth to dismantle the Treaty.

Reasons for the decline of Cumann na nGaedheal

1. During the 1920s the popularity of Cumann na nGaedheal declined.

2. It was regarded as **conservative and middle-class**, e.g. it did not tackle the housing problems of the 1920s; it cut old-age pensions and seemed to favour the better-off farmers.

3. It had **poor party organisation**; the leaders were mainly concerned with running the country and building the new state.

4. The failure of the Boundary Commission – partition was now fixed.

5. The **lack of dynamism** in the leadership, particularly by Cosgrave. The assassination of Kevin O'Higgins, an energetic and active leader, was a blow to Cumann na nGaedheal.

The rise of Fianna Fáil

1. Fianna Fáil was founded in 1926 when Sinn Féin continued with its policy of abstentionism. De Valera broke away from Sinn Féin and set up Fianna Fáil.
   - De Valera had the qualities of a leader; he was able to command **loyalty**.
   - Fianna Fáil had a very **good party organisation** based on cumann (branches); this was the work of Lemass and Boland, who went around the country organising.
   - The party had the broad appeal of its policy on **republicanism** and **social issues**; its economic policy was based on protectionism and self-sufficiency.
   - American and local money were used to found *The Irish Press* newspaper – it publicised Fianna Fáil policy.

2. The effects of the Great Depression on Ireland – it reduced exports and there was a rise in unemployment.

3. The hard-line image of Cumann na nGaedheal – it cut the salaries of civil servants to balance the budget.

The 1932 general election

1. The results of the 1932 general election were:
   - Cumann na nGaedheal – 57
   - Fianna Fáil – 72
   - Labour – 7

- Farmers – 3
- Independents – 14

2. De Valera and Fianna Fáil formed the next government with the help of the Labour Party.

11. State building and the consolidation of democracy: De Valera and Fianna Fáil in power, 1932–39

 In this section, you should understand:

- How de Valera handled Anglo-Irish affairs/pursued sovereignty (independence)
- How de Valera consolidated democracy (IRA and the Blueshirts)
- How de Valera managed the economy (Key personality, p. 131)

Anglo-Irish relations: Dismantling the Treaty

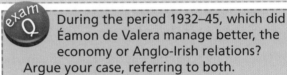 During the period 1932–45, which did Éamon de Valera manage better, the economy or Anglo-Irish relations? Argue your case, referring to both.

1. The **Statute of Westminster** (1931) gave power to change laws passed by Britain; now the Dáil could alter the Treaty, if it wished.

2. De Valera held the posts of president of the Executive Council and Minister for External Affairs; he adopted a step-by-step approach to dismantling the Treaty.

3. **The oath of allegiance**: de Valera brought in a bill abolishing the oath (March 1932); it was passed by the Dáil but rejected by the Senate; the oath was eventually abolished in May 1933.

4. **The Senate**: The Senate was dominated by Cumann na nGaedheal; it held up some of de Valera's bills; it was abolished in 1936.

5. The demotion of the **governor-general** (James MacNeill): government ministers boycotted functions attended by the governor-general; he was forced to resign and was replaced by Domhnall Ó Buachalla, a failed Fianna Fáil candidate.
   - Ó Buachalla did not live in the vice-regal lodge in Phoenix Park, but in a suburban house. The office was eventually abolished in June 1937.

6. **Privy Council**: The right of an Irish citizen to appeal from the Irish courts to the Privy Council was abolished.

7. The **king** in the constitution: The crisis in England caused by the abdication of Edward VIII in December 1936 was used by de Valera to abolish all the remaining functions of the king from the Free State Constitution.
   - He also passed the **External Relations Act**, which authorised the king to appoint diplomatic representatives on the advice of the Irish government.
   - De Valera had achieved external association within the Commonwealth.

8. **New Constitution**: By 1937 the Free State Constitution of 1922 had been changed so much that a new constitution was needed; de Valera wrote most of it. It made Ireland an independent republic in all but name.

9. **Main points:**

- The Irish people had the right to decide their own form of government.
- The territory of the state was 'the whole island of Ireland' (Article 2), but 'pending the reintegration of the national territory' (unification) its laws would apply only to the 26 counties (Article 3).

exam focus

Know the significance of certain key dates so that you can understand what is being asked in questions. For example:

- 1922–32 – Irish Free State, Cumann na nGaedheal in power
- 1932–39 – Fianna Fáil in power
- 1939–45 – Ireland during World War II

- The head of state was the president; it was mainly a ceremonial position.
- The Oireachtas (Parliament) was made up of the Dáil and the Senate.
- The Senate (60 members): Most members were elected by a system of vocational voting; the Senate was little more than a debating chamber.
- The head of government was the Taoiseach, elected by a majority of the Dáil.
- The Catholic Church was accorded a special position, but there was to be no religious discrimination.
- The place of women was 'within the home'; the family was the core of society and divorce was unconstitutional.

10. **Assessment**

- It was written by de Valera, but it was influenced by the encyclicals of the Catholic Church.
- It made the country republican in all but name but did not use the word 'republic', in order to avoid conflict with the British.
- It made Ireland liberal and democratic in political terms, but conservative in social matters, e.g. divorce and women.
- It strengthened partition.

11. The constitution was passed by 57 per cent of the voters in July 1937.

The economic war with Britain

1. De Valera refused to pay **land annuities** (valued at £3 million) to Britain in 1932. The British retaliated by imposing 20 per cent duties on Irish agricultural exports.
2. De Valera put 20 per cent duties on British (industrial) imports.
3. This meant increased prices for the consumer, but de Valera was able to blame these on Britain.
4. Agricultural exports collapsed from £36 million in 1931 to £18 million in 1934 (partly caused by the Great Depression).

- Calves were slaughtered; farmers suffered, especially cattle farmers; bounties were given by the government to compensate farmers.

5. The Irish economy suffered generally because of the economic war.
   - There was a serious reduction in the incomes of farmers.
   - There was a rise in unemployment from 29,000 in 1931 to 138,000 in 1935.
   - There was an increase in emigration to Britain.
   - There was a need to come to some agreement with Britain.

6. The **Coal–Cattle Pact (1935)** increased the numbers of Irish cattle allowed into Britain; the Free State took an extra 1.25 million tons of British coal.

7. **Anglo-Irish Agreement (1938)**
   - Relations with Britain improved after the Coal–Cattle Pact; the new Dominions Secretary, Malcolm McDonald, got on well with de Valera. This lead to the Anglo-Irish Agreement (1938).

8. The **terms** of the Agreement:
   - Ireland had to make a single payment of £10 million to pay off the land annuities.
   - The extra duties imposed by each country were withdrawn, but there was still protection of certain goods.
   - Britain gave up the three 'Treaty ports'.

9. **Significance** of the Agreement:
   - The economic war ended.
   - Irish neutrality was made possible during World War II by British withdrawal from the ports.

The economy – free trade to protectionism

1. Fianna Fáil policy was aimed at self-sufficiency. This would be achieved by protectionism and building up home industry. It was the old policy of Griffith's Sinn Féin.

2. Fianna Fáil was helped in implementing the policy by:
   - the economic war, when duties were put on British goods;
   - the Great Depression, when many countries introduced protection.

3. **Industry**: Seán **Lemass** was Minister for Industry and Commerce.
   - Fianna Fáil regarded industry as more important than agriculture (in contrast to Cumann na nGaedheal).

4. Tariffs and quotas on industrial imports provided **less competition**. There was the growth of some industries for the home market, e.g. car assembly, textiles, footwear.
   - But they were often **inefficient**; they charged higher prices and some companies had monopolies, so the consumer suffered.

5. The **Control of Manufacturers Act** said that Irish people must be involved in all new firms; as a result some foreign companies set up Irish subsidiaries.

6. **More industry**
   - The government set up the **Industrial Credit Corporation** (1933) to give loans to new industries.
   - State-sponsored industries (e.g. Aer Lingus, ICC, Irish Life) were developed because private industry would not invest in costly capital projects.

7. **Employment**
   - The **Housing Programme** – there was a serious shortage of houses; the government cleared slums and £10 million was spent between 1932 and 1940. An average of 12,000 houses were built each year (compared to 2,000 a year in the 1920s).
   - It was a labour-intensive industry, so it provided employment.

8. **Results**
   - There was increased employment in manufacturing industry (111,000 rose to 166,000). But industries were often inefficient; they had no competition. Ireland had few raw materials so they had to be imported – often the factories simply assembled imported parts.
   - Emigration stopped for a while during the Great Depression, but began again in the mid-1930s; 26,000 emigrated in 1937.
   - Export industries were hit; Jacob's, Guinness and Ford set up factories in Britain.
   - Poverty was widespread; average Irish income fell compared to the British in the 1930s.

9. **Agriculture**: Fianna Fáil planned to modernise farming and make farms bigger. It also wanted more tillage.

10. **Methods**: The government gave a guaranteed price for wheat; the acreage of wheat increased from 24,000 acres in 1932 to 254,000 acres in 1936. But the barley acreage was down, so only 10 per cent of extra acres were grown. Sugar factories were set up – more tillage.

11. **Results**: Agriculture was affected by the economic war – calves were slaughtered, production declined and exports fell.

The IRA and the Blueshirts

1. Fianna Fáil and the IRA were associated before the general election of 1932.
   - Fianna Fáil promised to release IRA prisoners. They were both republican and anti-Treaty.

Consolidating democracy

2. After the 1932 general election, IRA prisoners were released, the Public Safety Act was suspended and the ban on the IRA was lifted.

3. Cumann na nGaedheal meetings were broken up – 'No Free Speech to Traitors' – and Civil War tensions rose.

4. **Army Comrades Association** (ACA) was founded before the 1932 general election to safeguard ex-members of the army and to honour the memory of dead soldiers.

5. ACA was opened to public membership; its leader became Dr T.F. O'Higgins, a Cumann na nGaedheal TD and brother of Kevin O'Higgins.

6. ACA was committed to opposing Communism and upholding free speech; it had 30,000 members. It defended Cumann na nGaedheal meetings and this led to clashes with the IRA.

7. **Eoin O'Duffy** was dismissed as Commissioner of the gardaí by de Valera. He became leader of ACA. He was energetic and a good speaker, but he had little political ability.

8. ACA changed its name to the National Guard; it became known as the **Blueshirts**.

9. O'Duffy favoured vocational representation in Parliament – O'Duffy believed that party politics should be abandoned and that Parliament should be composed of representatives of professional and vocational groups (e.g. farmers, workers, etc.) He liked the corporate state set up by Mussolini in Italy.

10. In August 1933 O'Duffy planned a **march in Dublin** to commemorate the deaths of Collins, Griffith and O'Higgins. It was banned by de Valera, who feared that O'Duffy was planning a coup like the March on Rome (the 1922 event in which Benito Mussolini and his Fascist Party came to power in Italy); he also formed a special police force, nicknamed the **Broy Harriers**. O'Duffy gave in; the National Guard was declared an illegal organisation.

11. **Fine Gael** was formed: Cumann na nGaedheal, the Centre Party and the National Guard combined; the leaders feared that de Valera was heading towards dictatorship.
    - The National Guard was renamed the Young Ireland Association and became the youth organisation of the party. O'Duffy became leader of Fine Gael.

12. But O'Duffy was a poor leader:
    - he used extreme language – he talked about invading Northern Ireland
    - there was increasing violence in the countryside as farmers withheld rates and the government confiscated cattle and auctioned them off (the effects of the economic war).

13. There was dissatisfaction in Fine Gael with O'Duffy. O'Duffy failed to improve Fine Gael's position in the local elections (June 1934). O'Duffy told the farmers they should withhold rates.
    - He was deposed as leader and he went off to Spain to help Franco in the Spanish Civil War. The Blueshirts disintegrated.

14. **Assessment: Were the Blueshirts fascist?**
    - Their opponents called them fascists. They had the symbols of European fascism (e.g. salute, uniform). O'Duffy admired Mussolini. Corporative ideas were promoted.

    But:
    - The inspiration for the ideas came from papal encyclicals, especially *Quadragessimo Anno*. (These ideas were also used by de Valera in the 1937 Constitution.)

- The Blueshirts were opposed to dictatorship; they proclaimed their belief in democracy. They never believed in the use of violence as an end in itself (which fascists believed in).

De Valera and the IRA

1. The IRA began to criticise de Valera; the IRA did not like de Valera's policy of gradually dismantling the Treaty, they thought it was too slow.
2. There were divisions in the IRA between socialist republicans and traditional republicans.
   - The socialists believed that the IRA should involve itself in social and economic issues.
   - The traditionalists believed that the IRA should have one aim only – getting a 32-county republic.
   - The IRA was responsible for attacks, e.g. they killed 70-year-old Admiral Somerville in West Cork for giving references to young men who wanted to join the British Navy.
3. De Valera took action against the IRA.
   - The **Offences Against the State Act** was passed – internment without trial could be used. De Valera banned the IRA.
4. De Valera won over moderate republicans soon after coming to power – he gave pensions to men who had served in the anti-Treaty side in the Civil War.
   - The actions of de Valera had weakened the IRA by the beginning of World War II.

The achievements of de Valera, 1932–39

- He dismantled the Treaty (pursuit of sovereignty).
- He successfully dealt with the Blueshirts and the IRA; he showed his party could be relied on to protect the institutions of the state (consolidation of democracy).
- He brought in changes in the economy, especially by introducing protectionism. But the policy of self-sufficiency in agriculture and industry had failed.
- Social reform began (the Housing Act provided better houses; unemployment assistance was given for the first time in 1933; there were pensions for widows and orphans).
- He made neutrality possible by restoring the Treaty ports through the Anglo-Irish Agreement (1938) (pursuit of sovereignty).
- De Valera was involved in the League of Nations as President of the Council.

12. Language, religion, education and culture in the Free State

aims In this section, you should understand:
- How the state (government) promoted culture
- The role of language, religion and education in the promotion of cultural identity
- The Eucharistic Congress (1932)
- The role of Evie Hone (Key personality, p. 137)
- The link between state, education and culture in Northern Ireland (See p. 121)

Language, education and culture

The leaders of the new Free State, whether Cumann na nGaedheal or later Fianna Fáil, agreed with Pearse's idea that Ireland should be 'not free merely, but Gaelic as well'.

key point Promoting cultural identity

exam Q How was cultural identity promoted in Ireland, North and South, between 1920 and 1945?

1. The Free State government wanted to revive and restore **Gaelic culture**. The education system was the main instrument for achieving that.

2. In the early 1920s, the Minister for Education was **Eoin MacNeill**. The Department of Education changed the curriculum to achieve its aims.
   - The compulsory teaching of Irish history and language was introduced into **primary schools**; Irish had to be taught for at least one hour a day.
   - The emphasis in history teaching was to show 'examples of patriotism' and to analyse years of 'British oppression'.
   - Teachers had to pass an examination in Irish – special courses were set up for teachers to improve their knowledge of Irish.
   - A School Attendance Act was passed to ensure compulsory school attendance for children up to 14 years of age.

3. Only about 10 per cent of students attended **second-level schools**.
   - New examinations at Intermediate and Leaving Certificate level were introduced into secondary schools.
   - Special grants were given to schools that taught all subjects through Irish. Extra marks were given to students who did their examinations through Irish.
   - Knowledge of Irish became a compulsory requirement for civil service jobs.
   - History, with particular emphasis on Irish history, was a core subject up to Intermediate Certificate.
   - In the 1930s, the Fianna Fáil government made it necessary to pass Irish in the secondary schools examinations.

4. A new system of technical education was introduced under the **Vocational Education Act** (1930). Vocational Education Committees were set up to organise the schools. They geared students towards apprentices and the trades.

Assessment

1. The government also changed some place names, e.g. Kingstown became Dun Laoghaire.

2. However, the government's policies for reviving the Irish language failed.
   - The compulsory nature of Irish language teaching turned many students against the language. People continued to use English as their everyday language.

3. The promotion of a cultural identity was also the work of artists and writers.
   - The **writers** included W.B. Yeats, who was awarded the Nobel Prize for Literature in 1923. While Yeats supported the independence movement, he was critical of some aspects of the new Free State, such as censorship and the ban on divorce.
   - Another **writer** was the playwright Seán O'Casey. O'Casey's plays, such as *The Shadow of a Gunman*, *Juno and the Paycock* and *The Plough and the Stars*, were set in Dublin during the struggle for independence between 1916 and the Civil War. But O'Casey's portrayal of the times was not always acceptable to people; there were riots when the Abbey Theatre staged *The Plough and the Stars*.
   - The **artists** included Paul Henry, Jack B. Yeats and **Evie Hone**. Henry captured the way of life and the landscape of Achill Island; Yeats depicted Irish country life in the early decades of the twentieth century, which was a popular theme with nationalists; Hone produced outstanding stained-glass windows, mostly with a religious theme. (See Key personality: *Evie Hone*, p. 137.)

Religion

1. The Catholic Church took the pro-Treaty side in the Civil War because of their opposition to revolution.

2. The Church controlled most of the primary and secondary schools.

3. The Catholic Church was concerned with the state of **morals**, especially with the effect of cinema, radio and the English press on people's attitudes to sexual matters.
   - The bishops wrote pastorals attacking drinking, violence, gambling and modern dancing – especially jazz. Modern fashions were criticised because of the danger of immoral behaviour; 'company keeping' was heavily criticised.

4. The political leaders agreed with the Church on these issues; Cosgrave was an orthodox Catholic who supported the bishops' views.

5. Much of the legislation (laws) followed the views of the Catholic Church, for example on divorce, alcohol and censorship.
   - **Censorship of Films Act** – films were cut or rejected if they were 'subversive of public morality'.
   - **Intoxicating Liquor Act** – reduced the opening hours of pubs.
   - Divorce was banned.

- **Censorship of Publications Act** – banned the work of many important Irish and non-Irish authors.

6. When de Valera came to power in 1932, he followed the same pattern as Cumann na nGaedheal; de Valera was a devout Catholic.

   - The Eucharistic Congress (1932) was organised successfully. (See Case study: The Eucharistic Congress, 1932)

   - De Valera made a Holy Year pilgrimage to Rome in 1933.

   - The government put a tax on foreign newspapers.

7. The Fianna Fáil government also passed:

   - the Criminal Law Amendment Act, which banned the import of contraceptives
   - the Public Dance Halls Act, which required people to get a licence to hold dances
   - the 1937 Constitution, which recognised the 'special position' of the Catholic Church. On divorce, the role of mothers and the family, the Constitution followed the views of the Catholic Church.

8. But on political matters de Valera took an independent line, such as on the entry of the communist Soviet Union to the League of Nations, support for sanctions against Mussolini after his invasion of Abyssinia, and the Spanish Civil War.

9. After World War II, Catholicism was strengthened as it became more conservative. The bishops (hierarchy) became more critical of other aspects of Irish life, such as trade union affairs and the Health Act (1947).

> **key point**
>
> CENSORSHIP:
> Controlling the publication of books, magazines or newspapers or the showing of films in accordance with certain standards.

Case study: The Eucharistic Congress, 1932

1. In the early twentieth century, the Catholic Church was **very powerful** in Ireland.

   - Bishops and priests had considerable influence over their people.

   - The Catholic religion was associated with nationalism.

   - The Catholic Church was involved in healthcare (hospitals) and education (schools).

   - The influence of the Catholic Church increased with the establishment of the Irish Free State where Catholics were a dominant majority.

   - The political leaders agreed with the Catholic Church on many issues of public morality, such as censorship and divorce (see above 'Religion' p. 107).

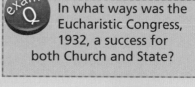

> **exam Q**
>
> In what ways was the Eucharistic Congress, 1932, a success for both Church and State?

> **key point**
>
> Promoting cultural identity

2. **Organisation:** The Eucharistic Congress was agreed with the Vatican by the Cumann na nGaedheal government under W.T. Cosgrave. The Eucharistic Congress was organised in honour of the Holy Eucharist, and it was held every two

years in different cities. Dublin was selected to honour the coming of Christianity to Ireland in 432.

- **Eoin O'Duffy**, Commissioner of the Garda, was put in charge of the government side of the organisation. But the main organisation was carried out by the Catholic Church through a committee of laymen and clergy, led by the director, **Frank O'Reilly**.

3. During the Irish Civil War, the Catholic Church was in conflict with republicanism, and now the Church was unsure of the new **de Valera** government which took over before the Congress was held.

- But de Valera looked on the Eucharistic Congress as an **opportunity to gain respectability** for Fianna Fáil, and to improve relations with the Catholic Church. De Valera was prepared to spend more money on the organisation of the Congress than the previous Cumann na nGaedheal government.

Events

4. The Congress was held over five days (22–26 June) and it began with the arrival of the Papal Legate, Cardinal **Lauri**.

- The streets of Dublin and other towns and cities were decorated with buntings and flowers. Aspects of Early Christian Ireland such as round towers and artwork featured prominently in decorations. Public buildings in Dublin were lit at night and the most advanced loudspeaker system was installed in the Phoenix Park and along the streets of Dublin. A new high-powered transmitter was installed in Athlone and the event was broadcast on 2RN (later Raidió Éireann). The Catholic Church raised money from parishes and businesses.

- The government passed the **Eucharistic Congress Act 1932** which gave powers to regulate traffic and gave special exemptions to hotels and restaurants.

- The huge crowds coming to Dublin were accommodated in large camps in the city, and in emergency accommodation in schools and town halls. Liners docked in Dublin accommodated many of the foreign visitors.

- Pilgrims came from European countries and Church leaders who were Irish-born of or Irish descent came from Australia, USA and Canada; Irish missionary clergy and bishops came from Africa and Asia.

5. In his **address of welcome** to Cardinal Lauri, de Valera associated Catholicism with the Irish people; he talked about the coming of Christianity to Ireland and the persecution that Irish people had suffered for their faith.

6. A week of **religious celebrations** followed, including public lectures on the Eucharist and exhibitions, especially highlighting Ireland's contribution to Catholicism.

- There were special days for men, women and children; on separate days there was the Men's Mass with 250,000 present; the Women's Mass, 200,000; and the Children's Mass, 100,000. During the week there were 20,000 voluntary stewards and 4,000 Catholic boy scouts involved.

7. The highlight was the open-air **High Mass** in the Phoenix Park with 1 million in attendance. Thousands travelled by road and rail from all over Ireland.

- There was a specially built altar, and John McCormack, Ireland's greatest tenor, sang 'Panis Angelicus'.
- The Pope, Pius XI, broadcast live from Rome to the people in the Phoenix Park.
- The mass was followed by a procession to the city centre for benediction where the crowds thronged O'Connell Street.

8. Cardinal Lauri sent a telegram to the Pope praising the Irish people's commitment to the Catholic religion and the Pope. The Vatican was delighted with the success of the Eucharistic Congress.

- After the Congress, Cardinal Lauri visited a number of Irish towns such as Armagh and Killarney.

9. **Assessment**

- The organisation of the Eucharistic Congress was a source of **pride** to the Irish government.
- Fianna Fáil showed the party's commitment to the Catholic Church. De Valera called a **snap election** soon after which resulted in a Fianna Fáil majority government.
- The Fianna Fáil government ignored the **Governor-general, James McNeill**, who was not invited to the government reception for the Papal Legate. This and other later boycotting of the Governor-general led to his resignation and replacement by a supporter of de Valera.
- The Congress helped heal **civil war divisions**; the army and gardaí worked well with the new government; and Cosgrave and de Valera were canopy bearers during the procession of the Eucharist.
- The Congress showed that **Catholicism** was strong in Ireland. It reinforced the idea of the South of Ireland being a Catholic State for a Catholic people. The Congress lessened the attraction of radicalism in Ireland.
- The power of the Catholic bishops increased, and the status of the Catholic religion was strengthened in the Irish Constitution of 1937.
- **Differences between North and South** were highlighted: About 100,000 Catholics travelled from Northern Ireland to the Congress in Dublin. But some were attacked by loyalists in Belfast, Lurgan, Coleraine and other towns as they travelled by buses and trains.

13. The war years, 1939–45: The Emergency

In this section, you should understand:

- Irish neutrality during World War II
- The impact of World War II on society and economy in the South
- Be able to link with developments in Northern Ireland, including the Case study: Belfast during the Second World War (see p. 122)

Neutrality

1. During World War II, de Valera and Fianna Fáil were in power.

2. The Dáil declared neutrality the day after war broke out in September 1939.

NEUTRALITY:
When a country does not take part in a war, e.g. Ireland's neutrality in World War II.

Pursuit of sovereignty

- The **Emergency Powers Act** was passed – this gave the government almost total power to secure public safety and the preservation of the state.
- The war years became known as The Emergency.

3. **Why did Ireland remain neutral?**
- Neutrality was an expression of Ireland's sovereignty or independence – the war could be seen as a 'British' war.
- The return of the Treaty ports: neutrality was now a practical proposition; Ireland would not get dragged into the war.
- Irish experience in the League of Nations: Owing to the ineffectiveness of the League, de Valera believed small nations should not be the pawns of big powers.
- Self-protection: Ireland was unable to defend herself – involvement in the war would result in great loss of life and enormous damage.
- Neutrality was the least divisive policy, because involvement in the war would cause deep divisions in Ireland with those who were strongly anti-British/pro-German.

National security

A **Department for the Coordination of Defensive Measures** was set up and it was headed by Frank Aiken.

- It increased the size of the regular army to 30,000 and the Local Defence Forces (LDF) to 100,000 members; there were a total of 250,000 soldiers in the armed forces.
- A coast watch was in operation.
- Gas masks were given to civilians; air-raid shelters were constructed.

- But the country had old-fashioned planes, and the navy had only six motor torpedo boats and two gunboats.

Strictly neutral

1. The outward signs of neutrality were maintained; there was press censorship and control of the radio.
   - There were no weather forecasts.
   - De Valera gave his condolences on the deaths of Roosevelt (America) and Hitler (Germany) in 1945.
2. But Ireland was **friendly to the Allied side**:
   - Information was given to Britain concerning all aliens (including Germans) in Ireland.
   - Ireland allowed infringement of Irish airspace over Donegal by British flying boats and US planes.
   - Weather reports were given secretly to the British.
   - Allied (British and American) pilots who crashed were allowed to return to Northern Ireland, while German pilots were interned.
   - British boats were allowed into Irish waters for air-sea rescue.

Neutrality in danger

1. The **IRA** held the traditional republican view that 'England's difficulty was Ireland's opportunity' – they put pressure on Britain because of the 'Six Counties'.
2. The IRA organised a bombing campaign in Britain in 1939.
3. The IRA raided the government magazine fort in Phoenix Park at the start of the war and took 1 million rounds of ammunition – the government later got most of it back.
4. The IRA cooperated with Germany – German spies landed to encourage IRA attacks on the border (e.g. Hermann Goertz, May 1940, who was later arrested and interned).
5. De Valera clamped down on the IRA – there was a special camp in the Curragh for internment; 500 IRA members were held there. De Valera broke the IRA hunger strikes (three died on hunger strike); there were five executions. The IRA had been almost wiped out by the end of the war.

The great powers

1. The most serious threat to Irish neutrality from great powers came between mid-1940 and the invasion of Russia in June 1941.
2. **Britain**: Sir John Maffey, the UK representative in Ireland, helped maintain relations between Ireland and UK; he got on well with de Valera.
3. **Churchill**, prime minister in 1940, saw the war as a great moral crusade against Nazi Germany.
   - He wanted the Treaty ports to be put at Britain's disposal; this was refused by de Valera.

- Churchill promised that if Éire entered the war, he would end partition at the end of the war.
- This idea was rejected by de Valera, because Britain would not be able to persuade the Unionists.

4. But Britain did not want to invade Ireland because:
   - Ireland provided food
   - Irish labour worked in Britain and Irish soldiers joined the British Army
   - Britain already possessed Northern Ireland, so it could patrol the North Atlantic from bases there.

5. Churchill's victory speech after the war criticised Ireland's failure to allow Britain to use the Irish ports; de Valera's reply appealed to Irish national sentiment.

6. **Germany**: Dr Eduard Hempel, German representative in Ireland, wanted to keep Ireland out of the war; he was against sending German spies to Ireland.

7. German spies dropped from planes or landed from submarines; most were easily caught. Only one – Hermann Goertz – escaped capture for 18 months.

8. Germany's '**Operation Green**' was a plan to invade Ireland, but it was not possible to put it into practice even if Hitler had wanted to invade the country.

9. German planes bombed Ireland – in Campile, Co. Wexford 3 people were killed; in the North Strand, Dublin (May 1941), 28 people were killed and 80 were injured.
   - Ireland was clear of the danger of invasion after Operation Barbarossa (June 1941).

10. **America**: After this the most serious danger to Irish neutrality came from David Gray, American representative in Dublin.
    - De Valera and Gray did not like each other.
    - Aiken went to the United States in 1941, but the US refused to supply Ireland with military equipment.
    - As the Americans prepared for D-Day, they feared that German spies in Ireland would report on preparations being made in Northern Ireland. In 1944 the Americans demanded the closure of the German and Japanese legations in Dublin; de Valera refused, which worsened relations between the US and Ireland.
    - De Valera expressed regret to the American representative on the death of President Roosevelt (April 1945).

The economy

1. The government was given wide powers to regulate supplies and prices.
2. Irish trade was dependent on British ships, which were now needed for the war effort; Seán **Lemass** was appointed as **Minister of Supplies**; he set up Irish Shipping and he bought eight ships and chartered five more.
3. 152 Irish seamen died during the war.
4. There was a general shortage of raw materials owing to the war.

5. **Effects**
   - Private motoring was ended – there was no petrol for ordinary people.
   - The trains slowed; there was just a single weekly train between Dublin and Cork.
   - Gas and electricity were rationed; use of 'glimmer men' (gas inspectors).
   - There was **rationing** of clothes, bread and tea; basic foodstuffs were in adequate supply, e.g. eggs, potatoes, meat and 'Lemass's Brown Bread'.
   - Turf was used instead of coal; there was a black market in rationed goods.

6. Wages were controlled (Wages Standstill Order, 1941) but inflation was high (70 per cent), so people were worse off. There was a fall in living standards.

7. **Industry** was hit: there was the loss of essential raw materials – Ireland got 25 per cent of petrol, 16 per cent of gas coal, no domestic coal. There was a limit on the use of gas and electricity. Industries dependent on imports were badly hit so the policy of self-sufficiency formed in the 1930s suffered.

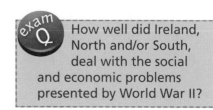

> **exam focus**
>
> When the question asks for 'and/or', you will not lose marks if you only answer one part. However, when the question says 'and' or 'both', you will lose marks if you do not refer to both parts in your answer.

8. **Agriculture**
   - There was an attempt at self-sufficiency during the war, but there were shortages of fertilisers (89,000 tons in 1939 – only 7,000 tons in 1941), feedstuffs (no imports) and machinery.

9. In 1940 the government introduced compulsory tillage – wheat = 0.25 million acres in 1939 rose to 0.6 million acres in 1945; overall tillage rose from 1.5m acres to 2.6m acres by 1945. But productivity (output per acre) fell.

10. Dairy, cattle and sheep production was not directly affected; they continued exports to Britain. But farmers were not sufficiently recovered from the Economic War to gain the full benefit of British demand. Also farms were hit by foot and mouth disease in 1941, and by British control of prices.

> **exam Q**
>
> How well did Ireland, North and/or South, deal with the social and economic problems presented by World War II?

11. **Unemployment** was high during the war; it was eased by demand for Irish labour in Britain and the numbers joining the British Army (50,000) and the Irish Army.
    - There was increased emigration, mostly to Britain – between 1936 and 1946, 187,000 (an average of 18,000 a year) emigrated. The increased emigration led to remittances (money) being sent back to families in Ireland. It eased unemployment in Ireland.

Assessment

1. Neutrality was maintained to some extent by playing the great powers off against each other, but mainly because the great powers felt the disadvantages of invading Ireland would outweigh the advantages.
2. Neutrality bolstered independence (sovereignty).
3. Greater divisions between North and South resulted, because the North had been part of the war.
4. The Northern economy prospered during the war.
5. Unionists felt greater attachment to Britain; they felt that Southern Ireland had neglected its duty during the war. (See *Northern Ireland – the Unionist Party in power and the war years*, pp. 117–22.)

14. The First Inter-Party government and the declaration of a republic

 In this section, you should understand:

- Why Fianna Fáil lost the 1948 general election
- Why the First Inter-Party government passed the Republic of Ireland Act (1949)

The 1948 general election

1. **Clann na Poblachta**, a republican party, was founded in 1946. It wanted a united Ireland, and it was committed to social and economic reform. It took support from Fianna Fáil.
2. De Valera called a snap election to surprise the opposition parties, especially Clann na Poblachta.
3. Result of election: Fianna Fáil was still the largest party (with 68 seats), but the First Inter-Party government was formed.

Reasons for the defeat of Fianna Fáil

1. Emergency conditions continued after World War II – there were shortages, rationing, low wages and strikes; as well as these, disease rates rose owing to bad living conditions; the Fianna Fáil government was blamed for these conditions.
2. Unemployment and emigration continued after the war: 120,000 people emigrated between 1945 and 1948. Government policies were blamed for this also.
3. A change was needed after 16 years – de Valera had been in power since 1932; people felt that it was time for a change.
4. Talks led to the formation of the **First Inter-Party government**. This was a coalition (combination) of Fine Gael, Labour, Clann na Poblachta, Clann na Talmhan,

National Labour and Independents. Richard Mulcahy, leader of Fine Gael, allowed John A. Costello to become Taoiseach because of objections to himself.

5. The First Inter-Party government laid the foundations for future economic progress by drawing up the first **Economic Plan**, and establishing Coras Trachtála to promote exports in the United States and Canada, and the Industrial Development Authority (IDA) to promote industry.

Anglo-Irish relations: Ireland declared a republic

1. On a visit to Canada, the Taoiseach, John A. Costello, announced that Ireland was going to repeal the External Relations Act (1936) and declare itself a republic.

Pursuit of sovereignty

   • The Minister for External Affairs, Sean McBride, a strong republican and former head of the IRA, favoured such a move.

2. The **Republic of Ireland Act (1949)** declared Ireland a republic; Ireland left the Commonwealth. Ireland formally became a republic at Easter 1949. Costello hoped that this would take the gun out of Irish politics.

REPUBLIC:
A completely independent Ireland.

3. The British Labour government, under pressure from Northern Unionists, passed the **Ireland Act** (1949), which said Northern Ireland would remain part of the United Kingdom as long as the parliament of Northern Ireland decided so.

4. **Impact:**

   Ireland had moved from dominion status within the British Commonwealth in 1922 to a republic outside the Commonwealth in 1949.

   • Partition between North and South was strengthened by the Republic of Ireland Act and the Ireland Act.

   • The Republic of Ireland Act did not take the gun out of politics – the IRA began border campaigns in the 1950s and the Troubles began in the North in the late 1960s.

   • The First Inter-Party government began an anti-partition campaign; but the efforts of Irish delegates to speak about the evils of partition at international conferences failed.

   • Ireland maintained its neutrality; Ireland was invited to join NATO (North Atlantic Treaty Organisation – a military alliance), but the Minister for External Affairs, Sean MacBride, refused because it would mean recognising Northern Ireland.

exam Q — How did Anglo-Irish relations develop during the period 1923–49?

Summary: Anglo-Irish relations, 1922–49

1. **Under Cumann na nGaedheal**
   - Cumann na nGaedheal and Anglo-Irish relations
   - The Boundary Commission
   - Relationship with the Commonwealth: the Balfour Declaration, 1926 and the Statute of Westminster, 1931
2. **Under Fianna Fáil**
   - Fianna Fáil and Anglo-Irish relations
   - Dismantling the Treaty
   - New Constitution
   - The economic war – the Coal–Cattle Pact, 1935, and the Anglo-Irish Agreement, 1938
   - World War II and Anglo-Irish relations
3. **Under the First Inter-Party government**
   - The First Inter-Party government – the declaration of the Republic and Anglo-Irish relations

15. Northern Ireland – the Unionist Party in power and the war years

aims In this section, you should understand:
   - How the Unionist government managed the affairs of Northern Ireland from 1920 to 1945
   - Case study: Belfast during the Second World War
   - The role of James Craig (Key personality, p. 125)
   - The role of Richard Dawson Bates (Key personality, p. 135)

Setting up of Northern Ireland

1. The **Government of Ireland Act (1920)** provided for Home Rule for the 32 counties of Ireland with one parliament in Dublin and one parliament in Belfast.

   exam focus

   The key dates here are:
   - 1920 – Northern Ireland set up
   - 1939–45 – World War II
   - 1945–49 – post-war period

   - The majority of power was reserved for the Westminster Parliament – Crown, war and peace, armed forces, foreign affairs, imports and exports.
   - The Government of Ireland Act was rejected by Sinn Féin, but it was put into operation in Northern Ireland; the Northern parliament opened in June 1921.
   - Partition was put in place.

key point

Unionists in power

2. The constitutional status of Northern Ireland:
   - The king of England was represented by the Governor; Parliament was divided into two Houses – the Senate and the Commons; the first prime minister was James Craig (later Lord Craigavon).
   - The House of Commons had 52 members who were elected by proportional representation (PR) until 1929. The Unionist Party won most of the seats.

Early crises

1. **Law and order**: In the early 1920s, there were tensions because of rising unemployment and IRA attacks; the boom of the First World War had ended and the War of Independence was in progress.
2. A rabble-rousing speech by Edward **Carson** in July 1920 led to the expulsion of Catholics – about 10,000 men and 1,000 women – from the shipyards and factories.
3. The Catholic response led to burnings, assaults and deaths; some Catholics were killed and driven from their homes in 1920 and 1921. The Dáil ordered a Southern boycott of Northern Irish goods. This increased tensions.
   - Overall, in 1920–22, 400 Catholics were killed and 1,200 were injured; about one-third of the people killed were Protestants.
4. The **Craig–Collins Pact (1922)** was agreed to ease tensions; even though Craig and Collins met three times, they failed to solve the conflicts.
5. In 1922 the IRA attacked police and Army barracks along the border, as well as Protestant businesses and homes.
   - The IRA wanted to provoke British retaliation and to end the Anglo-Irish Treaty.
6. The Unionists responded. The Minister of Home Affairs, **Richard Dawson Bates**, took severe action. Suspected IRA members were rounded up and interned in a ship in Belfast harbour. The **Ulster Volunteer Force** (UVF) was re-formed under the leadership of Basil Brooke to fight IRA border attacks. The **Civil Authorities Act** (or Special Powers Act) was passed; it gave powers of arrest and imprisonment, including internment, to the Minister for Home Affairs. The Royal Ulster Constabulary (RUC) was armed; they were supported by the '**B Specials**', a body of armed, part-time policemen; UVF members joined the 'B Specials' when they were set up.
   - Tough action by the Northern government and the start of the Civil War in the South led to less trouble in the North.
7. **The Anglo-Irish Treaty and partition:**
   - While the Anglo-Irish Treaty negotiations were going on, Northern Unionists were supported by Bonar Law, leader of the Conservative Party, and this ensured that the North did not become part of an All-Ireland Parliament.
   - Northern Ireland opted out of a united Ireland, as allowed for in the Anglo-Irish Treaty. Craig was afraid the **Boundary Commission** would take a large area from

Northern Ireland. He refused to appoint a Northern representative to the Boundary Commission, so one had to be appointed by Britain (Fisher).

- The **failure** of the Boundary Commission meant that the border was not changed and Craig's policy of not cooperating proved successful.

Unionist dominance

1. The Unionist Party was the governing party in Northern Ireland – Unionists controlled about 40 of the 52 seats in Parliament. The Parliament of Northern Ireland was a Protestant parliament for a Protestant people.

2. The Unionist Party was linked to the **Orange Order**.
   - The Orange Order united Protestants of all classes, from workers to industrialists.

3. To ensure their **domination**, the Unionist government:
   - redrew the boundaries of local government constituencies to guarantee unionist majorities in Catholic areas (called gerrymandering);
   - replaced PR in 1929 by simple majority vote and single-member constituencies for Commons elections;
   - had 26 members in the Senate, mostly elected by the Commons; in that way it was controlled by Unionists;
   - had 12 Members of Parliament representing Northern Ireland in Westminster; the Unionists won all the seats in each election.

4. **Local government**: Only ratepayers and owners of property could vote in local elections; this system favoured Unionists, who formed the majority of the property-owning classes. Unionist-dominated local councils often discriminated against Catholics, particularly in housing and jobs.

5. In the **Royal Ulster Constabulary (RUC)**, one-third of places were reserved for Catholics but few joined; the 'B Specials' were Unionist-controlled.

6. Nationalists were represented by the Nationalist Party and Sinn Féin.
   - Nationalists and Sinn Féin MPs did not take their seats in Parliament in the early 1920s. Nationalist MPs took their seats after the Boundary Commission ensured the border would not change – but they had little influence in Parliament.
   - Unionists believed the nationalists were trying to undermine Northern Ireland.

The economy: Finance

- The Northern government was often short of money, because taxation was controlled by Westminster.
- In the 1920s Northern Ireland was allowed to pay for its own services and give what was left over to pay 'the imperial contribution'.
- During the Great Depression, Northern Ireland had to pay for its own social welfare.
- In 1938 Britain agreed that it would make up any deficit (shortage) in the Northern Ireland budget.

Agriculture

1. A quarter of all workers were engaged in agriculture. Farmers were guaranteed access to the British market; as a result the pattern of agriculture changed away from cattle to sheep, pigs and poultry.

2. During the 1920s the Northern Ireland government passed laws to improve the quality of cattle, and to lay down minimum standards of quality and packaging for eggs, fruit, dairy and meat products.

> **exam Q**
> ● How well did the Unionist Party manage the affairs of Northern Ireland, 1920–39?
> ● What were the main social and economic challenges facing Northern Ireland, 1920–45?

3. Agricultural output rose significantly between 1926 and 1939.

Industry: Economic decline, 1920–39

1. The population of Northern Ireland was 1.5 million; over 60 per cent of people lived in Belfast and in the larger towns.

2. The North's two **main industries** were the textile industry, employing largely women, and the shipbuilding industry, employing largely men; both these industries depended principally on the British market.

3. Northern Ireland experienced high **unemployment** in the 1920s and 1930s, similar to the unemployment in the depressed areas of Britain.

4. The **textile industry**, especially linen, declined because:
   ● the boom of the First World War came to an end;
   ● the Great Depression and the change to man-made fibres led to unemployment averaging 25–30 per cent.

5. The **shipbuilding industry** declined because:
   ● after the First World War there was less demand in Britain for ships; the workforce declined from 15,000 to 7,500;
   ● the Great Depression (1929) reduced the number of ship workers to 2,000; one of the shipyards (Workman, Clark and Company) closed.

6. **Unemployment** remained high up until 1939. Social conditions were bad; there was a great deal of poverty; there was high infant mortality, tuberculosis (TB) and bad housing.

Education

1. Lord Londonderry was Minister of Education. He wanted to unite Catholics and Protestants, unionists and nationalists.

2. He passed the **1923 Education Act** – local councils were responsible for primary education; they had to build and maintain primary schools; schools that were part of the scheme received large grants. Religion was to be taught outside school hours.

key point

Promoting cultural identity

3. But pressure from the Protestant and Catholic churches led to the **failure** of his plan. Protestant schools became part of the government system and received full grants. Protestants and the Orange Order put pressure on the government, so that schools could provide Bible instruction during school hours.

- Catholic schools opted out of the local authority schools. They wanted only 'Catholic children . . . taught in Catholic schools, by Catholic teachers, under Catholic auspices' (support). They were given less government funding.
- As a result, Protestant schools were part of the government education system; Catholic schools were outside it. This contributed to **divisions** in Northern Ireland.

Education and culture

1. In Northern Ireland, the curriculum did not emphasise 'Ulsterness' in history or geography. Instead it concentrated on British history. Northern Unionists feared that teaching Ulster history would increase sectarian tensions.
2. However, Catholic secondary schools were able to teach southern Irish history.
3. The use of the Irish language was forbidden in addressing letters, for street names or other official uses.
4. But the Irish language or Irish history could be taught as an optional subject in primary schools.
5. Nationalist or Unionist identities were developed more through their religion, the newspapers and local organisations.

Sectarian conflict in the 1930s

1. In 1931 there were serious anti-Catholic attacks in a number of towns after the IRA attacked an Orange meeting in Co. Cavan. Later there were attacks on Catholics attending the Eucharistic Congress in Dublin. There was further trouble in the mid-1930s – burnings, looting and rioting. The British Army was called in to stop the riots.
2. The aim of the **Ulster Protestant League** was to safeguard jobs for Protestants.
   - Sir Basil Brooke, who was later prime minister, said: 'I have not one Catholic about my place.' Government ministers urged Protestants to employ Protestants.

The war years in Northern Ireland, 1939–45

1. Northern Ireland played an important part in World War II, because her ports and airports could be used as bases for **convoy protection**.
   - The North was used as a training ground for preparing for the D-Day invasions.
   - Conscription was not extended to Northern Ireland because of nationalist objections, but 5,000 from Northern Ireland died fighting in the war.

key point

The impact of World War II, North and South (see pp. 111–15)

- At the end of the war, Churchill congratulated Northern Ireland on its part.
- **Craig** died in 1940 – he was replaced as prime minister by **J.M. Andrews**, who refused to bring in younger ministers; he was forced to resign in 1943 and was replaced by Sir Basil Brooke.

2. **Northern industry** contributed to the war effort.
   - Ships – almost 700 warships and merchant ships were built during the war.
   - Harland and Wolff launched 150 warships and 123 merchant ships. It made 550 tanks, and Shorts built 1,500 bombers.
   - Engineering works made guns.
   - By 1945 the number of jobs in shipbuilding had increased to 21,000; other industries employed almost 21,000 workers, while the aircraft industry employed over 20,000.

3. Clothing factories made shirts, uniforms and parachutes.

4. Thousands of jobs were created when the North became a base for the US Navy and for training American soldiers.

5. Unemployment fell from 25 per cent to 5 per cent, and wages rose.

6. **Agriculture during World War II**
   - Agriculture supplied food to the British market; there were guaranteed prices for farm produce; production trebled.
   - Compulsory tillage orders increased the acreage under tillage; major crops were flax, oats and potatoes. By 1948 there were over 30,000 extra agricultural workers.

7. **Overall the Northern economy benefited greatly from World War II.**

Case study: Belfast during the Second World War

1. **War industry**: Belfast made a significant contribution to the war effort. Northern industry was centred mainly on the city.

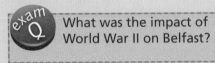

   What was the impact of World War II on Belfast?

   - **Harland and Wolff** produced warships, aircraft carriers, merchant ships and tanks; 140 warships, 123 merchant ships, 3,000 ships repaired.
   - **Short Brothers and Harland** produced aircraft; 1,500 Stirling bombers, 125 Sunderland flying boats. Engineering works produced armaments: 500 tanks, 75 million bullets and 50,000 bayonets.
   - The **linen industry** produced parachutes, uniforms and tents. Belfast exported food to Britain.

2. **Unemployment** fell as more workers were taken on, from 70,000 in 1941 to 10,000 in 1944.

3. **Defence**: Belfast was poorly defended from air attack:
   - It had only 24 anti-aircraft guns; the RAF in nearby Aldergrove did not have night fighters.

- The fire brigades were inadequate; blackouts were not enforced.
- There were only 4 public air-raid shelters because the government did not want to spend the money.
- Plans to evacuate children from the city failed.
- There were no searchlights and very few barrage balloons.

4. The Northern government failed to accept that there was a threat from the German Luftwaffe (air force) – **why**? Belfast was too far away; they would find it difficult flying over Britain and back; but some air-raid shelters were built when the British government warned about the danger of air attack.

5. The **German conquest of France** and the **Blitz of British cities** brought the threat closer. The new Minister of Public Security, **John McDermott**, was concerned about the danger.

6. Belfast was now within range of the Luftwaffe. The Luftwaffe did reconnaissance missions over the city and photographed targets around the docks (November 1940).

Bombings

7. Belfast was bombed **four times**: the first attack – the **Dockside Raid** – was on 7 April 1941, by seven German bombers. Thirteen people were killed and there were fires in the city.

8. A much more serious attack occurred on 15 April – the **Easter Raid**. Belfast was attacked for five hours by 180 aircraft as the anti-aircraft guns stopped firing.
- The bombers missed the docks and bombed mainly the working-class areas. 900 people were killed and about 600 were seriously injured.
- Public baths were used to lay out the bodies for identification.
- The Northern government requested **fire brigades** from the **south** which came from Dublin, Drogheda, Dundalk and Dun Laoghaire. This impressed the Northern Unionists but it endangered Irish neutrality.

9. After this people left the city for fear of attack: some left for the South of Ireland; others left the city each night for the suburbs and the countryside – these were called '**ditchers**'; the bombing revealed the terrible slum conditions; this influenced the development of the Welfare State after the war.

10. There were further raids in May 1941.
- In the **Fire Raid** (4–5 May), incendiary and high-explosive bombs were dropped on the harbour and on Harland and Wolff. Harland and Wolff was put out of production for six months. Almost 200 people were killed.
- Two bombers did very little damage in the **Fourth Raid** (5–6 May) but fourteen people were killed.

Results

11. In all the **attacks**:
- there were 1,100 people killed;

- half the houses in the city were destroyed; about 100,000 people were made temporarily homeless;
- there was **£20 million** of damage, but Belfast industries continued their contribution to the war;
- **Poverty** – the evacuations and the bombings revealed the poverty of the working class families in Belfast; this forced the Stormont Government to improve social welfare and to avail of the welfare state in Britain after the war.
- the government was criticised for poor defence preparations. It was one of the factors that led to the replacement of **J.M. Andrews** as prime minister by **Basil Brooke**.

12. Hitler's invasion of the Soviet Union in June 1941 ended the danger of further bombing of Belfast.

Northern Ireland after World War II

1. The post-war period saw the strengthening of the links between Northern Ireland and Britain.

2. **Politics**: The pattern of Unionist domination continued.
   - When the southern government passed the Republic of Ireland Act the British government passed the **Ireland Act (1949)**, which stated 'that in no event will Northern Ireland or any part thereof cease to be a part of his Majesty's dominions and of the United Kingdom without the consent of the Parliament of Northern Ireland'.

The economy

1. **Agriculture**
   - Exports of surplus eggs and milk continued to Britain.
   - Northern farmers were guaranteed prices and markets; farmers' incomes rose.

2. **Industry**
   - The traditional industries of shipbuilding, textiles and engineering continued their decline.

3. **Health**
   - The North benefited from the application of the **Welfare State**.
   - In 1948 the Northern Ireland Health Services Act was passed, which gave to Northern Ireland the same scheme of health service as in Britain; there was a comprehensive scheme of healthcare free for all citizens, with no means test. Because of the Health Services Act, Northern Ireland healthcare was well ahead of that in the South.

4. **Housing**
   - The extension of the Welfare State boosted the building of houses.

5. **Education**
- The extension of the Welfare State had a major effect on education in Northern Ireland. The **Education Act (1947)** raised the school-leaving age to 15, provided free post-primary education, gave increased grants to voluntary schools (i.e. Catholic schools), and provided more university grants.

6. As a result, numbers in secondary schools doubled. Other effects included:
- Secondary schooling was free in the North, but not in the South.
- Spending per pupil was much higher than in the South.
- It created a new, educated, Catholic middle class.

7. The improvements in health, housing and education changed Northern Ireland, brought her closer to Britain and widened the divisions between North and South.

Key personalities

James Craig

1. James Craig was born near Belfast in 1871, the son of a prosperous whisky distiller.

2. He was elected Unionist MP for East Down and later Mid-Down from 1906 to 1921.

3. As a Unionist he wanted to maintain the union with Britain.

4. Craig was the main organiser of **Ulster Unionist resistance** to Home Rule when it looked likely that the Third Home Rule Bill would become law, 1912–14.
- He was instrumental in Edward Carson becoming the leader of the Irish Unionist party.
- Craig organised Carson's tour of Ulster and provided his home, Craigavon, as the location for major anti-Home Rule speeches.
- He was the main organiser of the rallies all over Ulster at which Unionists pledged in the Ulster Solemn League and Covenant to fight Home Rule 'by all means which may be found necessary'.
- He backed the **Ulster Volunteer Force** and was involved in the purchase of arms in Germany, which were landed through the ports of Larne, Bangor and Donaghadee.

5. By 1914, he had begun to take a different view from his leader, Carson.
- While Carson did not favour partition, Craig and many Ulster Unionists were not concerned about Unionists in Southern Ireland and were prepared to accept partition.
- Craig was prepared to allow Home Rule for the South of Ireland provided Ulster remained part of Britain.

6. Craig and Carson represented the Ulster Unionists at the **Buckingham Palace Conference** called by King George V to find a solution to the Home Rule question. But Craig and Carson would not agree with the Home Rulers.

7. When the operation of the Home Rule Act was suspended until after the First World War, Craig encouraged Unionists to join the British Army in defence of the Empire and union with Britain.

8. Craig failed medical tests to join the Army. Instead he was a junior minister in the British government between 1917 and 1921.

9. He influenced the terms of the **Government of Ireland Act** (1920). He insisted that a six-county Northern Ireland would be better, in opposition to British ministers and some Unionists, who favoured nine counties.

10. Craig became the first prime minister of Northern Ireland after the Act came into operation.

11. He ensured that Northern Ireland overcame the IRA campaign in 1920–22 with the passage of the Special Powers Act, the setting up of the 'B Specials' and the armed RUC.

12. The **Craig–Collins Pact** (1922) was agreed to ease tensions; even though Craig and Collins met three times they failed to solve the conflicts.

13. While the Anglo-Irish Treaty negotiations were on, he worked for the support of Bonar Law, leader of the Conservative Party, and this ensured that the North did not become part of an All-Ireland parliament.
    - Northern Ireland opted out of a united Ireland, as allowed for in the Anglo-Irish Treaty.

14. Craig was afraid the Boundary Commission would take a large area from Northern Ireland.
    - He refused to appoint a northern representative to the Boundary Commission, so one had to be appointed by Britain (Fisher).
    - The failure of the Boundary Commission meant that the border was not changed and Craig's policy of not cooperating had been successful.

15. He maintained **Unionist dominance** in Northern Ireland through electoral victories and changes to the electoral laws for local and parliamentary elections.

16. He made no real effort to integrate the nationalist minority into Northern Ireland.

17. He was often absent from Ulster during the 1930s and his wartime leadership was ineffective.

18. He remained as prime minister until his death in 1940.

Patrick Pearse

1. Patrick Pearse was born in Dublin in 1879. His father was an English stonemason, his mother was Irish.

2. He was educated by the Christian Brothers in Westland Row and at University College, Dublin. He qualified as a barrister at King's Inn.

3. Pearse took an early interest in the **Gaelic Revival**; he joined the Gaelic League at 16 and became editor of its newspaper, *An Claidheamh Soluis*, at 23.

4. Pearse wrote poems and plays in Irish and English. He took a keen interest in Irish history, beginning with the legendary heroes such as Cuchulainn. Later, he studied the lives of the republican leaders Wolfe Tone and Robert Emmet.

5. Pearse founded his own school, St Enda's, because he believed the school system was important in preserving the Irish language and culture.

6. In November 1913 Pearse attended the opening meeting of the Irish Volunteers, formed to ensure the passage of Home Rule.

7. He became a member of the **Irish Republican Brotherhood** (IRB) in 1914, dedicated to the use of force to achieve a republic.

8. Pearse became the Director of Military Organisation of the **Irish Volunteers**. He believed that the IRB could use the Volunteers to stage a rebellion. He opposed Ireland's involvement in the First World War and was part of the minority Irish Volunteers who broke away from the main body of the Volunteers (who supported Redmond).

9. In 1915 he made a **speech** at the graveside of an old Fenian, O'Donovan Rossa: 'Life springs from death; and from the graves of patriot men and women spring living nations . . . [The English] think they have purchased half of us and intimidated the other half . . . but, the fools, the fools, the fools! – they have left us our Fenian dead, and while Ireland holds these graves, Ireland unfree shall never be at peace.'

10. Pearse was a member of the IRB's Supreme Council and also its **Military Council**, which planned the 1916 Rising.

11. **Blood sacrifice:** Pearse believed military success was not needed; instead their deaths would change people's attitudes and revive the spirit of the Irish nation.

12. The Military Council appointed him President of the Irish Republic and Commander-in-Chief. He was part of the Military Council which decided to go

ahead with the Rising on Easter Monday even though the arms from Germany were captured and the manoeuvres for the Irish Volunteers were cancelled.

13. He read the **Proclamation** of the Irish Republic from the steps of the GPO, where he and others had set up their headquarters for the Rising. It was mainly written by Pearse, but he had been influenced by some of Connolly's thinking.

14. At the end of a week's fighting, Pearse gave the order to surrender.

15. Pearse and 14 others, including his brother, Willie, were executed after the Rising.

Arthur Griffith

1. Arthur Griffith was born in Dublin in 1871. He was educated by the Christian Brothers and became a member of the Gaelic League and the Irish Republican Brotherhood.

2. He put forward his ideas in a book called *The Resurrection of Hungary* (1904). Here he proposed:

   - **parliamentary abstention** – a policy that Irish MPs should withdraw from Westminster and set up their own Parliament in Dublin;
   - the idea of a **dual monarchy** – a shared monarch between Britain and Ireland;
   - a policy of **self-sufficiency** based on protectionism (the use of tariffs to protect Irish industry from British competition).

3. He founded **Sinn Féin** to put forward his ideas, but Sinn Féin did not become popular.

   - However, his ideas had an important influence on later Irish history.

4. Griffith joined the **Irish Volunteers** in 1913 and was involved in the Howth gunrunning in 1914.

   - He opposed the involvement of Irishmen in the First World War, but he was also opposed to the use of force to establish a republic in Ireland.

5. He did not take part in the 1916 Rising. Even though he had no involvement in the planning, the Rising became known as the Sinn Féin Rising or Rebellion. As a result, Griffith was arrested and jailed in England.

6. When he was released he began to rebuild Sinn Féin.

   - He proposed his abstentionist policy.
   - He proposed to appeal to the post-war Peace Conference to recognise Ireland's right to self-government.

7. But his party was gradually taken over by Republicans. He stepped aside and de Valera became president of Sinn Féin in 1917.
  - The policy was based on Griffith's ideas, but dual monarchy was dropped in favour of the republic.

8. Griffith was **arrested** again during the 'German Plot'. While in jail he was elected as MP for East Cavan.

9. He was in jail when the First Dáil met in January 1919; but in setting up the Dáil, Sinn Féin was following his policy of parliamentary abstentionism.
  - He was appointed **Minister for Home Affairs** by de Valera at the next meeting in April.
  - He also became acting president of the Dáil while de Valera was in America during the War of Independence. He was involved in setting up the Sinn Féin courts.

10. Griffith was again arrested in late 1920, but was released before the Truce which ended the War of Independence.

11. He led the Irish delegation in London in talks with the British government. He supported the **Anglo-Irish Treaty** as the best that could be achieved.

12. He became President of the Dáil when de Valera resigned after the Treaty debates. The strain of involvement in establishing the new Free State and the beginning of the Civil War affected his health. He died of a brain haemorrhage in August 1921.

Michael Collins

1. Michael Collins was born in Sam's Cross, near Clonakilty, Co. Cork, in 1890.

2. At 15 he went to work in the British Post Office in London. There he joined the GAA, the Gaelic League, Sinn Féin and the IRB.

3. He returned to Ireland and took a small part in the **1916 Rising**, defending the GPO.
  - He was critical of the military tactics of the Rising, in which major buildings were captured and defended.

4. After the Rising Collins was not court-martialled but was jailed in an internment camp in Wales. Here he rose to prominence when he showed his leadership skills.

5. When he was released in December 1916 he returned to Ireland, intent on reviving the independence movement.
  - He became secretary of the Irish National Aid and the Irish Volunteer Dependants' Fund.

- Collins began to rebuild the Irish Republican Brotherhood (IRB).
- He was also active in Sinn Féin.
- By late 1917 Collins was a member of the Sinn Féin Executive and Director of Organisation for the Irish Volunteers.

6. Through his network of spies, he warned the Sinn Féin leadership about the 'German Plot'. But de Valera refused to heed the warning and, like others, was arrested.

7. Collins was elected as **Sinn Féin MP** for South Cork in the 1918 general election. He did not attend the meeting of the First Dáil in January 1919 because he was planning the escape of de Valera from Lincoln jail.

8. He was appointed **Minister of Finance** at the next meeting of the Dáil. He organised the National Loan, which helped to fund the activities of the Sinn Féin government during the War of Independence.

9. **War of Independence**
   - Collins became the **chief organiser** of the conflict in Ireland; he held the key posts of Adjutant-General of the Volunteers, Director of Organisation and Director of Intelligence. He was also president of the IRB.
   - The IRA looked to Collins rather than Brugha (Minister for Defence) for instruction.
   - Collins was determined that spies and informers would not betray the IRA. He established his own spy network, with contacts among civil servants, typists, maids, railwaymen and hotel porters.
   - The British government offered a bounty of £10,000 for information leading to his capture or death – but he managed to evade arrest.
   - Collins had his '**Squad**' of men, 'the twelve apostles' – this was a group of specially selected gunmen. The Squad tracked down and murdered detectives, especially the G-men (members of 'G division' of the Dublin Metropolitan Police who were charged with subverting the republican movement) working in Dublin Castle.
   - He planned the assassination of government spies sent to capture him on Bloody Sunday, November 1920.

10. Collins came into conflict with Brugha, who did not like his popularity, and with de Valera, who was envious of his power when he returned from America late in the War of Independence.

11. After the truce in 1921, Collins reluctantly agreed to go on the **Irish delegation** to talks with the British government in London. He accepted the terms of the Anglo-Irish Treaty as a **stepping stone** to Irish independence. But he believed he had signed his own death warrant, because he knew some would not accept the Treaty.

12. After the Treaty debates he was appointed President of the provisional government, which began the process of taking over from the British government.

13. Collins made many attempts to avoid civil war, including making an Election Pact with de Valera and not attacking the anti-Treaty forces who took over the Four Courts.

14. He ordered the shelling of the Four Courts when the Irregulars there captured a Free State general, O'Connell. He became Commander-in-Chief of the National Army.

15. Collins was killed in an **ambush** by anti-Treaty forces at Beal na mBláth, Co. Cork, in August 1922. He was buried in Glasnevin Cemetery.

Éamon de Valera

1. Éamon de Valera was born in New York in 1882. He was brought to Ireland at the age of 2 and reared in Co. Limerick by relatives of his mother.

2. He was educated by the Christian Brothers in Charleville, Co. Cork, and graduated in mathematics from the Royal University of Ireland. He got a job as professor of mathematics in Carysfort Teachers' Training College, Dublin.

3. De Valera joined the **Gaelic League** in 1910, where he met his future wife. He joined the Irish Volunteers in 1913 and rose through the ranks of the Dublin Brigade. He was sworn into the IRB by Thomas MacDonagh.

4. He took part in the **1916 Rising** in charge of Boland's Mills.
   - He showed characteristics of leadership and planning, but also suffered a nervous breakdown.
   - After the surrender, he was court-martialled and sentenced to death.
   - But his sentence was commuted to life imprisonment, partly because the British government decided to stop executions and also because he was an American citizen.

5. After release from jail in 1917, he was elected as a **Sinn Féin candidate** in East Clare. He became president of both Sinn Féin and the Irish Volunteers.

6. He was arrested in the '**German Plot**' in 1918. He was in jail when the First Dáil met in January 1919, but became President of the Dáil at the second meeting in April, after his escape from Lincoln Jail was organised by Michael Collins.

7. He spent most of the War of Independence in **America** organising a large loan and winning public support from Irish-Americans – but he failed to get official recognition for the Irish Republic.

8. When he returned he organised a truce with Lloyd George, the British prime minister. He had discussions with him, but failed to get agreement.

9. De Valera refused to become a member of the Irish delegation to negotiate with the British government, because he said he:
   - was the head of state;
   - was needed in Dublin to keep more extreme or militant republicans in check;
   - would give the delegation an excuse to refer British proposals to Dublin and to resist British pressure.

10. De Valera **rejected the terms** of the Anglo-Irish Treaty. He led the anti-Treaty side in the debates on the terms of the Treaty.

11. He contributed to the causes of the Civil War by means of the inflammatory speeches he made and in which he talked about 'wading through Irish blood'. But he played little part in the actual fighting and could not control the IRA.

12. After the Civil War, he followed the Sinn Féin abstentionist policy in relation to the Dáil, because of the Oath of Allegiance. When Sinn Féin refused to change its policy, de Valera founded **Fianna Fáil**.

13. De Valera became President of the Executive Council after the 1932 general election. In the 1930s he was involved in **dismantling the Treaty**, writing a new constitution, the economic war with Britain and taking action against the Blueshirts and the IRA. He also attended the League of Nations and was elected President of the Council and later President of the Assembly.

14. He maintained Irish **neutrality** during World War II, although it was a neutrality that was friendly to the Allies. After the war he rejected Churchill's criticism of Irish neutrality.

15. After 16 years in government, de Valera was defeated in the 1948 general election when the First Inter-Party government was formed.

W.T. Cosgrave

1. W.T. Cosgrave was born in Dublin in 1880. He joined Sinn Féin when it was founded in 1905 and was elected a Sinn Féin councillor for Dublin Corporation in 1901.

2. He joined the **Irish Volunteers** in 1913. He played an active part in the **1916 Rising**, serving under Eamonn Ceannt at the South Dublin Union.

3. After the Rising he was sentenced to death, but had his sentence commuted to life imprisonment when the British

government stopped its policy of execution. He was sent to an internment camp in Wales.

4. He won a seat for Sinn Féin in a by-election in Kilkenny in 1917.

5. After his release from prison, he was arrested again in the '**German Plot**' in 1918. He was re-elected for Kilkenny in the 1918 general election, but was unable to attend the first meeting of the Dáil in January 1919. Instead he was appointed Minister for Local Government by de Valera at the second meeting.

6. During the **War of Independence**, he worked for Sinn Féin success in the local elections where the party won control of 28 of the 33 local councils. The councils refused to cooperate with the British government, instead giving their loyalty to the Dáil and to Cosgrave as Minister for Local Government.

7. Cosgrave was in favour of the terms of the **Anglo-Irish Treaty**. He was part of the majority in the cabinet which voted to accept the Treaty. He defended the Treaty in the Treaty debates.

8. After de Valera resigned when the Treaty was accepted, Cosgrave was a member both of Griffith's Dáil government and Collins' provisional government.

9. After the deaths of Griffith and Collins during the Civil War, Cosgrave became **President** of the provisional government. Along with Kevin O'Higgins, he worked to ensure the survival of the Free State.

   - He passed the Special Powers Act, which set up military tribunals. He used the death penalty – Erskine Childers was executed for having a gun. In revenge for the death of Hales, four Irregular prisoners were executed without trial.

10. Cosgrave became **President of the Executive Council** when the Free State was officially established in December 1923. He became leader of the new party, Cumann na nGaedheal, formed by the pro-Treaty TDs in 1923.

11. As President of the Executive Council, Cosgrave worked for the next ten years to establish the new state and to expand its independence.

12. He was faced by the crisis of the **Army Mutiny**. Much of the work in stopping the mutiny was done by Kevin O'Higgins because Cosgrave was sick in hospital.

13. Cosgrave also had to deal with the problem of the **Boundary Commission**. The Irish representative, Eoin MacNeill, failed to inform Cosgrave of the progress of the Commission, so he was very surprised when the news of the Commission's findings was leaked to a London newspaper. Cosgrave rushed to London to prevent the publication of the report and maintain the border or partition as it was.

14. Cosgrave's government worked:
   - to build up the structure of the new state, maintaining its democratic tradition;
   - to develop the Shannon Scheme;
   - to expand Irish independence at the Imperial Conferences in London and to win the Statute of Westminster in 1931;
   - to gain international recognition for the Free State.

15. But the popularity of Cosgrave and Cumann na nGaedheal declined and they were beaten in the 1932 general election by de Valera's Fianna Fáil. Cosgrave ensured that power was handed over democratically to de Valera.

16. After the election, he handed over power briefly to Eoin O'Duffy when Cumann na nGaedheal, the Centre Party and the National Guard joined together to form Fine Gael. He was very much opposed to O'Duffy's ideas, and when O'Duffy was deposed Cosgrave resumed as leader. However, he was an **ineffective leader** of the opposition and the popularity of Fine Gael continued to decline.

17. He fully supported the policy of **neutrality** during World War II, but his party lost seats in the 1943 and 1944 general elections. He resigned as leader of the party and retired from politics in 1944.

Countess Markievicz

1. Constance Gore-Booth was born in London in 1868 into an Anglo-Irish family. She was reared at the family home in Lissadell, Co. Sligo.

2. She studied art in London and Paris, where she met and married a Polish count, Casimir Markievicz, in 1900.

3. Countess Markievicz became involved in **radical politics in** Dublin. She was active in the suffragette movement and she joined **Sinn Féin**. She joined Maud Gonne's Inghinidhe na hÉireann. She founded Fianna Éireann, a nationalist boy-scout organisation that taught boys military drill and the use of weapons.

4. In 1913 she supported the Dublin workers in the **Strike and Lockout**, and worked in a soup kitchen in Liberty Hall. She also became a member of James Connolly's Irish Citizen Army, which he set up to defend workers.

5. Countess Markievicz took part in the **1916 Rising** as an officer of the Citizen Army. She was second-in-command to Michael Mallin in St Stephen's Green. They were involved in the fighting all week and surrendered only when shown a copy of Pearse's surrender order.

6. After the Rising, Markievicz was the only woman to be court-martialled. She was sentenced to death, but the sentence was commuted to life imprisonment on account of her gender. She was jailed in Ireland and England until her release in 1917.

7. Shortly after her release, Markievicz converted to Catholicism.

8. Markievicz was arrested during the '**German Plot**' in 1918. While she was in jail she was elected as a Sinn Féin candidate for a Dublin constituency in the 1918 general election. She was the first woman to be elected to the Westminster Parliament. But following Sinn Féin's policy of abstention, she refused to take her seat there. She could not attend the meeting of the First Dáil in January 1919 because she was in jail – but she was appointed Minister of Labour by de Valera at the next meeting in April. She was the first Irish woman Cabinet member.

9. Markievicz opposed the terms of the **Anglo-Irish Treaty** in the Treaty debates. She was President of Cumann na mBan, which was very much opposed to the Treaty. She resigned from government after the Treaty was accepted. She fought actively on the anti-Treaty side in the Civil War, being involved in the fighting in Dublin. She toured America to raise funds for the republican cause.

10. Markievicz was elected as a Sinn Féin candidate to the Dáil in the new Free State, but refused to take her seat. She joined Fianna Fáil when it was founded and was elected as a Fianna Fáil candidate in the 1927 general election.

11. She died shortly after and was buried in Glasnevin Cemetery after a huge funeral.

Richard Dawson Bates

1. Richard Dawson Bates was born in Belfast in 1876. He became a solicitor, but he was more interested in politics.

2. Bates became secretary to the **Ulster Unionist Council** in 1905, a position he held until 1921.

3. He assisted James Craig in the organisation of Ulster Unionist resistance to Home Rule between 1912 and 1914. He was particularly involved in organising the Balmoral and Craigavon anti-Home Rule meetings and the rallies for the signing of the Ulster Solemn League and Covenant.

4. Bates was committed to a hard-line defence of the Union and opposition to Home Rule.

5. He was a founder member of the **Ulster Volunteer Force** and played a leading part in the Larne gunrunning in 1914. He worked with Southern unionists in defending the union, but he was, like Craig, prepared to agree to partition to preserve Ulster Unionism at the expense of Southern unionism.

6. His bad health prevented him serving in the First World War.

7. Bates believed in building links with the Ulster Protestant working class. During the Belfast general strike in 1919, he warned against the influence of Sinn Féin and promoted instead the Ulster Unionist Labour Association.

8. Bates was elected to the new Northern Parliament for East Belfast in 1921. He

continued to represent this area when it became the Victoria constituency, until he retired in 1945.

9. Craig appointed Bates the **Minister of Home Affairs** in 1921, a position he held for 22 years. As such he was in the forefront of defending the Northern state against IRA attacks.

- Suspected IRA members were rounded up and interned in a ship in Belfast harbour.
- The Ulster Volunteer Force (UVF) was re-formed under the leadership of Basil Brooke to fight IRA border attacks.
- A Civil Authorities Act (or Special Powers Act) was passed; it gave powers of arrest and imprisonment, including internment, to the Minister of Home Affairs.
- The Royal Ulster Constabulary (RUC) were armed; they were supported by the 'B Specials', a body of armed part-time policemen; UVF members joined the 'B Specials' when it was set up.
- He redrew the boundaries of local government constituencies to guarantee unionist majorities in Catholic areas (called gerrymandering).
- In 1929 he replaced PR by simple majority vote and single-member constituencies for Commons elections.
- In this way he played a key role in maintaining Unionist dominance in the North.
- But after his actions in 1921 he had a permanent police escort wherever he travelled in Northern Ireland.

10. Bates showed his **dislike** of Catholics.

- He had his officials intervene with magistrates not to impose prison sentences on those found guilty of attacking Catholics travelling from the Eucharistic Congress in Dublin in 1932.
- He did not want to see any increase in the numbers of Catholics serving in the RUC.
- He refused to use his office phone while a Catholic was employed as a telephonist at Stormont.

11. Bates was often a weak and incompetent Minister of Home Affairs. This showed when he failed to deal with corruption in Belfast Corporation. In the 1930s his bad health made matters worse. He failed to prepare the defence of Belfast in World War II, but survived a vote of censure in Parliament.

12. Bates continued to serve in J.M. Andrews' government after Craig's death in 1940; but he was not appointed by Basil Brooke in 1943.

13. He moved to England after the war and died there in 1949. He was buried in Portrush, Co. Antrim.

Evie Hone

1. Evie Hone was born in Co. Dublin in 1894. She was physically disabled after a fall in a local church when she was 9.

2. In 1914 she began to study art in London under Walter Sickert, Byam Shaw and Bernard Meninsky. Here she met her lifelong friend, the painter Mainie **Jellett**.

3. Between 1920 and 1930 she, along with Mainie Jellett, studied at various times in **Paris** under the semi-cubist painter André Lhote and later Albert Gleizes, both influenced by Braque and Picasso. Here Hone moved away from perspective to a two-dimensional surface.

4. Hone and Jellett had a joint exhibition in Dublin in 1924. This surprised the public, who were not used to abstract art.

5. Hone was a **very religious person** and her art was influenced by early Christian art, as well as cubism. She withdrew for a brief period to an Anglican community in Cornwall in 1925.

6. She later converted to **Catholicism**.

7. Hone had other exhibitions in Paris, London and Dublin again. In 1930 her role in introducing abstract art to Ireland was recognised in the Brussels Exhibition of Irish Art.

8. Developments in her painting led her to **stained glass**. She learnt the skills of the craft in London with Wilhelmina Geddes. There she produced her first stained-glass panels, which were leaded, as 'The Annunciation' in Taney Church, Co. Dublin, in 1933–34.

9. Hone joined the co-operative of glass and mosaic works founded by Sarah Purser, called 'An Túr Gloine'.
   - She used her cubist style to introduce new elements and styles into stained glass.
   - She showed the influence of the religious art of El Greco (Spanish Renaissance) and Georges Roualt (twentieth-century French).

10. From the mid-1940s she produced her stained-glass windows in a studio next to her home in Marlay Grange, Rathfarnham. Here she developed full-scale windows for the Jesuit Chapel, Tullabeg, Co. Offaly, and the University Hall Chapel, Dublin. She also produced 'My Four Green Fields' for the CIE offices in Dublin.
    - Her best-known work was the huge window for Eton College Chapel, the 'Crucifixion and Last Supper' window. A short film, *Hallowed Fire*, was recorded as she worked on the window.

11. Hone produced over a hundred small stained-glass panels as well as the larger windows. Her work can be seen in churches throughout Ireland, England and the United States and is in the Victoria and Albert Museum, London, the National Gallery of Ireland and the Ulster Museum, Belfast.

12. She died in 1955.

James J. McElligott

1. James J. McElligott was born in Tralee, Co. Kerry, in 1893. He graduated with a BA in classics from University College, Dublin in 1913. He was appointed to the civil service in 1913 and worked with the Local Government Board in Dublin.

2. McElligott joined the Irish Volunteers in 1913. He was returning from Fairyhouse Races on Easter Monday when he became involved in the **Easter Rising**. He fought in the GPO and led a small group of insurgents across Sackville Street (O'Connell Street) under fire.

3. As a result of his involvement in the Rising, he lost his job and was jailed in England.

4. On his release from jail in 1917, McElligott completed a postgraduate degree in **economics**. He became a freelance financial journalist and then managing editor of *The Statist*, a London financial weekly.

5. He was invited to join the new **Department of Finance** when the Free State was set up. He became assistant secretary to the Department and succeeded the secretary, Joseph Brennan, when he retired in 1927.

6. McElligott and Brennan believed in **sound finances**. This involved cuts in spending that were sometimes criticised for their severity, but which put the new state on a sound financial footing. They wanted to keep taxes low and avoid borrowing.

   ● His views were supported by the Minister of Finance, Ernest Blythe. They resulted in cuts in civil service pay during the Great Depression and increased the unpopularity of the Cumann na nGaedheal government.

7. McElligott served on the **Banking Commission**, where he produced a minority report which favoured the setting up of a central bank.

8. The Department of Finance set up the **Fiscal Enquiry Commission** to decide on whether the Free State should introduce **protectionism**. Even though McElligott was not a member of the Commission, he was opposed to protectionism and believed in free trade. The Commission also was opposed to protectionism.

- McElligott became chairman of the **Tariff Commission** and, given his views, it is not surprising that only a few tariffs were introduced.
- In the 1930s McElligott clashed with Seán Lemass, Minister of Industry and Commerce, over the question of protectionism.

9. In the mid-1920s McElligott supported the **Shannon Scheme** to harness the river for electricity.

10. He was a member of the **Currency Commission**, which later became the Central Bank under the Central Bank Act (1942).

11. McElligott constantly defended the power and influence of the Department of Finance within the structure of government.

12. He served under Sean MacEntee in the 1930s and exerted influence over him. He disapproved of the economic war in the 1930s and his assessment of its influence on the Irish economy contributed to de Valera negotiating an agreement with Britain.

13. McElligott did not favour the new Keynesian economics that began to spread from the late 1930s.

Key concepts

Allegiance: Loyalty to a person's own government or country.

Blood sacrifice: The conviction of Pádraig Pearse that he and others would be prepared to sacrifice their lives to rise up the spirit of Irish people for independence.

Censorship: Controlling the publication of books, magazines or newspapers or the showing of films in accordance with certain standards.

Conformity: When people behave in accordance with certain rules, practices or customs.

Discrimination: When a group of people are treated unfairly because of their colour, religion, sex or age.

Dominion status: Countries that were members of the British Commonwealth but had a degree of power over their own affairs.

Free trade: The elimination of tariffs (taxes) on imports to encourage trade between countries.

IRA: Irish Republican Army, the military wing of Sinn Féin, which grew out of the Irish Volunteers and which fought in the War of Independence to establish an independent Ireland.

IRB: Irish Republican Brotherhood or Fenians, a secret organisation aimed at establishing an Irish republic by force of arms.

Neutrality: When a country does not take part in a war, e.g. Ireland's neutrality in World War II.

Partition: The border dividing Northern Ireland and Southern Ireland based on the Government of Ireland Act (1920).

Physical force: The use of violence (force of arms) to achieve political aims.

Protectionism: Using tariffs (taxes) to protect home industry against competition from foreign industries.

Republic: A completely independent Ireland.

Sovereignty: The authority of a state to control itself, and to be free of outside control.

Ulster Unionism: The belief of those in Ulster that Ulster should continue to be part of Britain in accordance with the Act of Union.

Northern Ireland 1949–93: Timeline

1689	Siege and Relief of Derry
1690	Battle of the Boyne
1920	Government of Ireland Act
1943	Basil Brooke Prime Minister
1947	Education Act
1949	Ireland Act
1963	Terence O'Neill Prime Minister
1963	**Lockwood Committee on Higher Education in Northern Ireland appointed**
1964	**University for Derry Committee founded**
1965	**Lockwood Committee report published**
1967	Northern Ireland Civil Rights Association (NICRA) founded
1968	Civil rights march in Derry
	Opening of **university** at Coleraine
1969	Terence O'Neill resigned as PM, succeeded by James Chichester-Clark
1969 (Aug)	**Apprentice Boys parade in Derry, Battle of the Bogside, riots in Belfast; British army brought in**
1969 (Dec)	Split in IRA
1970 (Aug)	SDLP formed
1971 (Feb)	Chichester-Clark resigned as PM; Brian Faulkner Prime Minister
1971 (Aug)	Internment introduced
1972 (Jan)	Bloody Sunday in Derry
1972 (March)	Direct Rule from Westminster imposed on Northern Ireland
1973 (Dec)	**Sunningdale Conference and Agreement**
1974 (Jan)	**Power-sharing Executive in operation; Faulkner resigned as leader of Ulster Unionist Party**
1974 (Feb)	**British general election**
1974 (May)	**Ulster Workers' Council strike; collapse of power-sharing Executive**
1976	Political prisoner status removed from paramilitary prisoners
1980–81	Hunger strikes
1981	Republican 'Armalite and ballot box' strategy
1983	New Ireland Forum in Dublin
1984	Amalgamation of Ulster Polytechnic and New University of Ulster to form University of Ulster
1985	Anglo-Irish Agreement
1993	Downing Street Declaration

The Government of Northern Ireland, 1949–93

Prime Ministers of Northern Ireland

1943–63 Sir Basil Brooke (Lord Brookeborough)

1963–69 Terence O'Neill

1969–71 James Chichester-Clark

1971–72 Brian Faulkner

The counties of Northern Ireland

1. From Brookeborough to O'Neill, 1949–69

 In this section, you should understand:

- Brookeborough as Prime Minister
- O'Neill as Prime Minister (Key personality, p. 197)
- Economic and social development in Northern Ireland
- Case study: The Coleraine University Controversy

Background

 Who was the more effective leader, Brookeborough or O'Neill? Argue your case, referring to both.

1. Northern Ireland was set up under the **Government of Ireland Act** 1920.
   - It had two houses of Parliament: the Senate and House of Commons. These were based in Stormont, which was opened in the early 1930s.
2. The Northern Ireland government controlled internal affairs – law and order, education, health, local government.
   - The Westminster government controlled war and peace, trade and taxation.
3. The Northern Ireland parliament and government was controlled by a unionist majority.

Divided society

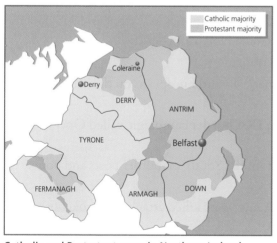

Catholic and Protestant areas in Northern Ireland

BIGOTRY:
Intolerance of other creeds or political beliefs.

TOLERANCE:
A fair and objective attitude to other people's views and opinions (intolerance – a refusal to accept other's views and opinions).

1. Protestant and Catholics were divided over **religion and politics**.
2. Protestant and Catholics were also divided along **class lines**.
   - The business and professional classes (lawyers, doctors, etc.), larger farmers, and skilled craftsmen were largely Protestant.
   - They felt superior to Catholics, who were largely smaller farmers and unskilled workers.

3. The unionist majority used the Special Powers Act, the 'B-Specials' (reserve policemen) and the straight vote in elections to control the North.

4. There was discrimination against Catholics in jobs and housing.

Post-Second World War: The Brookeborough Years, 1949–63

1. Sir Basil Brooke (later Lord Brookeborough) was Prime Minister of Northern Ireland from 1943 to 1963.

2. At the end of World War II, unionists felt secure because the British government was grateful for the part Northern Ireland had played in the war.

Ireland Act (1949)

1. In 1949, the Inter-Party government passed the **Republic of Ireland Act**, which declared the South to be a republic and took it out of the British Commonwealth.

2. Brookeborough got guarantees from the new Labour government (under Clement Attlee), which took power in Britain.
   - The British government passed the **Ireland Act** (1949), which said Northern Ireland would remain part of the United Kingdom so long as a majority in the Northern Ireland Parliament wanted it.

Threats to unionism

1. The Unionists felt threatened by the **Anti-Partition League** and the IRA border campaign.

2. The Anti-Partition League was formed in Dungannon, Co. Tyrone in 1945. It aimed to end partition (the border) between North and South.

3. It got the support of the Southern governments

4. The League tried to influence Irish-Americans and Europeans on the issue of the partition of Ireland.

5. Brookeborough faced a threat from the **IRA border campaign**, called Operation Harvest, between 1956 and 1962.
   - The IRA launched attacks, mostly from the South, on border posts and police barracks.

6. In one of those attacks, 2 Limerick IRA men were killed attacking Brookeborough RUC barracks.

7. But the Southern and Northern governments clamped down on the IRA; there were increased patrols and internment was used in both North and South.

8. By the time the border campaign was called off in 1962, 12 IRA and 6 RUC had been killed and 200 IRA convicted and jailed.

Impact of the Welfare State

1. The **Welfare State** was introduced in Britain after the Second World War. The government provided free healthcare, social welfare and education.

2. It was introduced to Northern Ireland because of the agreement that Northern Ireland would have the same level of social services as Britain ('parity').

Education reforms

3. The changes in education were brought in under the **Education Act**, 1947.
   - At the end of primary school, pupils sat an 11-Plus exam.
   - This decided whether pupils went to grammar school (more academic) or secondary school (more technical).
   - Student numbers in second-level schools doubled between 1947 and 1952. Many new schools were built.
   - There were grants available for students in third-level education.

4. Educational changes were opposed by the Catholic Church, which said the state was exercising too much control over education.

5. But the educational reforms benefited Catholics – they created an educated Catholic leadership who later opposed discrimination and led the civil rights movement in the 1960s.

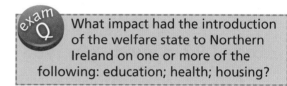

exam Q

What impact had the introduction of the welfare state to Northern Ireland on one or more of the following: education; health; housing?

6. However, Protestant and Catholic schools remained segregated (separated).

Health

7. The **National Health Service** was set up in Northern Ireland in 1948.
   - Free medical care was available to everybody.

8. The government refused to fund the Mater Hospital, a Catholic-owned and operated hospital, because it wanted complete control of the hospital.

9. Tuberculosis (TB) was responsible for half the deaths in the 15–25 age group during the 1940s. Health check-ups and the use of new drugs (e.g. BCG) reduced the death rate by 1954.

Social welfare and housing

10. A **National Insurance Scheme** was introduced – workers paid into a social insurance fund. This meant they were covered for unemployment, sickness, widows' benefit, and old age pensions.

Public housing

1. Half of Belfast's housing stock was bombed in the Second World War; over 100,000 new houses were needed.

2. After the war, the **Northern Ireland Housing Trust** was set up. It built 113,000 houses between 1945 and 1963.
   - It allocated the houses fairly between Protestants and Catholics.

3. Local councils also built houses, but there was **discrimination** in the allocation of local council houses.

- Unionist-controlled councils favoured Unionists and Protestants; nationalist-controlled councils favoured nationalists and Catholics.

The Northern economy under Brookeborough

(See *Economic and social developments in Northern Ireland up to 1969*, pp. 148–153).

1. **Agriculture** was the most important industry, but numbers working in agriculture declined during the 1950s due to mechanisation (tractors and machinery).
2. There was also a decline in the traditional industries of the North – linen and shipbuilding.
3. But new jobs were created with government incentives in synthetic fibre factories, for example, as foreign companies were attracted to Northern Ireland. But the jobs created could not match the decline in agriculture and the traditional industries.
4. Northern Ireland was a disadvantaged area. It had 7 per cent unemployment, which contrasted with the prosperity of Britain and Western Europe.
5. Unemployment was higher in Catholic areas, especially Derry and Newry.

End of Brookeborough, 1963

1. During Brookeborough's long premiership, there was relative **political stability** in the North.
2. Some people later looked on this time as a lost opportunity to bring in reforms.
3. Brookeborough failed to bring Catholics/nationalists more into the political system due to a number of factors:
   - the British government policy of not getting involved in the North
   - Brookeborough's own attitude – he regarded nationalists as potential traitors
4. Brookeborough was replaced as Prime Minister by Terence O'Neill in 1963.

The O'Neill years, 1963–69

1. As Prime Minister, Terence O'Neill was committed to the modernisation of Northern Ireland. He also wanted 'to build bridges between the two traditions' (Protestant and Catholic).
2. **Economic plan:** O'Neill appointed Professor Thomas Wilson to draw up an economic plan for Northern Ireland. The **Wilson Plan** set targets for economic expansion.
3. The economy progressed – there was a 4 per cent growth rate per year; 40,000 new jobs were created in the 1960s, but 25,000 were lost in the declining traditional industries of shipbuilding and linen. (See *Economic and social developments in Northern Ireland up to 1969*, pp. 148–153).
4. **North–South relations:** O'Neill invited Seán Lemass, Taoiseach, to the North (January 1965) to improve relations. O'Neill made a return visit to the South in February 1965.
   - They discussed mostly economic co-operation.
5. There were protests in the North over O'Neill's contacts with the South, led especially by Ian Paisley.

Coleraine University controversy

6. There was a need for a second university in the North to add to Queen's University, Belfast, due to the greater numbers going to secondary school and the economic development of Northern Ireland. (See *Case study: The Coleraine University Controversy*, p. 150)

7. O'Neill appointed the **Lockwood Committee** (November 1963) to report on third-level education.
   - They investigated Londonderry, Armagh, Craigavon and Coleraine.

8. The Lockwood Committee favoured Coleraine. This led to protests among unionists and nationalists in Derry.
   - They organised a **University for Derry Committee**, chaired by John Hume. They led a motorcade to Stormont.
   - The O'Neill government backed the Lockwood Report but did not close Magee College, Derry.

9. The university opened in Coleraine in October 1968.

Civil rights

10. There were nationalist grievances over gerrymandering, multiple votes and discrimination in jobs and housing. This was especially so west of the Bann – for example, in Derry, Dungannon and Enniskillen. (See *The Civil Rights movement in Northern Ireland*, pp. 154–160)

> **CIVIL RIGHTS:**
> The rights that people are entitled to, including free speech and movement, equality before the law and freedom to practise religion.

11. In Dungannon, the Homeless Citizens' League was organised by **Patricia and Conn McCluskey** to protest over housing shortages and discrimination.

12. They later (January 1964) established the Campaign for Social Justice in Northern Ireland, which concentrated on civil rights.

13. These actions inspired the setting up of the **Northern Ireland Civil Rights Association** (NICRA), founded in Belfast in January 1967.

14. The O'Neill government was faced by organised protest marches, e.g. Coalisland to Dungannon over the Caledon affair (August 1968) and the Derry Civil Rights March (5 October 1968).

15. The O'Neill government, through William **Craig**, Minister for Home Affairs, banned the civil rights march because a counter-Apprentice Boys march was planned.
   - But the civil rights march went ahead; marchers were batoned by police, and these attacks were shown on TV worldwide.

16. The British government got the O'Neill government to introduce a five-point reform programme, which was opposed by unionists inside and outside his party, the Unionist Party.

17. O'Neill's appeal for peace on the streets in his television address, 'Ulster at the Crossroads', appeared to work.

18. But the **People's Democracy march** (January 1969) from Belfast to Derry through loyalist areas put an end to the temporary peace.

19. O'Neill called a general election in the hope of defeating his enemies within his party.
   - But he did badly and failed to defeat them.

20. **Ulster Volunteer Force** (UVF) bombings of water pipes near Belfast eventually brought about O'Neill's resignation.
   - O'Neill was replaced as Prime Minister by James Chichester-Clark. (See also Key personality: *Terence O'Neill*, p. 197)

2. Economic and social developments in Northern Ireland up to 1969

 In this section, you should understand:
   - How the Northern Ireland economy developed up to 1969

The Brookeborough years, 1949–63

 How successful was the government of Northern Ireland in responding to social and economic problems, 1949–69?

1. In 1950, shipbuilding, linen and agriculture were the main economic activities.

2. After the Second World War, **agriculture** was the North's largest industry – it depended on guaranteed prices and the British market. Output grew by 2 per cent a year in the 1950s.

3. By 1960, 14 per cent of the labour force was occupied in agriculture; it declined from 100,000 in 1945 to 73,000 in 1960 due to mechanisation and the elimination of smaller holdings, e.g. the number of tractors doubled in the 1950s.

4. **Manufacturing industry**: There was a slow growth of manufacturing industry in the 1950s due to the decline of traditional industries.
   - The Northern economy suffered from remoteness from the main markets, higher transport costs and lack of domestic raw materials for industry.

5. The linen industry remained strong up to the early 1950s. This was due to demand after the Second World War, and the Korean War.
   - There was a serious collapse after the Korean War – in 7 years 25,000 jobs were lost due to competition from synthetic fibres such as rayon and Terylene.

Shipbuilding

1. Shipbuilding employed a skilled male labour force.
   - Harland and Wolff employed 21,000 in 1950 – there were still 22,000 employed in 1960. There was **post-war demand** for merchant ships, oil tankers and passenger liners; engineering works produced turbines.

2. But the launching of the passenger liner *Canberra* in 1960 was the end of an era; employment dropped by 40 per cent (11,500 jobs) between 1961 and 1964.
   - Harland and Wolff now faced competition from Japanese and continental European shipyards and an oversupply of ships on the world market.
3. **Problems facing the government**: There was a need for more jobs because of a natural increase in the population during the 1950s, a decline in farming jobs, and a decline in traditional industries.
4. **Government policy**: the Northern Ireland government led by Brookeborough had a policy of attracting foreign industry with advanced factories, improved infrastructure and grants for capital investment; by 1961 48,000 new jobs were created. Newer industries such as Courtauld's rayon factory were attracted.
5. **Social developments**: But because of the increasing workforce, there was still high unemployment – an average of 7.4 per cent, four times higher than the UK as a whole at that time. There was also emigration from the North of about 9,000 a year.
   - Northern Ireland was the most disadvantaged region of the United Kingdom.
   - However, social welfare payments were high as they were on a par with Britain.
   - Northern Ireland unemployment, sickness and maternity benefits and old age pensions were equal to those in the United Kingdom.

The O'Neill years, 1963–69

1. When O'Neill succeeded Brookeborough as Prime Minister, he wanted to improve the Northern economy.
2. O'Neill used a series of plans and reports to introduce his policies:
   - **The Benson Report (1963)** proposed the modernisation of the railways.
   - **The Matthew Plan (1964)** proposed a new city between Portadown and Lurgan, later named as Craigavon.
   - **The Wilson Plan (1965)** proposed:
     - a new Ministry of Development
     - new growth centres, mostly east of the Bann.
3. New motorways, schools and houses were also built, and there was more manpower training.
   - There was also a new university to be built in Coleraine, which opened in 1968.
4. In the 1960s manufacturing grew faster in Northern Ireland than in the UK as a whole.
   - Multinational companies such as Goodyear, Michelin and ICI were attracted to Northern Ireland.
   - But there was only a small increase in employment because of the decline in other industries – shipbuilding and linen.
5. The Northern Ireland economy was still far behind the UK economy.
   - Household incomes in 1968–69 were 89 per cent of the UK average.

- Unemployment was 7 per cent in 1970, but it was even higher in Derry and other towns – 18 per cent.
- The gap between the North and South closed in 1960s, partly because of the improved economy in the South.

Case study: The Coleraine University controversy

Need for a second university

> Why was the choice of Coleraine as the site for Northern Ireland's second university controversial?

1. In the early 1960s, Queen's University, Belfast, was the North's only university. **Magee College**, Derry, was not a university, but a university college. It provided two years' university education, but students had to complete their degree at Trinity College, Dublin.

2. After the **Education Act** (1947), there was a growth in numbers attending secondary schools in the 1950s. More university places were also needed if Northern Ireland was to attract new industry to replace the declining shipbuilding and linen industries.

3. Terence O'Neill was Prime Minister – his government was faced with the decision to either expand Queen's or found a second university.

Setting up the committee

4. The British government set up the Robbins Committee to review third-level education in Britain. The Northern Ireland government asked if the Robbins Committee would extend its enquiries to cover Northern Ireland. The Committee did not do so because it was too far advanced in its inquiry.

5. Instead, in 1962 the Northern Ireland government set up a Committee for Northern Ireland called the **Lockwood Committee**.

The Lockwood Committee

6. An eight-member committee was set up by the Northern Ireland government in November 1963 to enquire into third-level education.

7. The Committee was chaired by Sir John Lockwood, the Master of Birkbeck College, London. Other members were drawn from Northern Ireland and Britain.

8. The terms of reference: The Committee was asked to 'review the facilities for university and higher technical education in Northern Ireland having regard to the report of the Robbins Committee, and to make recommendations'.

Eliminating Queen's University

9. The Lockwood Committee decided that Queen's University should not be expanded because Queen's University itself was opposed to this idea. Also, the existing site of Queen's was too small and it would be too costly to acquire the extra land needed in Belfast.

- The Committee decided that the better alternative was to set up a second university in Northern Ireland.

Location

10. Four possible locations were considered: Armagh, Craigavon, Derry and Coleraine.

11. The Lockwood Committee heard representations from each of the locations.

- Armagh was eliminated because the population was too small to service a university and it was too close to Belfast.
- Craigavon, a proposed new city, was only in the planning stages.

12. **Derry representations:** The case for Magee College, Derry, was supported by submissions from the Londonderry City Council and the Londonderry branch of the Association of University Teachers. There was also a meeting with Londonderry councillors. The Lockwood Committee visited Magee and met with representatives there.

13. **Coleraine representations:** The case for Coleraine was supported by a submission from the Coleraine Promotions Committee and a meeting with them.

The Report

14. The Lockwood Committee report was published in February 1965.

- The Committee recommended Coleraine as the site for a second university because it believed it 'satisfies the criteria better than any of the other areas we have considered'.

15. The Committee's criteria were:

- 'a site of adequate magnitude (size) to accommodate its proposed activities and to allow for future growth . . .
- ample provision of space for halls of residence, college houses and students' flats should be made in planning . . .
- a site of about 300 acres . . . for a new university . . . (of) 6,000 students . . .
- but if the new university is to develop . . . agriculture, very much more space than this will be required . . .
- it is of paramount importance in our view that the university develops . . . within the boundaries of a single site.'

16. **Coleraine's criteria:** The criteria that Coleraine fulfilled were:

- It could provide residential facilities.
- It had suitable accommodation for students because summer boarding houses in the local towns of Portrush and Portstewart could be used. This would eliminate the need for expensive student accommodation.
- Coleraine was not a competitor with Belfast for urban industry, so therefore would not have faculties/departments which would weaken Queen's.
- It was an area which would attract first-rate staff, and could offer housing accommodation to rent on a short-term basis and good sites on which to build.
- It was convenient to Belfast, and to Northern Ireland's civil airport at Aldergrove.
- Conferences and seminars would flourish there as ample accommodation would be available for academic visitors.

- It had the support of the sponsoring local authorities.
- It was suitable for marine biology studies.

17. **Rejection of Magee**: The Lockwood Committee rejected the case for setting up the second university in Derry because of the inadequacy of Magee.
   - The site was too small.
   - Its governing structure was poor since there was no academic representation on the board of trustees who ran the college.
   - There was a shortage of private accommodation in Derry, so there would be a need to build expensive student accommodation.
   - There was opposition to Derry from officials in the Ministry of Commerce. They said Derry was too remote for industry.
   - Derry had never lost the 'siege mentality', and the local sectarian tension would impact on the development of a university.

18. The report also recommended the **closure** of Magee College, Derry, because it would only be a drain on resources needed for the new university.

Derry protests

19. Even before the report was published rumours of its conclusions led to protests in Derry.
   - A **University for Derry Committee** was set up by **John Hume**.
   - It was supported by unionists and nationalists, e.g. unionist mayor Albert Anderson and Eddie McAteer, nationalist MP.

20. They argued that:
   - Magee College could be the basis for a new university – it had been in existence since the mid-nineteenth century.
   - If Magee was not suitable other sites in Derry could be used.
   - Derry had historic claims to be 'The Site'.
   - Derry was the North's second city – the only one large enough to sustain a university.
   - There was a need to build up Derry and the north-west as a counterbalance to Belfast, to attract more industry.
   - There would be a brain drain from Derry if there was no university.
   - A university in Derry could increase cross-border co-operation with Donegal.
   - There was a need to treat the nationalist community fairly.
   - There was no Catholic on the Lockwood Committee.
   - Nationalists (and Derry unionists) said the decision to site in Coleraine was evidence of more neglect of Derry.
   - Nationalists said it was deliberate decision in order to build up unionist areas to maintain unionist power.

21. A delegation from Derry, including John Hume, met Terence O'Neill, the Prime Minister, who did not give any commitments.

22. A huge Derry protest went to Stormont with a motorcade of 2,000 cars as businesses in the city closed for the day.

23. In the debate in Stormont, O'Neill's government supported the Lockwood recommendations, except the closure of Magee. The government won the debate by 27 votes to 19 – 2 Unionists voted against the government.

Further controversy over Lockwood

24. In May 1965, a Unionist MP, Dr Robert Nixon, said that **'nameless, faceless men from Londonderry'** had gone to Stormont and advised against the locating of the second university in Derry.

- Named members of this group were prominent local Unionists and members of the Apprentice Boys of Derry
- It was said they feared losing control of Derry if Catholics benefited from a new university.

25. Nationalists were angry about this information. It led to a split between nationalists and unionists.

26. Unionists defended the decision to locate the university at Coleraine. They said Lockwood:

- would not be influenced by prejudice
- had followed the criteria he set down.

New university

27. Opposition to the closure of Magee led to a government decision that Magee should not be closed. Instead it became a constituent college of the university.

28. The university at Coleraine was built rapidly on a greenfield site. The first student intake took place in October 1968.

29. The opening of the university coincided with the beginning of the Troubles, so student numbers in the 1970s were not as high as projected.

30. In 1985 Magee College was incorporated into the University of Ulster.

Conclusion

31. Lockwood denied that his committee was influenced by anyone.

32. The committee followed criteria used in England for siting universities.

33. The decision to locate the new university in Coleraine was a bad political decision.

- It angered nationalists and they lost trust in O'Neill.
- Nationalists saw the decision as further proof that the west of Northern Ireland was badly treated.
- They said this was in line with the Benson, Matthew and Wilson Reports, which made proposals which either downgraded Derry or built up the area east of the Bann around Belfast.
- They said Coleraine was selected because it was a largely Protestant town.
- John Hume said the Coleraine University controversy was the spark that ignited the civil rights movement.

3. The Civil Rights movement in Northern Ireland

 In this section, you should understand:
- How and why the Civil Rights movement developed
- The impact of the Civil Rights movement

What were the origins of the Civil Rights movement?

 Why did the Civil Rights movement emerge in Northern Ireland and was it successful?

There were many factors that influenced the origins of the Civil Rights movement in Northern Ireland.

Catholic/nationalist grievances – discrimination

1. Nationalists accused unionists of discriminating against them in politics, housing, jobs, education and regional development.

2. Nationalist said unionists used **gerrymandering** (drawing of ward and constituency boundaries to achieve a majority) to maintain their power

   - e.g. Londonderry – there was a nationalist majority in the city, but unionists organised the wards so that they achieved a majority in the city council.

3. **Housing:** Catholics accused unionist-controlled councils of discriminating in the allocation of council houses, favouring Protestant tenants.

   - This was especially the case **west of the Bann** (other councils did not discriminate) so as to maintain unionist power in those areas.
     - e.g. in Dungannon, Co. Tyrone, by 1963 no new Catholic family had been allocated a permanent house in the previous 34 years.

> **key point**
>
> GERRYMANDERING:
> Rigging the boundaries of constituencies (electoral areas) to ensure a majority of seats at elections.

Derry
39% Catholic voters
61% Protestant voters
8 Unionist Councillors
NORTH WARD
River Foyle
Ward Boundary
N ↑
SOUTH WARD
Creggan
Bogside
Walled City
WATERSIDE WARD
90% Catholic voters
10% Protestant voters
8 Nationalist Councillors
33% Catholic voters
67% Protestant voters
4 Unionist Councillors
City Boundary

4. **Jobs:** Catholics accused unionists of discriminating in relation to public employment by councils or government.

   - Overall the proportion of Catholics in public employment was roughly the same as the proportion in the population, but Catholics tended to be employed in the lower ranks of public service, while Protestants dominated the higher grades. (Catholic-controlled councils also discriminated against Protestants.)

5. Catholics said there were examples of discrimination in private employment: The Harland and Wolff workforce was dominated by Protestants – only 400 out of 10,000 workers were Catholic.

6. Catholics said that as a result of this discrimination, unemployment was worse in Catholic areas (e.g. Londonderry) than in Protestant areas.

7. **Education**: Nationalists complained that the Lockwood Committee (Lockwood Report (1965)) chose Protestant-dominated Coleraine as the location for Northern Ireland's second university over Derry, the second-largest city.

8. **Regional development**: Nationalists complained that areas west of the Bann were discriminated against in regional development because that is where most Catholics lived.

- The **Benson Report** (1963) led to the closure of one of Derry's two railway lines.

- The **Matthew Report** (1964) said that a new city should be developed joining Lurgan and Portadown, later named Craigavon.

> **key point**
>
> SECTARIANISM:
> Adherence to a particular sect or group and hatred for an opposing group, usually based on religious differences.

- The **Wilson Report** (1965) designated growth centres for Northern Ireland, which were mainly concentrated in the east.

- Catholics complained that industries were mainly attracted to the strongly Protestant areas east of the Bann. (Of 111 factories built between 1945 and the mid-1960s, only 16 were built in Fermanagh, Londonderry and Tyrone.)

Growth of a Catholic middle class

9. As a result of the **Education Act** (1947), there were more educated Catholics. They became teachers or other professionals (doctors, lawyers).

- They provided new leadership and they were not prepared to accept discrimination.

Unionist resistance to reform

10. **Attitudes:** Extreme unionists such as Reverend Ian Paisley put pressure on the Unionist Party not to introduce reforms for Catholics.

11. **Role of Brookeborough:** He favoured Protestant domination. He resisted Catholic employment in the higher levels of the civil service and the judiciary.

12. **Role of O'Neill:** He raised nationalist hopes with visits to Catholic schools. He raised hopes that he would introduce reforms, but failed to do so, e.g.:

- he did not appoint a Catholic to the Lockwood Committee
- he accepted the recommendation of the Lockwood Committee that Coleraine should be the site of the new university.

13. **Role of the Westminster government**: Traditional British policy from the 1920s was not to interfere in Northern Irish affairs; they left it to the Northern government.

14. **Campaign for Democracy in Ulster** (CDU) was founded in 1965 and included some left-wing Labour MPs who were interested in civil rights in Northern Ireland.
    - They believed that the Government of Ireland Act (1920) gave Westminster power over all matters in Northern Ireland.
    - They were encouraged by the victory of **Gerry Fitt**, Republican Labour MP for West Belfast, in the Westminster elections in 1966.

15. **Failure of the Nationalist Party**: The Nationalist Party (led by Eddie McAteer) was badly organised. It was opposed to direct-action tactics such as squatting in houses – it was afraid that a confrontational strategy would lead to conflict.

Events in Dungannon, Co. Tyrone

16. The failure of the Nationalist Party resulted in the development of pressure groups. The **Homeless Citizens' League** was set up in Dungannon in 1963 under the leadership of Patricia McCluskey (a social worker) and her husband, Conn (a local doctor).
    - It complained to the Dungannon Urban District Council that Protestants got houses even before Catholics who were living in crowded or unsanitary conditions.

17. Soon after, in January 1964, the **Campaign for Social Justice** (CSJ) was founded by Conn and Patricia McCluskey.
    - It wanted to pressurise British public opinion about discrimination in Northern Ireland.
    - It publicised its case in pamphlets: *Londonderry: One Man, No Vote* and *Northern Ireland: The Plain Truth*.

From civil rights to civil strife

1. The **Northern Ireland Civil Rights Association** (NICRA) was founded in Belfast in January 1967. Its aims were to:
   - defend the basic freedoms of all citizens
   - protect the rights of the individual
   - highlight all possible abuses of power
   - demand guarantees for freedom of speech, assembly and association.

2. **Austin Currie's sit-in in Caledon, Co. Tyrone**: In June 1968, Austin Currie, a Nationalist MP for East Tyrone, staged a sit-in in a house allocated to a single young Protestant woman. (She was secretary to a member of the local Unionist Party.)
   - He said it should be given to couples with children.
   - He was removed by police, and the event was filmed by television news cameras.

Civil rights marches

3. A civil rights march was organised by CSJ and NICRA from Coalisland to Dungannon to highlight discrimination against Catholics.
   - Marchers carried placards, 'One Man, One House, One Job' and 'Jobs on Merit' – this was the beginning of a campaign of non-violent civil disobedience.
4. A **Civil Rights March in Derry** in October 1968 was organised by NICRA.
   - It was banned by William Craig, Minister for Home Affairs, when the Apprentice Boys said they would hold a march along the same route at the same time.
5. The civil rights march went ahead; it was stopped by the police (RUC). An RTÉ news film showed police batoning marchers (including Gerry Fitt and Eddie McAteer) and using water cannon.
   - Some Labour MPs were present and they were shocked by the police action.
   - News was splashed around the world – Northern Ireland was seen as a police state.

British government pressure

6. Harold Wilson, British Prime Minister, was now forced to intervene more actively in Northern Ireland.
   - He brought O'Neill, Craig and Brian Faulkner to London.
   - He forced the Northern Ireland government to introduce a programme of reforms.
7. O'Neill announced a **five-point programme of reform**. He promised:
   - the introduction of a points system in the allocation of houses
   - the reform of local government elections
   - the repeal of parts of the Special Powers Act
   - the suspension of Derry Corporation.
8. **Mixed reaction**: Moderate nationalists saw the reforms as a victory; more militant nationalists felt the reforms were not enough and wanted more.
   - Unionists felt the government had been forced to give in by nationalists.
   - Extreme unionists ('hard-liners'), including Ian Paisley, were opposed to any reforms.

Ulster stands at the crossroads

9. O'Neill gave a television address in December 1968. He said, '**Ulster stands at the crossroads**'.
   - He asked civil rights leaders to stop their demonstrations.
   - He told unionists that the British government would rule Northern Ireland directly from Westminster.
10. Civil rights leaders agreed to end demonstrations for the moment.
11. But extreme unionists, including William Craig, said O'Neill was selling out to nationalists. O'Neill sacked Craig.

People's Democracy march

12. The People's Democracy (PD) was founded by radical (left-wing) students in Queen's University, Belfast, including Michael Farrell and Bernadette Devlin.

13. The People's Democracy proposed a **march** from Belfast to Derry. (This was modelled on the American civil rights marches from Selma to Montgomery, Alabama, in 1965.) It would go through strong loyalist (unionist) areas.

14. They did not want to give O'Neill's 'miserable reforms' a chance.

15. There was a serious attack on the march by loyalists at Burntollet Bridge near Derry, where the marchers were not protected by the RUC.

16. Thousands supported the marchers when they got to Derry. Anti-RUC riots broke out, and later the RUC attacked Catholics in the Bogside.

17. **Impact of the march:** the PD march increased tensions in Northern Ireland. It marked the end of the civil rights period, and the beginning of more serious conflict.

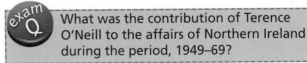
exam Q | What was the contribution of Terence O'Neill to the affairs of Northern Ireland during the period, 1949–69?

Downfall of O'Neill

18. O'Neill defended the actions of the RUC during the march.
   - He appointed the **Cameron Commission** to enquire into the causes of the riots in Derry.

19. There was pressure from the British government to bring in more reforms.

20. There were further riots in Derry. An innocent local man, Samuel Devanney, was injured in an RUC attack. Now there were complaints about RUC behaviour.

21. O'Neill called a general election to try to strengthen his position.

22. The majority of Unionist MPs elected favoured O'Neill, but some opposed him and wanted his resignation. O'Neill won his own seat, but beat Ian Paisley by only 1,000 votes.

23. There were bomb attacks on Belfast's water supply – these were blamed on republicans, but were carried out by loyalists (the Ulster Volunteer Force (UVF)) to undermine O'Neill.

24. **O'Neill resigned** as Prime Minister and was succeeded by Major James Chichester-Clark.

Apprentice Boys March and the Battle of the Bogside

25. There was conflict between Catholic and Protestant groups during July 1969 in various parts of Northern Ireland.
   - Tensions were high in Derry due to rioting and clashes between working-class Catholic youths and the RUC.

26. The Apprentice Boys planned their annual march for August 1969.

27. Derry civil rights leaders, including John Hume, wanted to get the march banned because they feared trouble; the Northern Ireland government refused.

28. The Apprentice Boys (12,000) marched in Derry in August 1969.
    - Nationalist youths from the Bogside stoned the police (RUC).
    - Barricades were erected in the Bogside to prevent the RUC from entering.
    - The police chased youths into the Bogside.
    - The Battle of the Bogside began.

29. Thousands of milk bottles were used for petrol bombs; the RUC responded with CS gas, a powerful form of tear gas. 'Free Derry' was painted on a gable wall.

Southern government intervention – the Republic's response

30. During the **Battle of the Bogside**, the Taoiseach, Jack Lynch, gave a television address. He said:

    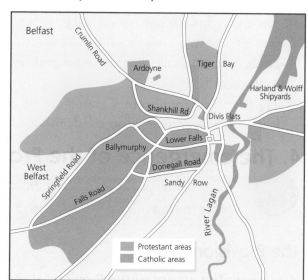

    - the Irish government 'can no longer stand by and see innocent people injured and perhaps worse'
    - 'the reunification of the national territory can provide the only permanent solution for the problem'
    - the Irish government would set up army medical camps in Donegal to care for the injured.

31. **Reaction:** Unionists were very angry at Lynch's speech – it increased tensions. Some nationalists hoped the Irish army would invade.

Rioting and sectarian attacks in Belfast

32. During the Battle of the Bogside, NICRA called on other areas to demonstrate to relieve the police pressure on the Bogside.
    - There was rioting in Belfast; Catholics erected barricades there and Protestant mobs petrol bombed Catholic houses.

33. The IRA had only old weapons; they were accused of running away and failing to defend the Catholic/nationalist areas: IRA – 'I Ran Away'.

Arrival of British troops

34. The British army was brought in to the streets of Derry and Belfast to replace the RUC. They were welcomed by the nationalist people, who gave them tea.

35. This was a defeat for the Northern Ireland government and the RUC.

36. The British Home Secretary, James Callaghan, visited the Bogside and Belfast; he received a great welcome.

Chichester-Clark and the British government

37. Chichester-Clark went to London to meet Wilson. They issued a declaration which said:
    - Northern Ireland would remain part of the United Kingdom so long as the majority wished it
    - the British Army was on the streets only as a temporary measure
    - reforms in Northern Ireland should be maintained
    - the Hunt Committee was appointed to inquire into policing.

The situation in Northern Ireland in 1969

1. The civil rights demonstrations had given way to wider civil strife (communal conflict) between Catholics and Protestants.
2. Nationalists/Catholics had won most of their civil rights, but now there were conflicts with the RUC.
3. The British government took greater control of Northern Ireland but did not bring in 'Direct Rule' – nationalists still demanded the end of Stormont.

4. The emergence of the Provisional IRA

In this section, you should understand:
- How the Provisional IRA developed

The Provisional IRA

What were the origins of the Provisional IRA?

1. The Provisional IRA changed the nature of the Northern Ireland conflict from a clash of cultures to an attack on the British state in Northern Ireland.

IRA Campaign 1956–62

2. At the end of the IRA campaign in 1962, there was a move away from violence and republicans placed more emphasis on (Marxist) political activity. They were concerned with the social and economic conditions of people.
3. Belfast riots, August 1969: the IRA was largely taken by surprise by these riots. There were fewer than 60 men in the IRA, with no arms training and few weapons.
    - Insults were shouted by local people at IRA members: 'IRA – I Ran Away'.

IRA Army Convention, December 1969

4. There was a split in the IRA between 'Official' IRA and 'Provisional' IRA. The breakaway Provisional IRA was led by Séan MacStiofáin. A Provisional Army Council was elected.
5. Provisional Sinn Féin, led by Ruairi Ó Bradaigh and Daithi Ó Conaill, was the political wing of the Provisional IRA.
6. **Aims of the Provisional IRA and Sinn Féin**: to overthrow British rule and establish a free Gaelic Republic of All Ireland by force of arms.

The role of the Irish government

- 'The Irish Government did not create the Provisional IRA but it nurtured them.' (Hennessey)
7. There was conflict in the Southern government led by the Taoiseach, Jack Lynch, over policy in relation to Northern Ireland.
   - Some ministers wanted Irish army intervention in the North or to provide weapons to the Provisional IRA.
   - Some encouraged the establishment and development of the Provisional IRA.
8. The government authorised Charles Haughey, Minister for Finance, to give £100,000 to the Irish Red Cross. More than £30,000 vanished and was used to import arms for the IRA.
   - **The Arms Trial:** These events later led to the sacking of Charles Haughey and Neil Blaney as ministers by Jack Lynch, the resignation of another minister, Kevin Boland, in protest, and an Arms Trial. Haughey and Blaney were charged with attempting to smuggle arms into the North. The charges against Blaney were dropped while Haughey and others were put on trial. They were found not guilty. (See *The Republic – responses to the Troubles*, pp. 180–84.)

Policy and activities of the security forces helped the IRA

9. The Northern government refused to ban Orange marches in 1970; these led to clashes with Catholic youths.
10. The Provisional IRA realised the significance of deliberately provoking confrontation with the army.
    - Originally, Catholics looked on the British army as protectors – now that changed.

The Falls Road curfew by the British Army

11. This event was the single greatest boost in the growth of the Provisional IRA.
12. Protestants rioted after Orange marches in June 1970 and this led to gun battles between the Provisional IRA and Protestants.
13. The British Army imposed a 24-hour curfew on the Falls Road to search for arms and ammunition – guns, home-made bombs and explosives were found.
14. Local people were very angry; Catholic opinion was alienated from the Army.
    - The Provisional IRA grew from a few hundred to 800 by the end of 1970.

IRA targets

15. The IRA carried out a bombing campaign – their targets were mainly commercial or economic or government buildings.
16. There were also attacks on the RUC, including targeting off-duty police and the bombing of police barracks – the IRA killed the first unarmed RUC man in August 1970.
17. They began to target British army personnel – the first British soldier was killed in February 1971.

- Three off-duty soldiers were lured to their deaths by the Provisionals in March 1971. (See *Republican and loyalist terrorism*, pp. 172–76.)

Relations with the Official IRA

18. The Official IRA was involved in the street fighting, but it was also in conflict with the Provisional IRA.
    - Cathal Goulding, Chief-of-Staff of the Official IRA, declared a ceasefire in 1972 – he criticised the Provisional IRA bombing campaign as inhuman.

5. Political developments leading to the fall of Stormont

 In this section, you should understand:
- Why Stormont fell and why Britain brought in Direct Rule from Westminster

Political change

1. The continued disturbances led to political change in Northern Ireland in 1970.
2. **Ian Paisley** was elected MP to Stormont in the Bannside by-election in April 1970 after O'Neill was appointed to the House of Lords.
3. In this election, the Conservative Party took office in Britain with **Edward Heath** as Prime Minister and Reginald Maudling as Home Secretary.
    - Maudling showed little interest in Northern Ireland – 'What a bloody awful country,' he said.
4. The **Alliance Party** was formed by moderate unionists in favour of union with Britain but against sectarianism.
5. On the nationalist side, the **Social Democratic and Labour Party** (SDLP) was formed. Gerry Fitt was leader and John Hume was Deputy Leader.

> **exam Q**
> - What factors contributed to the fall of Stormont and how did unionists react to its fall?
> - Why was Direct Rule (from London) introduced in 1972, and why did it last so long?

- The SDLP:
    - favoured the unity of Ireland by consent
    - opposed the use of violence
    - was against all forms of discrimination
    - intended to contest elections to sit in the Stormont Parliament.
- The SDLP became the main voice of the Catholic minority.

The downfall of Chichester-Clark

6. Chichester-Clark was criticised by unionists for giving into reform and for not clamping down on the IRA. He resigned on 20 March 1971 when he failed to get permission for further security measures from the British government.

7. Brian **Faulkner** was elected leader of the Unionist Party and Prime Minister.

Faulkner and internment

1. Because of the increased violence, Brian Faulkner introduced internment (arrest without trial) on 9 August 1971.

2. Thousands of British soldiers in arrest squads accompanied by members of the RUC Special Branch raided houses in the early morning to arrest suspected IRA men – 342 men were seized, but 104 were later released.

3. Internment was **one-sided** – they did not try to arrest loyalist suspects from the Ulster Volunteer Force (UVF).

4. The government failed to capture the leading members of the Provisional IRA because their information was flawed.

Impact of internment

5. Internment led to a massive increase in violence:
   - 2 soldiers and 8 civilians were killed on the first day
   - Protestant and Catholic families fled their homes as houses were burned.
   - Nationalists and the SDLP called for a rent and rate strike as a protest.

6. 7,000 Catholics fled to the South for refuge and hundreds of Protestants moved to Liverpool for safety.

7. Catholics were also angered because of the treatment of suspects – some were tortured; conditions were bad in the prison ship, *Maidstone*, and at the internment camp at Long Kesh.

8. The British Army were now a greater target for Catholic/nationalist resentment.

9. **Growth of the IRA:** There was a boost to IRA recruitment; there was increased support from the United States, providing money and arms.

10. The IRA used the 'no-go' areas in Belfast and Derry to plan attacks, make bombs, and recruit and train members.
    - There were increased bombings, some on economic targets, to force Britain to abandon Northern Ireland.

Unionists' reaction

11. Ian Paisley founded the **Democratic Unionist Party** (DUP) to put pressure on the Unionist Party.

12. The **Ulster Defence Association** (UDA) was formed as a loyalist paramilitary group.

Bloody Sunday, 30 January 1972

13. The Civil Rights Association organised a protest march against internment in Derry, but it was banned. However, 15,000 took part in the march.

14. Catholic youths stoned the British army. Then soldiers from the 1st Parachute Regiment opened fire on the crowd, killing 13 and injuring another 13. Another man died later.

15. Later the army accused the IRA of firing the first shots.

16. Catholics in Derry and nationalists all over Ireland were very angry at the killings.

17. Relations between Britain and Ireland worsened.
    - An angry crowd attacked and burned the British Embassy in Dublin.

18. Unionists reacted against the nationalists' claims on Bloody Sunday – the Ulster Vanguard Association, led by William Craig, held a rally of 70,000 people in Belfast.

The fall of Stormont – Direct Rule imposed

19. The British Prime Minister, Ted Heath, told Brian Faulkner that control of security (including the RUC) was being transferred to Westminster. Faulkner and his government resigned in March 1972.

20. Stormont was closed and **William Whitelaw** was appointed Secretary of State for Northern Ireland.
    - This was the beginning of **Direct Rule** from Westminster, which lasted for 20 years.

Summary: Reasons for the collapse of Stormont

- Nationalists organised campaigns in favour of civil rights reform.
- Efforts to bring in civil rights reforms frightened the unionists; Paisley and extreme unionists put pressure on the unionist government to resist further reform – they could not adjust to the changed times.
- Civil rights marches drifted into civil strife and then open violence; there was continued street violence by both nationalists and unionists; the IRA bombing campaign caused deaths and disruptions that the Stormont government could not deal with.
- Events such as the Apprentice Boys march and the Battle of the Bogside, the introduction of the British Army and internment heightened tensions.
- The British government began direct involvement in the problems of Northern Ireland too late.

Reaction to the fall of Stormont

21. Unionists were very angry – it was the end of 50 years of Stormont rule and unionist control.
    - They were afraid of the future – some feared there would be a united Ireland; some wanted Northern Ireland to go it alone (an independent Ulster).
    - Nationalists and the IRA looked on the fall of Stormont as a victory – it was the end of the 'Orange State'.
    - It allowed the British government to bring in a process of reform from above.

6. Direct rule from Westminster – 1

aims In this section, you should understand:

- How the British government dealt with Northern Ireland
- Case study: The Sunningdale Agreement and the power-sharing Executive, 1973–74
- The role of Brian Faulkner (Key personality, p. 199)
- The role of Ian Paisley (Key personality, p. 201)
- The role of John Hume (Key personality, p. 202)

Government of Northern Ireland

1. After the fall of Stormont, Northern Ireland was **ruled directly** from Westminster. The Stormont government was replaced by William Whitelaw as Secretary of State.

2. British policy rejected the full integration of Northern Ireland with the United Kingdom; it favoured 'community government' or **power sharing** between Protestants and Catholics.

3. Whitelaw had to balance the demands of unionists and nationalists. He wanted to phase out internment and negotiate an end to the IRA campaign. He also wanted to end Catholic no-go areas.

Unionist reaction to Direct Rule

4. There were huge unionist protests: there was a protest strike, power supplies were cut, and public transport was closed down.

5. There was a huge meeting of 100,000 outside Stormont, addressed by Unionist Party leaders Faulkner and Craig.
   - Loyalists matched IRA violence with assassinations. Murder gangs killed Catholics at random, often after severe torture.

Nationalist reaction to Direct Rule

6. The IRA said 'the war goes on'; they believed that if they continued to put on pressure, the British government would withdraw from Northern Ireland.

7. The SDLP and the Irish government welcomed the end of unionist rule in Stormont.

8. Peace organisations grew in response to the death of innocent civilians – Women Together and the Central Citizens Defence Committee. They called on both the Official and Provisional IRA to end violence. The Official IRA called a ceasefire in May 1972.

9. Whitelaw hoped to get the Provos (Provisional IRA) to end violence. The Provisional IRA called a ceasefire for late June 1972.

10. The Provisional IRA leaders, including Gerry Adams, were taken to London; they met Whitelaw there.

- They demanded Britain to pull out troops from Northern Ireland within 3 years.
- These demands were rejected by Whitelaw.
- The IRA ceasefire ended shortly afterwards.

11. On **Bloody Friday**, 21 July 1972, 20 IRA bombs were exploded in Belfast, more in Derry – 9 people were killed, 130 injured.
    - Overall, 1972 proved to be the worst year of the Troubles: 496 people were killed.

Operation Motorman – eliminating no-go areas

12. Whitelaw used the increased bombing to get rid of the **no-go areas**; the British army took over nationalist and unionist no-go areas in both Belfast and Derry, e.g. the Bogside.

13. Whitelaw said Operation Motorman was aimed at removing 'the capacity of the IRA to create terror and violence'. This was a defeat for the IRA – they could not now move around as easily.

14. Loyalists also carried out violent attacks. This led to the introduction of internment for loyalists in March 1973.

Case study: The Sunningdale Agreement and the power-sharing Executive, 1973–74

Background

> **exam Q** Which factors contributed to the formation of a power-sharing Executive in Northern Ireland in May 1974?

1. **British policy**: The British government saw the introduction of the army as a temporary measure; they wanted to bring in a power-sharing government in Northern Ireland.
    - Their policy was aimed at attempting to find a political solution to the Northern problem.

2. The British government was involved in three major initiatives to find a political solution:
    - The Sunningdale Agreement and the power-sharing Executive in 1973–74.
    - The Anglo-Irish Agreement in 1985.
    - The Downing Street Declaration in 1993.

Darlington Conference (1972)

3. The British government called the **Darlington Conference** in 1972. It was chaired by William Whitelaw, Secretary of State for Northern Ireland.
    - The Unionist Party, the Northern Ireland Labour Party (NILP) and the Alliance Party attended.
    - The SDLP did not go. They said there would be 'no talks while internment lasts'.

4. After the conference, the British government published a discussion paper, *The Future of Northern Ireland.*
    - It reaffirmed the status of Northern Ireland as long as a majority of the people wished it.

- It was opposed to the integration of Northern Ireland with Britain.
- But it also said the Republic of Ireland should be involved in future co-operation. The SDLP and the Taoiseach, Jack Lynch, were pleased with this.

Constitutional proposals

5. The British government published a White Paper on **Northern Ireland constitutional proposals**. This proposed:
   - Self-government for Northern Ireland (devolution of power).
   - An assembly elected by proportional representation (PR).
   - A power-sharing executive in Northern Ireland between unionists and nationalists.
   - A Council of Ireland for co-operation between Northern Ireland and the Republic of Ireland (an Irish Dimension).

Border Poll

6. A referendum (the **Border Poll**) was held in March 1973 to decide whether or not Northern Ireland should be part of the United Kingdom.
   - The poll was boycotted by Catholics.
   - Ninety-eight per cent of the voters were in favour of union with Britain.

Unionist reaction to the constitutional proposals

7. Faulkner supported the White Paper as the only chance to end violence; it also guaranteed Northern Ireland's position in the UK.
8. The Ulster Unionist Council also supported the White Paper.
9. But the Unionist Party was split – some were opposed to the constitutional proposals.
   - **Craig** left the Unionist Party and set up the Vanguard Unionist Progressive Party.
10. Craig, Paisley, the Orange Order and the Ulster Defence Association (UDA) wanted to restore Stormont.

Nationalist reaction

11. The constitutional proposals were rejected by the IRA, who would accept nothing less than a united Ireland.
12. The SDLP welcomed the proposals because they were very much in line with their thinking.
13. In the South, the new coalition government of Fine Gael and Labour were in favour of the proposals.

Assembly elections, June 1973

14. The Unionist Party was divided before the elections between pledged (pro-power sharing/Faulkner Unionists) and unpledged (anti-power sharing) Unionists.

- As a result of the Assembly elections, there was a good overall majority in favour of the

Party	Power sharing?	Seats	% votes
Faulkner Unionists	For	24	29.3
Other Unionists	Against	26	32.6
SDLP	For	19	22.1
Alliance	For	8	9.2
NILP	For	1	2.6

power-sharing proposals; but only a small majority among Unionists.

Inter-Party talks on power-sharing executive

15. Talks were held between the Unionist Party, the Alliance Party and the SDLP to form a **power-sharing executive**.
    - They reached an agreement on a power-sharing executive in November 1973.
    - The 11 members/ministers of the Executive (government) would be divided as follows: 6 Ulster Unionist Party ministers, 4 SDLP ministers, and 1 Alliance Party minister. Brian Faulkner, leader of the Unionist Party, would be Chief Executive, and Gerry Fitt, leader of the SDLP, would be Deputy Chief Executive.

POWER SHARING:

Sharing political power between different groups (e.g. unionists and nationalists in Northern Ireland).

16. The question of the Council of Ireland was left for discussions with all parties and the British and Irish governments.

Opposition to power sharing

17. But there was growing **anti-power-sharing feeling** among Ulster Unionists.
    - A motion against power sharing was barely rejected in the Ulster Unionist Council.
    - 5 out of 7 Ulster Unionist MPs in Westminster went against Faulkner.
    - Members of the Unionist Party, Craig's Vanguard, Paisley's Democratic Unionist Party and the Orange Order formed the **United Ulster Unionist Council** (UUUC) to oppose power sharing and the Council of Ireland.

The Sunningdale Conference, 6–9 December 1973

18. Representatives of the Faulkner Unionists, the SDLP, the Alliance Party and the British and Irish governments (Fine Gael-Labour Coalition) met at Sunningdale in England.
19. Heath, the British Prime Minister, led the British delegation; Cosgrave (the Taoiseach) and FitzGerald (Minister for Foreign Affairs) led the Irish government delegation; Faulkner led the UUP, Fitt and Hume led the SDLP, and Napier led the Alliance Party.
20. William Whitelaw was replaced by Francis Pym as Secretary of State for Northern Ireland shortly before the conference.

21. Loyalist opponents to power sharing (e.g. Paisley, Craig) were not invited to participate in the Conference.

The negotiations

22. The views of the SDLP (especially those of Hume) were supported by the Irish government; they wanted an improved role for the Council of Ireland; they stressed the significance of the '**Irish Dimension**'.

23. But Fitt and Paddy Devlin (SDLP) wanted to play down the role of the Council of Ireland. They did not want to upset Unionists – Devlin said he did not want his Unionist friends hung from lamp posts on their return to Belfast.

24. Faulkner had no support; Heath saw him as an old-style Unionist, and he favoured the views of the SDLP.

25. Faulkner wanted the South to delete Articles 2 and 3 (claiming jurisdiction over Northern Ireland) from the Irish Constitution; he also wanted the Southern Irish government to take measures to tackle the IRA in the South.

26. But the Irish government said there would have to be a referendum on Articles 2 and 3, and that it would be defeated.

The Sunningdale Agreement, December 1973

27. After 4 days of negotiations, an agreement was signed. The **Council of Ireland** would include:
   - A Council of Ministers with 7 members from Northern Ireland and 7 members from the Southern Irish government.
   - It would have 'executive and harmonising functions'.
   - A Consultative Assembly with 30 members from the Northern Ireland Assembly and 30 members from the Dáil.
   - A Permanent Secretariat to carry out duties and functions.
   - An Anglo-Irish Special Commission to discuss amending laws on extradition, the creation of a common law area with all-Ireland courts.
   - There were two police authorities, North and South.
   - The Irish Government 'fully and solemnly declared' that there would be no change in the status of Northern Ireland until a majority of the people of Northern Ireland said so.
   - The British government gave a similar declaration.

Reaction to the Sunningdale Agreement

28. Faulkner thought that the Unionists came out best.
   - The South recognised Northern Ireland's power to decide for itself on unity.

29. Faulkner believed that the extra bits about the Council of Ireland were only '**necessary nonsense**' to get the cooperation of the SDLP and the Irish government.

30. Paddy Devlin said the SDLP strategy was to get all-Ireland institutions established, which would lead eventually to a 'single state of Ireland'. They were happy with Sunningdale.

31. The Provisional IRA was opposed to the Sunningdale Agreement.

32. Anti-power-sharing Unionists feared the Sunningdale Agreement meant the end of the union with Britain; they rejected the South as a 'safe sanctuary' for the IRA.

Northern Ireland power-sharing Executive

33. The power-sharing Executive was installed on 1 January 1974. The Executive found it very difficult to govern Northern Ireland; there was widespread violence, demonstrations and riots.

34. In January 1974, the **Ulster Unionist Council** (UUC) rejected the Council of Ireland by 427 to 374 votes. Faulkner resigned as leader of UUC (he was succeeded by Harry West) and set up his own party.

35. There was also trouble in the Assembly as loyalist members, such as Paisley, caused disruption; the RUC were used to remove them.

Resistance to Sunningdale Agreement grows

36. **Boland case:** In the South of Ireland, Kevin Boland, a former Fianna Fáil minister, challenged the

> **exam Q** What factors contributed to the downfall of the power-sharing Executive in Northern Ireland in May 1974?

legality of the Sunningdale Agreement in the High Court. His case was defeated, but the Irish government had to argue in its own defence that the South's constitutional claim to Northern Ireland was still in force.

37. A British **general election** was called by Heath in February 1974.

- Anti-power-sharing Unionists used the slogan, 'Dublin is just a Sunningdale away'.
- The United Ulster Unionist Council candidates won 11 of the 12 seats and 51 per cent of the vote (the last seat was won by Fitt). They saw the Council of Ireland as being a vehicle for bringing about Irish unity by gradually transferring powers to it.
- After the election, the Northern Ireland Executive did not reflect the wishes of the majority of the people of Northern Ireland.

Ulster Workers' Council

38. In March 1974, a new Unionist group, the **Ulster Workers' Council** (UWC), threatened civil disobedience unless new Assembly elections were held; they pledged to fight 'Irish Republicanism and all forms of Communism'. They aimed to:

- preserve the union between Ulster and Britain
- oppose and resist all attempts to merge Ulster with the Irish Republic.

39. The UWC was a committee of workers from Harland and Wolff, the power stations, and engineering works.

UWC strike

40. The UWC called a loyalist strike for 14 May – electricity was reduced, but the strike was slow to get going until the UWC got the help of the Ulster Defence Association (UDA) led by Andy Tyrie.

41. UDA men and youths visited businesses and used intimidation to force them to close; barricades were built.

    - There were power cuts; farm machinery closed roads; road blocks encircled central Belfast; all areas of Northern Ireland were affected. In many areas there were shortages of food.

42. Tension was also heightened by car bombs in the South of Ireland. Car bombs planted by the Ulster Volunteer Force (UVF) killed 22 people in Dublin and 5 in Monaghan.

43. Efforts by trade union leaders to get workers back to work failed badly.

44. The British Army said the strike was too big for them to try to break it – they only took over some fuel supplies. They feared that there would be a complete shutdown if they tried to take over the power stations.

    - They did not want to take on the loyalists at the same time as they were fighting the IRA.

45. **'Spongers' speech:** Harold Wilson, the British Prime Minister, made a TV broadcast which caused great anger among loyalists. He said:

    - 'British taxpayers have seen the taxes they have poured out, almost without regard to cost . . . Yet people who benefit from all this now viciously defy Westminster . . . people who spend their lives sponging on Westminster . . . Who do these people think they are?'

46. As matters became worse, Faulkner wanted to negotiate with the UWC; the SDLP executive members were opposed to negotiation – they wanted the army to come in and break the strike.

47. When Faulkner resigned on 27 May, loyalist areas celebrated; the power-sharing Executive had collapsed; the strike had lasted 15 days.

Assessment

48. There had been a steady increase in Unionist opposition to power sharing and the Council of Ireland, so that by the time the power-sharing Executive took over in January 1974, most Unionists were opposed to it.

49. Decisive action by the army on the first day might have broken the strike, but it was too late after that; the strike won the widespread support of Protestants, including the middle classes.

50. The Sunningdale initiative was ended – Direct Rule from Westminster was brought back. But all future British initiatives followed the Sunningdale framework – a power-sharing government and an Irish Dimension.

51. Loyalists felt they could wreck any future British government initiatives – this led to political stalemate in the North.

7. Republican and loyalist terrorism

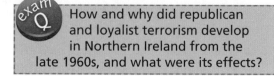

aims In this section, you should understand:

● How republican and loyalist terrorism developed and their impact

Republican terrorism

The Provisional IRA

exam Q How and why did republican and loyalist terrorism develop in Northern Ireland from the late 1960s, and what were its effects?

1. The main republican terrorism was carried out by the Provisional IRA (Provos).

2. After the Provisional IRA was formed in 1969, its support increased due to:
   ● attacks by Protestants on Catholic areas
   ● the Falls Road curfew by the British Army (July 1971)
   ● the introduction of internment (1972)
   ● Bloody Sunday in Derry (1972)
   ● economic problems in Northern Ireland and increased unemployment.

Aims of the Provos

3. The Provisional IRA wanted a **32-county republic.**
   ● They believed that this could be achieved by armed struggle (violence) – they wanted to force the British out of Northern Ireland.

key point

TERRORISM:
The use of violence and threats to achieve political aims.

4. During 1970, the Provisional IRA built up its organisation. They created active service units and membership grew in Belfast to over 1,000 by the end of 1971. Their campaign was largely defensive, to protect the Catholic communities.

IRA attacks

5. In the summer 1970, the IRA launched a **bombing campaign**. They aimed at 'economic targets' – hotels, telephone exchanges and public houses.

6. The Provos launched a massive bombing campaign in 1971, continuing to target Protestant businesses and shops (so-called 'economic targets').

7. They also began attacks on British soldiers and the RUC. The first British soldier was killed in February 1971. The IRA attacked off-duty RUC officers and bombed police stations.

8. By 1971, the spread of communal violence helped the IRA. Catholic youths in working-class areas rioted against the British Army, throwing petrol and nail bombs. The army responded by searching houses – the British Army and the RUC overreacted, which upset nationalists.

9. The bombing campaign continued – attacks became more frequent and vicious as bombing public houses resulted in the deaths and injury of civilians (usually Protestants).

10. The introduction of internment helped the IRA. Younger and newer leaders escaped internment, and recruitment increased.

11. The IRA increased its bomb attacks: in the four months before internment, 4 soldiers and 4 civilians were killed; in the four months after internment, 73 civilians, 30 soldiers and 11 RUC were killed.

12. The IRA campaign was criticised by Cardinal Conway, Archbishop of Armagh. The bombings which resulted in atrocities led to criticism of the IRA campaign.

13. In December 1971 an explosion at a Shankill Road furniture store resulted in the deaths of 2 children and 2 adults.

14. On 30 January 1972, **Bloody Sunday** occurred in Derry. Thirteen civilians were killed by the Parachute Regiment. This alienated the Catholic community.

15. The republican paramilitaries responded:
    - The Official IRA planted a bomb in Aldershot, HQ of the Parachute Regiment, which killed 7 people.

16. **Direct Rule, March 1972**: The IRA welcomed the fall of Stormont and the imposition of Direct Rule from Westminster. This encouraged them to believe that if they gave one more push, the British would be out of Northern Ireland. 'The war goes on,' they said.

17. In May 1972 the **Official IRA** called a ceasefire – they now concentrated more on politics.

18. The **Provisional IRA** called a ceasefire in June 1972. A group of Provisional IRA leaders, including Gerry Adams, was flown to London to meet the Secretary of State, Whitelaw. The Provos demanded the withdrawal of Britain's troops from Northern Ireland within three years. Whitelaw would not agree and the ceasefire ended.

19. In 1973 and 1974, the Provisionals bombed the British mainland, aiming at economic, military, political and judicial targets. The intention was to force British public opinion to get British withdrawal from Northern Ireland.

20. At this time, the Provos largely ran some of the Catholic areas – extortion and racketeering were common, and petty crime was dealt with by punishment beatings.
    - They were also involved in bitter sectarian killings with the UVF.

21. The **Shankill Butchers**, a group of UVF led by Lennie Murphy, were responsible for the brutal killing of many Catholics in the winter of 1975–76. Provisional IRA men responded by killing Protestants.

22. From 1976 onwards, the Provos improved their bombing technology – they used remote-controlled devices – these were used against the army, the RUC and prison officers.

23. The IRA used a variety of other tactics: they used snipers against the British army and RUC.

24. By the end of the 1970s, the British Army concluded that the Provos had 'the dedication and the sinews of war' to maintain violence 'for the foreseeable future'.

25. But neither could the Provisional IRA achieve its aims of forcing the British army out of Northern Ireland. Its influence was mainly negative.

26. The British government used its security forces to maintain what it called 'an acceptable level of violence'.
    - They had success against the IRA through informants and the use of the SAS.
    - The Provos lost some public support, especially when the Peace People was set up in the mid-1970s. (See *Direct rule from Westminster – 2*, p. 177–80)

Killings by the main republican paramilitary organisations (1969–2001)	
Irish Republican Army (IRA)	1,822
Official Irish Republican Army (OIRA)	55
Irish National Liberation Army (INLA)	123

(Sutton Database, CAIN)

    - Of the total number of people killed in Northern Ireland, republican paramilitaries were responsible for over 70 per cent of the deaths.

Reorganisation of the IRA – the role of Gerry Adams

27. Gerry Adams was mainly responsible for the reorganisation of the Provisional IRA in the late 1970s. Instead of the formal brigades, battalions and active service units, they were now organised into **small cells** of three or four activists which operated independently of each other. This made it more difficult for the army and RUC to infiltrate and spy on them.

28. Adams said that there would be no immediate British withdrawal and the IRA should prepare for a '**long war**'. He also said that the Provisionals should be more involved politically.

29. **Hunger strikes:** Support for the Provos increased with the 'dirty protest' and the hunger strikes.
    - The Provisional IRA demanded special-category status for their prisoners in the Maze Prison. When this was refused, they began a blanket protest ('on the blanket'). This escalated to a dirty protest, when they rubbed excrement on the walls of their prison cells. When this failed, they began hunger strikes. These were led by Bobby Sands.

30. The hunger strikers received huge support in Ireland, North and South. They also gained great publicity in the United States. The IRA got support from Noraid, which provided money and weapons from the US.

31. Bobby Sands was elected MP for Fermanagh and South Tyrone. This success and the popular interest in the funerals after the deaths of the hunger strikers led the Provisional IRA leadership to move to political methods.

32. Danny Morrison said in 1981 that they would pursue power with the **ballot paper** in one hand and the **Armalite** in the other.

33. They got a huge supply of weapons and explosives from Libya towards the end of the 1980s. This ensured that it would be very difficult to defeat the Provos.

Loyalist terrorism

Ulster Volunteer Force

1. The **Ulster Volunteer Force** (UVF) was revived in 1966 in response to nationalist celebrations of the 1916 Rising.
   - It was a highly anti-Catholic and anti-nationalist organisation.
2. The UVF was responsible for the bombing of Belfast's water supply, which brought about the resignation of O'Neill as Prime Minister.
3. The UVF planted a bomb in McGurk's Bar in December 1971 which killed 15 people.
4. It was responsible for the Dublin and Monaghan bombings in May 1974, which resulted in the deaths of 33 people – the largest loss of life in a single day in the Troubles.
5. Later in 1974 the British government lifted the ban on the UVF in the hope that it would become more political. But after further deaths in October 1975, it was again banned.

Killings by the main loyalist paramilitary organisations (1969–2001)	
Ulster Volunteer Force (UVF)	482
Ulster Defence Association (UDA) (includes UFF and LRDG)	261

(Sutton Database, CAIN)

Ulster Defence Association

6. Local loyalist defence associations came together to form the **Ulster Defence Association** (UDA) in September 1971.
7. The aim of the UDA was the 'Defence of Ulster against all who would destroy her'.
8. The UDA was based in Protestant working-class areas. At its peak in 1972, it had about 40,000 members.
9. In 1972, UDA members began a campaign of random sectarian killings. Some Catholics were killed indiscriminately. Some Protestants who had Catholic girlfriends were also killed.
   - The murders were usually claimed in the name of the **Ulster Freedom Fighters** – a cover name for the UDA.
10. The Provisional IRA responded to these sectarian attacks by killing Protestants. In July 1972, 19 Catholics and 17 Protestants were killed.
11. The UDA organised Protestant no-go areas in imitation of nationalist areas.
12. Inevitably, this led to clashes with the British Army.
13. **Andy Tyrie** became leader of the UDA in May 1973. He created greater unity in the UDA.
14. The UDA was opposed to power sharing and the Council of Ireland as proposed by the Sunningdale Agreement (1973).
15. The **Ulster Workers' Council** organised the loyalist strike against the Sunningdale Agreement in May 1974. The organising committee included Andy Tyrie, leader of the UDA, and Ken Gibson, leader of the UVF.

- The UDA intimidated Protestant businesses on the first day and this led to the closure of many shops. It also manned road blocks during the strike, which brought Northern Ireland to a standstill.

16. The UDA opposed the Anglo-Irish Agreement (1985), but it was not in favour of a national strike over the issue.

17. The UDA moved to a more political view during the mid-1980s.

18. In January 1987 the UDA published the document *Common Sense*, which set out plans for a future political settlement in Northern Ireland.

19. Soon after the UDA became more militant; Andy Tyrie was removed as leader of the UDA.

20. During 1988 large quantities of arms were secured by the UDA, some of which came from South Africa. In October 1988 both the UDA and the UFF were included in the direct-broadcasting ban.

21. The UDA had access to security files on republicans and suspected members of republican paramilitary groups, which they used to target victims.

22. During the 1990s the UFF stepped up its attacks on Catholics and republicans. It also attacked SDLP politicians and councillors.

23. The UDA and the UFF joined other loyalist paramilitary groups in calling a ceasefire on 13 October 1994 in response to the earlier IRA ceasefire.

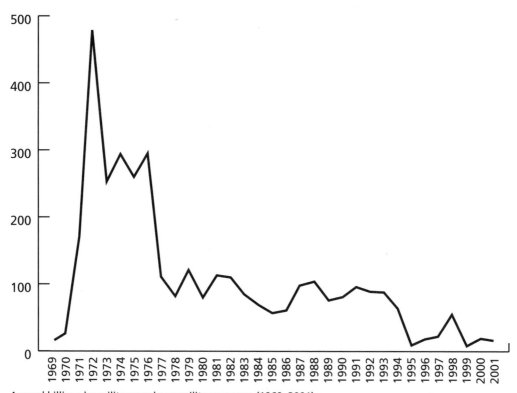

Annual killings by military and paramilitary groups (1969–2001)

(Sutton Database, CAIN)

8. Direct rule from Westminster – 2

In this section, you should understand:

- The various attempts to create agreement in Northern Ireland
- The Anglo-Irish Agreement, 1985
- The Downing Street Declaration

Direct Rule continues

1. After the UWC strike, Direct Rule from London continued. The Secretary of State for Northern Ireland represented the British government. Holders of this post included **Merlyn Rees** and **Roy Mason**.

2. The British government was faced with a number of problems:
   - the continued violence of republican and loyalist paramilitaries
   - the necessity of finding a political solution for Northern Ireland.

Security measures

3. Beginning in 1973 the Provisional IRA took their bombing campaign to Britain. This was followed by more serious explosions in 1974 – e.g. a 'no-warning' bomb in Guildford, bombs in two public houses in Birmingham.

4. The Labour government passed the **Prevention of Terrorism Act** (1974), which allowed them to prevent suspects from any part of Ireland entering Britain.

> **exam Q**
> What moves were made towards finding a peaceful resolution of the Troubles, 1973–93, and how successful were they?

5. After this the Provos largely confined their campaign to Northern Ireland because of the effectiveness of the police in Britain, the difficulty of operating in Britain, and the bad propaganda arising from the bombings.

Ulsterisation

6. The British government wanted to reduce the role of the British Army in Northern Ireland. They began the process of **Ulsterisation**.

7. The RUC was increased in size; they had an increased budget; new fleets of armoured patrol cars were provided.

8. The army still retained a role in difficult areas such as 'Bandit Country' in South Armagh, a predominantly nationalist region, where there were constant battles with the IRA.

9. Other security measures which began to have an impact included:
   - increased co-operation between the security forces on both sides of the border
   - the FBI and CIA worked together to stop IRA gun-smuggling from America.

10. The IRA went on the defensive in 1976 and began a re-organisation into smaller active service units. They now began to plan for the 'long war'.

Peace People

11. The increased level of violence and the bitter sectarian murders in the middle of the 1970s led to the foundation of Peace People by Mairead Corrigan and Betty Williams.

12. They, along with journalist Ciaran McKeown, organised peace rallies all over Northern Ireland as Protestants and Catholics came together to demand an end to the violence.

   - But the movement failed because of the bitter divisions in society.

Political initiatives – peace initiatives after Sunningdale

1. The British government attempted various political initiatives to bring peace to Northern Ireland. These failed for a variety of reasons:
   - Violence – IRA and loyalist paramilitary violence continued.
   - Moderate unionist and nationalist politicians failed to agree because of pressure from extreme loyalist and nationalist groups.

2. **Constitutional Convention (1975–76):** This was convened to allow elected representatives from Northern Ireland to propose solutions.
   - The Unionists wanted a return to majority rule.
   - But this was rejected by the British government and the SDLP.

3. **Rolling Devolution (1982–84):** This proposed an elected assembly and a committee system which would be given more and more power by the British government.
   - But the SDLP rejected it because it did not provide for power sharing.

The Anglo-Irish Agreement (1985)

4. This was the most important peace initiative during these years.

5. There were regular meetings in the early 1980s between the British Prime Minister, **Margaret Thatcher**, and the Irish governments of **Charles Haughey** and **Garret FitzGerald**.

6. **Garret FitzGerald** organised the **New Ireland Forum** to bring together Southern and Northern (nationalist) political parties to suggest solutions for Northern Ireland.

7. The governments were concerned about the level of violence in Northern Ireland and the increasing support for Sinn Féin.

8. Thatcher believed that the solution to Northern Ireland's problems would have to involve the Republic of Ireland. Unionists were worried about this possibility.

9. Thatcher and FitzGerald signed the **Anglo-Irish Agreement** in Hillsborough Castle in November 1985.

10. **The Terms of the Anglo-Irish Agreement**
    - An intergovernmental conference was set up.
    - The intergovernmental conference would have its own civil service drawn from both North and South.
    - The Northern Ireland secretary and the Republic's minister of foreign affairs would meet regularly.

- There would be cross-border cooperation on security, legal and political matters.
- The British government accepted there might be a united Ireland in the future, but only with the consent of the majority of people in Northern Ireland.
- The Irish government accepted partition and the principle of consent.

Reaction

11. The agreement was well received in Britain and the South of Ireland

12. In Northern Ireland, it was supported by the Alliance Party and the SDLP.

13. Sinn Féin and the IRA rejected the agreement because they said it reinforced partition.

14. Unionists and loyalists were very angry – they had not been consulted and they felt betrayed by London. They were angry at Dublin having a say in Northern Ireland affairs.
    - They organised huge demonstrations – one in Belfast had a crowd of over 100,000 people. It was addressed by Ian Paisley and Jim Molyneaux (Unionist Party leader) as part of their '**Ulster Says No**' campaign.

15. Thatcher ignored the protests – there was little support in Britain for the unionist cause.
    - By mid-1987, the loyalist protests had lost their impact.

16. The Anglo-Irish Agreement helped the SDLP in local and national elections in 1986–87 – the Sinn Féin vote dropped.

17. The IRA and loyalist paramilitaries kept up their campaign of violence.

18. **Phased talks (1991–92):** It was proposed to involve the Northern political parties in talks, to be followed by the involvement of the Irish government.

Downing Street Declaration (1993)

19. **Peace demands:** There was a desire for peace among the people of Northern Ireland.

20. **Hume–Adams Talks:** There were secret talks between John Hume and Gerry Adams. Hume hoped to persuade Sinn Féin and the IRA that their view of the problems of Northern Ireland was wrong.
    - While the talks failed initially, the contacts between Hume and Adams continued.

21. The SDLP defeated Sinn Féin in the West Belfast election in 1992 when Gerry Adams lost his seat to Joe Hendron.

22. **The Downing Street Declaration (1993)** was agreed between the British Prime Minister, John Major, and the Taoiseach, Albert Reynolds.

23. **Terms of the Downing Street Declaration**
    - Talks would be set up to decide on a new form of government for Northern Ireland.
    - The new Government would respect all traditions in Northern Ireland.
    - Only parties that rejected violence would be allowed take part in the talks.

- The British government said it had no selfish political or economic interest in Northern Ireland.
- The British government accepted that Irish unity was an issue for Irish people.
- The Irish government accepted the principle of consent for Irish unity.
- The Irish government accepted it might have to drop some articles in its constitution which claimed jurisdiction over Northern Ireland.

Reaction

24. The Alliance Party and the SDLP welcomed the Downing Street Declaration and Ulster Unionists accepted it.
25. Sinn Féin rejected it.
26. Ian Paisley said Major had 'sold out Ulster'.
27. Republican and loyalist paramilitaries asked the British government to clarify details so they did not openly reject it.
28. But the Downing Street Declaration helped move the peace process on – it eventually led to IRA and loyalist ceasefires (1994).
   - But there were many more difficulties before the Good Friday Agreement (1998) was signed.

9. The Republic – responses to the Troubles

 aims In this section, you should understand:
   - How the Republic of Ireland responded to events in Northern Ireland

The Troubles

exam Q How did the Republic of Ireland react to events in Northern Ireland from the development of the Civil Rights movement to the Anglo-Irish Agreement (1985)?

Before the Troubles

1. **Attitudes to the North:**
   In the South, some believed that unity between North and South would be achieved through North–South co-operation, with help from London.
   - But there was very little interest in events in the North until the civil rights march in Derry in October 1968.

2. **O'Neill and Lemass:** Terence O'Neill, Prime Minister of Northern Ireland, believed
   - he should develop economic co-operation with the South.
   - He invited Seán Lemass to the North in January 1965.
   - O'Neill made a return visit to Dublin in February.
   - Lemass believed co-operation with the North would eventually lead to unity.

Civil Rights movement

3. Civil disturbances in the North (especially Derry) in 1968 led to a strain in relations between North and South. **Jack Lynch**, the Taoiseach, said that partition was the root cause of the disturbances in Northern Ireland. This upset unionists.

4. After the Apprentice Boys march in August 1969, more serious trouble erupted in Derry, which led to the Battle of the Bogside.

5. In a TV address, Jack Lynch said the Northern Ireland government was no longer in control of the situation.
   - He said the Irish government could 'no longer stand by and see innocent people injured and perhaps worse'.
   - He said the Irish army would set up field hospitals along the border.
   - Lynch's speech caused great anger among unionists.

6. Some ministers in his government favoured sending troops across the Border. But Lynch resisted this.

Formation of the Provisional IRA

7. Trouble in the North between Catholics and Protestants became more widespread.
   - Some ministers formed an alliance with extreme republicans, which led to the formation of the Provisional IRA.

8. £100,000 was put under the control of **Charles Haughey**, Minister of Finance, to help victims of unrest in the North.
   - Some of this money was used to finance a nationalist newspaper, *The Voice of the North*.
   - Some money was also used to train Derry republicans in the use of arms.
   - These and other actions encouraged some Northern republicans to set up the Provisional IRA.

Arms crisis

9. Efforts were also made to import arms through Dublin airport for the North.

10. Jack Lynch sacked two ministers, Haughey and Blaney, from the Cabinet because of suspicion that they were involved in the **importation of arms**. Another minister, Kevin Boland, resigned in protest.

11. Haughey and Blaney were arrested and charged. Charges against Blaney were dropped, and Haughey was acquitted.

12. Most people in the South supported Lynch's actions – he believed in seeking unity through agreement. The Irish government was opposed to using force in Northern Ireland.

Security actions

13. The South feared the spread of Provisional IRA violence southwards.
   - Des O'Malley, Minister for Justice, used the **Offences against the State Act** to create a special criminal court to deal with subversion. The Act also allowed the imprisonment of those suspected of membership of an illegal organisation.

14. The South did not want unity because it could not afford to maintain the level of social services, education and roads that the North enjoyed.
   - Jack Lynch said 'if we were given a gift of Northern Ireland tomorrow we could not accept it'.

Bloody Sunday (1972)

15. 13 civilians were shot dead, 17 wounded by the Parachute Regiment in Derry – another died later.
    - There were anti-British demonstrations in the South, including a huge demonstration in Dublin which led to the burning of the British Embassy.
    - Relations between North and South were at their worst.

IRA actions in the South

16. In 1973, the *Claudia* was captured off the Waterford coast with a shipment of arms. The IRA also used the South as a location for arms dumps, training, funds from bank robberies and kidnappings. Some local people supported them.

17. The IRA killed the British ambassador, Christopher Ewart-Biggs, with a landmine. They also killed Billy Fox, a Fine Gael senator and a Presbyterian, in a sectarian murder.

18. The government used the **Broadcasting Authority Act** to give the Minister of Posts and Telegraphs the power to prevent members of certain organisations, e.g. Sinn Féin/IRA, being interviewed on RTÉ. The government feared that their authority would be undermined by the spread of violence from the North.

Divisions in the government

19. There were some divisions in the coalition government of Fine Gael–Labour about their approach to Northern Ireland.
    - Conor Cruise O'Brien, Minister for Post and Telegraphs, wanted the question of Irish unity dropped. Instead he believed that reforms in the North and better North–South relations would lead to peace there.
    - Justin Keating, Minister for Industry and Commerce, favoured immediate British withdrawal.

Sunningdale and the power-sharing Executive

20. The British government proposed an **Irish Dimension** – this was a Council of Ireland which would develop co-operation between North and South.
    - The details of the Council of Ireland were sorted out at the Sunningdale Conference (1973). (See *Case study: The Sunningdale Agreement and the Power-sharing Executive, 1973–74*, p. 168.)

21. Heath (British Prime Minister), Cosgrave (Taoiseach), FitzGerald (Irish Minister of Foreign Affairs), and the main Northern political parties (Unionist Party, SDLP, Alliance Party) were represented at the conference.
    - They agreed the Council of Ireland would have a Council of Ministers and a Consultative Assembly with members from both North and South.
    - The Southern government supported the views of John Hume on the Council of Ireland.

22. **Boland Case:** Kevin Boland, a former Fianna Fáil minister, challenged the legality of the Sunningdale Agreement in the High Court. His case was defeated, but the Irish

government had to argue in its own defence that the South's constitutional claim to Northern Ireland was still in force.

- This claim confirmed the fears of unionists about a united Ireland, and it weakened support for the power-sharing government in Northern Ireland.

23. Unionists bitterly opposed the Sunningdale Agreement. The Ulster Workers' Council strike in May 1974 led to the downfall of the power-sharing Executive and the Council of Ireland.

24. During the strike, car bombs in Dublin and Monaghan killed 33 people and injured over 120 people. The bombing was carried out by the Ulster Volunteer Force (UVF).

Hunger strikes

25. The British government (led by Margaret Thatcher) refused to give political status to prisoners.

- IRA members in Long Kesh prison (the H-Blocks) went on hunger strike; 10 died.

26. There was support from the Republic for the hunger strikers, and marches supporting them when they died; two of them were elected to the Dáil in the general election of June 1981.

27. The growth in the popularity of Sinn Féin led the Irish government to fear that Sinn Féin would replace the SDLP as the representatives of Northern Catholics. This brought the Irish and British governments closer together.

28. Charles Haughey, Taoiseach, and Margaret Thatcher, British Prime Minister, agreed that they would consider the '**totality of relationships**' between the two countries.

29. The government of Garret FitzGerald, Taoiseach, set up the **New Ireland Forum** to discuss solutions to the Northern problem. The report of the Forum proposed three possible solutions:

- a united Ireland
- a federal state
- a joint authority.

30. These were rejected by Margaret Thatcher.

The Anglo-Irish Agreement (1985)

31. The Irish government, led by the Taoiseach, Garret FitzGerald, negotiated with the British government led by Margaret Thatcher. FitzGerald was concerned about the growing influence of Sinn Féin/IRA; he wanted to support the ideas of John Hume and the SDLP (constitutional nationalism).

- The Irish government used Irish-American influence to put pressure on the British government.

32. The negotiations led to the **Anglo-Irish Agreement** (1985). Margaret Thatcher and Garret FitzGerald signed the Agreement in Hillsborough, Co. Down.

- The Anglo-Irish Agreement set up an Inter-Governmental Conference which gave the Irish government some say in the running of Northern Ireland.

33. Unionists were very much opposed to the agreement, but they could not stop it.

Downing Street Declaration (1993)

34. A further step on the road to peace in the North was taken with the **Downing Street Declaration**. This was agreed by John Major, British Prime Minister, and Albert Reynolds, Taoiseach.

    • The Irish government agreed that Irish unity would come about only by the consent of the people of Northern Ireland.

    • The British government said that they had no strategic interest in Northern Ireland.

Conclusion

35. Through the various agreements from 1973 onwards, the Irish government had increased its role in Northern Ireland's affairs.

36. It also meant that the Irish government could not ignore Northern Ireland as it had before the 1970s.

37. Many in the South also changed their attitude to the North.

    • At the beginning of the Troubles, it was commonly held view that partition and the British presence in the North was the core of the Northern problem.

    • By the 1990s, many saw the problem as the divisions between the two communities in the North. The solution had to be found in Northern Ireland.

10. The impact of the Troubles – economy and society

 In this section, you should understand:

   • How the Troubles impacted on economy and society in Northern Ireland

Economy

 What were the social and economic effects of the Troubles?

1. The Northern economy grew in the 1960s, but it went into decline after 1973.

    • It was affected by recessions in Britain, the world oil crisis, the continuing decline of traditional industry and the impact of the Troubles.

2. Industrial **employment fell** during the 1970s. Older industries such as shipbuilding and linen continued to decline. Harland and Wolff declined from 20,000 employees in the 1960s to fewer than 4,000 in the 1980s.

3. Newer industries established in the 1960s, such as synthetic fibres, were very dependent on oil and were badly affected by the oil crises of the 1970s.

4. Along with these developments, it is estimated that the Troubles prevented the creation of 40,000 jobs because companies feared the impact of the violence in the North.

5. **Unemployment**: unemployment was low in the 1960s at 5 per cent. But unemployed numbers doubled in the 1970s, and again by the early 1980s.

6. Northern Ireland had the highest unemployment rate in the United Kingdom at an average of 14 per cent.

- Long-term unemployment posed a particular problem.
- Youth unemployment was also high.

7. Overall, rising unemployment contributed to rising **tensions** in working-class Protestant and Catholic areas. Catholic males were more likely to be unemployed than Protestant males. This fuelled Catholic grievances.

8. From the early 1970s, Northern Ireland was highly dependent on state employment.
- There was growth in the public sector – especially health, the civil service, education and the security services.

9. By the 1980s, public sector employment stood at 42 per cent of the workforce, up from 27 per cent a decade earlier.

10. There was increased government spending – it was 50 per cent higher per head in Ulster compared to the UK overall.

11. There was a huge increase in the **subvention** paid by Westminster (this was the difference between what was raised in taxes in Northern Ireland and what it cost to run the area). By the mid-1990s, it was almost £4 billion each year.

12. In the 1970s the British government established agencies to promote and encourage industrial development, e.g. Northern Ireland Development Agency.

13. The government also set up the Fair Employment Agency (1976) and passed the Fair Employment Act (1989) to outlaw discrimination in employment. But change was slow.

Society

Education

1. Schools remained **segregated** with the vast majority of Protestant and Catholic students educated separately.

2. Schools largely followed their traditional games – Catholic schools played Gaelic games, while Protestant schools played those of British origin, e.g. rugby, cricket. But soccer and basketball cut across religious lines.

3. Schools were involved in building up community relations, especially from the 1980s onwards.
- The Department of Education set up the Education for Mutual Understanding (EMU) programme.
- Schools had to include themes on community relations in their curriculum.

4. **Integrated schools** were developed. They were attended in roughly equal numbers by Protestants and Catholics. The first such school was Lagan College, which began in 1981.
- By 1993, there were 21 integrated primary and secondary schools. But only 1 per cent of the school population went to these schools.

5. The main area of education which was integrated was third-level and further education.

Housing

6. Housing was a key issue in the rise of the civil rights movement. Nationalists accused local councils of discriminating against them in the allocation of houses.

7. The **Housing Executive** was set up in 1971 with full responsibility for house building.

8. The Executive faced many problems; it was called 'the largest slum landlord in Europe'.
   - During the Troubles, houses were burnt, and families moved, creating bigger ghettos. By 1975, 25,000 houses in Belfast had been destroyed.
   - By 1974, 20 per cent of houses were unfit for living in; this figure was much higher in some areas of Belfast.

9. There was a **rent and rate strike** amongst nationalist tenants because of internment.

10. In spite of these problems, the Housing Executive built and improved houses during the 1970s so that by the end of the decade there were fewer uninhabitable houses.

11. But new houses followed the segregated pattern for the sake of stability.
   - e.g. in Derry, there was a very long waiting list for houses. With the building of new houses, west of the River Foyle was largely Catholic, and east of the Foyle largely Protestant.

12. The **Housing Executive** got more money in the early 1980s – construction was labour intensive, so it provided employment. It also depended on local materials.

13. The Housing Executive spent £2.4 billion on building new houses or renovating older ones.
   - It improved the quality of houses and changed the layout of estates.
   - The Divis Flats complex (Belfast) was pulled down, except for one tower, and replaced by houses.
   - New suburbs were created on the edge of Belfast.
   - These developments may have contributed to lowering the levels of violence.

14. By 1992, the housing crisis was over.

Health

15. The control of health was taken from the local councils and given to Health Boards.

16. Health provision in Northern Ireland was even better than in Britain: There was relatively more spent on health in Northern Ireland than in Britain and there were more hospital beds per thousand of the population in Northern Ireland.

11. Religious affiliation and cultural identity

Religious affiliation

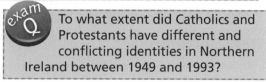

To what extent did Catholics and Protestants have different and conflicting identities in Northern Ireland between 1949 and 1993?

1. Protestants made up the majority of Northern Ireland's population of 1.5 million.
   - They comprised about two-thirds of the population in the 1950s.
   - Protestants were in a greater majority in the counties of Antrim and Down, and in the city of Belfast (east of the Bann).
2. Catholics comprised one-third of the population in the 1950s and 1960s.
   - The main Catholic majorities were west of the Bann, in counties Derry and Tyrone.
3. The Catholic population rose from the 1960s onwards so that by the early 1990s it comprised over 40 per cent of the population. This was due to a higher birth rate.

Protestant identity

4. Protestants and Catholics maintained **different and conflicting identities**. These separate identities had a long history.
5. Protestants were largely **unionists**; they proclaimed their loyalty to the Queen and the union with Britain.
6. They had their own schools and social clubs, and played sports such as soccer and rugby. In the cities they lived in different areas from Catholics.
7. They felt **under siege and threatened** by the Catholic majority in the island of Ireland.
   - They looked on Catholics in Northern Ireland as an internal threat to their government.
   - They also felt insulted by propaganda against them; they wanted to maintain their majority in Northern Ireland in order to maintain their way of life.

> **key point**
>
> PROPAGANDA:
> Spreading information and ideas to support one's own side and undermine the other side with the aim of achieving political power.

   - The Unionist government passed the **Flags and Emblems Act** (1954) to allow people fly the Union flag – the flag of the Crown and constitution – in support of the British way of life.
   - The Act gave power to the RUC to remove any emblem or flag whose display might cause disturbance. In particular, unionists saw the tricolour as the flag of a country that claimed jurisdiction over their country.

8. Protestants celebrated different traditions and historic events from Catholics. The main events were the **Siege of Derry** and the **Battle of the Boyne**, which were seen as Protestant triumphs over Catholics. They also commemorated participation in the First and Second World Wars.

> **key point**
>
> CULTURAL IDENTITY:
> The patterns, beliefs and activities of a group of people that mark them out from other groups.

The Loyal Orders

9. Protestants celebrated their culture through associations such as the Orange Order, the Apprentice Boys of Derry and the Royal Black Institution. These were known as the **Loyal Orders**.

10. The largest of the Loyal Orders was the **Orange Order**, which had up to 100,000 members drawn from all classes in Northern society.

11. The Orange Order celebrated the victory of the army of the Protestant King William III over the Catholic King James II at the **Battle of the Boyne** in 1690. Huge parades on 12 July ('The Twelfth') each year celebrated King Billy's victory.
    - Over the years some of these parades resulted in attacks on Catholic areas.

12. There were close ties between the Orange Order and the ruling Unionist Party. Most Unionist politicians and government ministers were members of the Order. The Order also had representation in the Ulster Unionist Council, the ruling body of the party.

Catholic identity

13. Catholics celebrated a **different history** – they commemorated the 50th anniversary of the 1916 Rising, for example.

> **key point**
>
> CULTURAL TRADITIONS:
> The patterns, beliefs and activities that form part of the way of life of a people.

14. They favoured Irish unity and the end of partition – very often they flew the Irish tricolour rather than the Union flag.

15. Catholics relied on their own organisations. They followed games organised by the Gaelic Athletic Association and played the Irish national anthem before matches.
    - Members of the RUC and British Army were excluded from the GAA.

16. The **Ancient Order of Hibernians** was a Catholic organisation which mirrored the Protestant Orange Order. It promoted Irish unity and its banners carried symbols of Irish nationalism – the 1916 Rising, Pádraig Pearse. But it was never as strong among Catholics as the Orange Order was among Protestants.

17. Some nationalists/Catholics supported soccer teams, but these were different from the soccer teams supported by Protestants; for example, Catholics supported Glasgow Celtic and Protestants supported Rangers.

18. Catholic schools taught the Irish language and Irish history.

19. Catholics felt discriminated against by the Protestant majority – they believed they were treated as second-class citizens in the North.

12. Ecumenism in Northern Ireland

In this section, you should understand:
- How various groups reacted to ecumenism in Northern Ireland

1. Ecumenism promotes understanding between different Christian religions, with the eventual aim of Christian unity.

What problems and opportunities did ecumenism present to society in Northern Ireland between 1965 and 1993?

2. In 1948, the World Council of Churches was set up as an international ecumenical organisation to promote common action by the churches and to promote co-operation in study and ecumenism. The World Council of Churches was composed mostly of Protestant churches – the Catholic Church did not join.

3. The British Council of Churches was linked to this organisation. The BCC worked to promote ecumenism in Northern Ireland.

Paisley and opposition to ecumenism

4. In Northern Ireland, Rev. Ian Paisley was the most vocal **opponent** of ecumenism.

> **key point**
>
> ECUMENISM:
> A movement promoting understanding between religions, with the eventual aim of unity.

   - He founded the Free Presbyterian Church in the early 1950s and was immediately involved in protests against ecumenism.
   - He picketed outside a meeting in Belfast of the British Council of Churches.
   - He used his monthly church magazine, *The Revivalist*, to attack any signs of ecumenism, even among Protestant churches.
   - He attacked the BBC (British Broadcasting Corporation) for being under the control 'partly of Romanists'.

5. Paisley attacked the World Council of Churches for inviting the 'Roman Antichrist' to join their organisation.

6. He attacked the Presbyterians, Methodists and Church of Ireland for their membership of the World Council of Churches.

7. In spite of Paisley's fears, there was **little progress in ecumenism** in the 1950s. In particular, relations between the Protestant churches and the Catholic Church were still governed by mistrust between the two sides.
   - Protestants viewed Catholics as part of an international empire, under the control of the Pope.
   - Catholics looked on themselves as being oppressed.
   - Protestants complained about the involvement of priests in politics, while Catholics complained about the involvement of Protestant clergy in the Orange Order.

8. Changes occurred in the Catholic Church with the advent of Pope John XXIII and the **Vatican Council** (1961–64). This council decreed that the restoration of unity

among all Christians was one of its principal concerns. It encouraged discussion with the World Council of Churches.

9. Even though the changes agreed at the Vatican Council were slow to take effect in Ireland, some clergy led the way in attempting to improve relations with the Protestant churches.

10. There was also movement by the Protestant churches for greater co-operation.
   - The Methodists and the Church of Ireland shared church buildings.
   - In 1964 the Church of Ireland proposed to begin talks on church unity with the Methodist and Presbyterian Churches. The Presbyterian Church welcomed this.

11. The Methodist Church agreed to hold talks between Methodist groups and Catholics on questions of social and religious concern.

12. In 1964, the Presbyterian Church said that while they were still opposed to the doctrine of the Catholic Church, they welcomed movements towards reform in the Catholic Church.

Further opposition to ecumenism

13. All these and other examples of ecumenical progress led to even further objections by Paisley and others who agreed with his anti-ecumenical views.
   - They saw ecumenism as a movement of unity with the Catholic Church.
   - They feared that ecumenism would lead to Irish unity.

14. They were concerned about the dangers of **mixed marriages** in Ireland between Protestants and Catholics because of the Catholic Church's *Ne Temere* decree that the children of such marriages should be brought up Catholic.

15. They saw this as an explanation for the falling numbers of Protestants in the South of Ireland as shown by the 1961 census figures. Among some Northern Ireland unionists there was a fear of being out-bred by Catholics.

16. They were also opposed to papal infallibility and they looked on Catholics as being dominated by the Pope.

17. They looked on the South as a **Catholic-dominated state**.
   - They pointed to the Catholic Church's ban on Catholics attending Trinity College, Dublin, as evidence of the power of the Catholic Church.

18. Paisley protested against the visit of the Church of England Archbishop of Canterbury, Archbishop Ramsey, because of his 'Romanising activities'.

19. While anti-ecumenical protests were mostly about religious issues, there was also a political side to them. Paisley protested against the visit of O'Neill, Prime Minister, to Catholic schools.

20. Paisley also published his own newspaper, the *Protestant Telegraph*, because he felt that the existing newspapers, especially the *Belfast Telegraph*, were in favour of ecumenism.

21. Paisley went to Rome to protest at the presence of the WCC at the Vatican Council.

22. **The Orange Order** was also concerned about ecumenism. The Order agreed a motion which was passed during 12 July parades in 1966. This condemned the visit

of the Archbishop of Canterbury to Rome and the influence of the World Council of Churches on the progress towards 'one united Church'.

23. Anti-ecumenism and fear of Catholics was used by Paisley to move into politics.
    - He also wanted to recruit new members for his Free Presbyterian Church from the Presbyterian Church of Ireland.

24. In 1966 Church of Ireland Bishop McAdoo had to withdraw from the Anglican–Roman Catholic Preparatory Commission because of the situation in Northern Ireland. Pressure came from Paisley due to Northern hostility to ecumenism.
    - Overall, there was still great opposition to ecumenism in Northern Ireland in the mid-1960s.

The impact of the Troubles on ecumenism

25. The coming of the Troubles in 1968–69 led to greater divisions between Protestants and Catholics but they also brought about inter-church co-operation in three ways:
    - meetings of church leaders and their representatives
    - pleas for peace
    - meetings of the Joint Group on Social Problems (e.g. poverty and drug addiction) (1970).

26. The **Irish Council of Churches** (ICC) worked for ecumenism. Its eight Protestant member churches worked to improve relations with the Catholic Church to achieve better community relations.

Appeals for peace

27. PACE (Protestant and Catholic Encounter), a non-political organisation, was set up in 1968 to promote harmony and goodwill between different communities in Northern Ireland.

28. At the height of the Troubles, 8,000 Protestants and Catholics went to Ulster Hall in February 1971 to pray for peace.

Ballymacscanlon Meeting

29. The first meeting of all the member churches of the ICC and the Catholic Church took place at Ballymacscanlon Hotel, Dundalk, on 26 September 1973.
    - This was the first time the Catholic Church in Ireland had become involved in ecumenical dialogue at an official level.
    - Horror of the communal conflict in Northern Ireland forced the churches together.
    - At this time, while the church leaders had more contact with each other, the people had less contact. But in the long term, the example set by the church leaders helped to improve relations between the two communities in Northern Ireland.

13. Cultural responses to the Troubles

aims In this section, you should understand:
- How nationalists and unionists expressed their cultural identity
- Case study: The Apprentice Boys of Derry

Symbols and murals

exam Q How true is it that divided societies such as Northern Ireland between 1949 and 1993 are sometimes culturally productive?

Symbols

1. Each side – unionist and nationalist – had their own symbols to represent their ideas and culture.

2. The **Unionist** colours were largely orange (from the Orange Order and King William of Orange), and red, white and blue (from the British Union flag). The Apprentice Boys of Derry used crimson.

3. Unionists also used the **Crown** to represent the British monarchy, and the poppy on Remembrance Day to commemorate those who died in the First and Second World Wars.

4. The biggest blaze of colour and symbolism was seen around the main day of celebration in the unionist calendar, the **Twelfth**, when flags were flown from buntings, and colours were painted on kerbstones and lamp posts.
   - The Orange sash was worn in the parades.

5. The **nationalists** were more associated with green, and green, white and orange from the tricolour flag of the Republic of Ireland. In contrast to the poppy, republicans wore the Easter Lily to commemorate those who died for Irish independence.

6. One symbol, the **Red Hand**, was used by both sides, but it represented different things – to unionists it symbolised the six counties, while to nationalists it represented the traditional nine counties of Ulster.

7. These symbols were used more frequently as the Troubles progressed. Apart from the parades, most were used on the **murals** – gable-end paintings – which became a feature of Northern Irish politics.

Murals

8. **Loyalist** (unionist) murals dated back to the early 20th century. They were mostly painted around the time of the Twelfth celebrations. They largely represented figures from the unionist view of their history – King William, the Battle of the Boyne, the Siege of Derry.

9. After Stormont was closed and Direct Rule was imposed from London, the themes and symbols changed. The Red Hand of Ulster featured more often.

10. There were more changes after the Anglo-Irish Agreement (1985), when unionists felt betrayed. Military men in balaclavas firing weapons featured and the tone became more anti-nationalist and anti-Catholic.

11. Murals were initially not important in **nationalist** culture. Irish dancing, music and Gaelic sports were more important. These were conducted in GAA clubs and local halls.

12. Nationalist murals date largely from the **Hunger Strikes** of 1981. They depicted coffins, black flags, and H-Block symbols. They also depicted the armed struggle of the IRA using military images.
    - Nationalists used different historical images from unionists, and they also used Celtic imagery.

Parades and marches

1. Parades and marches had been an important part of unionist and nationalist culture since the 18th century. But during the Troubles the number of parades increased considerably as each side felt threatened.
   - Most of the parades were held during the so-called marching season, from Easter Monday to the end of August.
2. Parading was more part of the unionist culture than the nationalist. By the 1990s, unionists had a much higher proportion of parades (over 70 per cent) than nationalists (about 10 per cent). (The rest were church parades, trade union marches, etc.)
3. The key organisations involved in parading were the **Loyal Orders** – the Orange Order, the Royal Black Institution and the Apprentice Boys of Derry.
4. The Orange Order organised the parades on 12 July to commemorate the victory of King William over King James at the Battle of the Boyne.
   - The Black Institution organised marches on the following day and later in August.
   - The Apprentice Boys of Derry marched in August to celebrate the lifting of the Siege of Derry, and in December to mark the closure of the gates at the beginning of the siege. (See *Case study: The Apprentice Boys of Derry*, p. 194)
5. On the **nationalist** side, the Ancient Order of Hibernians organised parades on St Patrick's Day and on 15 August, Our Lady's Day. They were defending the Catholic religion and supporting Irish nationalism.
6. Parades represented a **public display of the culture and symbols** of each side.
7. Parades were often flashpoints for conflict between the two communities. Sometimes Orange parades broke off into attacks on Catholic neighbourhoods.
   - Unionists viewed parades as part of their tradition. Nationalists viewed unionist parades as threatening.
8. By the 1980s, power was given to the RUC to regulate the parade routes to minimise the danger of conflict.

Poetry and drama

1. There was a revival of poetry in Northern Ireland before the Troubles, which owed its origins to the Education Act (1947).
2. When the Troubles began in 1968–69, poets responded. Poets such as Seamus Heaney, Michael Longley, Seamus Deane and John Montague wrote on many different aspects of the Troubles.
3. These aspects included:

- the origins of the Troubles and the clash of cultures
- the discrimination and injustice between the establishment of Northern Ireland in 1921 and the beginning of the Troubles
- the victims of the Troubles
- the conflict between the artist and politics.

4. Poems such as Ciaran Carson's 'Belfast Confetti', Michael Longley's laments for the dead like 'The Civil Servant', Derek Mahon's 'A Disused Shed in Co. Wexford', and Paul Muldoon's 'Gathering Mushrooms' were examples of the poetry inspired by the Troubles.

5. Many poets wrote full-length collections of poetry dealing with the Troubles: these include *North* by Seamus Heaney, *An Exploded View* by Michael Longley and *The Rough Field* by John Montague. (See Key personality: *Seamus Heaney,* p. 219)

6. The most important dramatist to write about the North was **Brian Friel**. He was reared in a middle-class Catholic family in Derry at a time when Catholics suffered high unemployment and discrimination. Some of the plays he wrote after the Troubles began, such as *The Freedom of the City*, *Volunteers* and *Aristocrats*, had strong political themes.

7. In 1982, he set up the **Field Day Theatre Company** in Derry, along with Stephen Rea (actor), Seamus Heaney and others, to put on plays which would change the mood of Northern Ireland.

- Its first production was a play written by Friel, *Translations*. Even though it was set in the 1830s, it dealt with the clash of English and Irish cultures, and the spread of English colonialism. However, he wrote without condemning either side.

Case study: The Apprentice Boys of Derry

Historical background

1. The Apprentice Boys of Derry is the oldest of the Loyal Orders. Its first club was founded in 1714 to commemorate the Siege of Derry in 1688–89.

- What was the contribution of the Apprentice Boys of Derry to the celebration of religious and cultural identity among that city's unionist minority?
- To what extent were the activities of the Apprentice Boys of Derry and/or the choice of Coleraine as the site of Northern Ireland's second university divisive?

2. **The Siege**: In 1688, the armies of King James II, a Catholic king, surrounded the city of Londonderry, which supported the armies of King William of Orange. The population of the city grew from about 3,000 to 30,000 as Protestants from surrounding areas took refuge behind Derry's high walls.

- 13 apprentice boys closed the gates of the city against James in December 1688.
- The governor of the city, Robert Lundy, favoured surrender, but he was replaced by George Walker.

3. For the next 105 days Derry refused to surrender – **'No Surrender'** – in spite of hunger, and constant bombardment by James's army from the hills around the walled city.

4. James's army also erected a boom across the River Foyle to block any ship supplying the city. But in the summer of 1689, William sent three ships to break the boom. The *Mountjoy* eventually broke through and the city was relieved in August 1689.

5. The Siege of Derry became a powerful **symbol of Protestant resistance** against Catholic domination.

The Apprentice Boys of Derry

6. Derry Protestants celebrated the Siege during the 18th century. But the main clubs that formed the Apprentice Boys were not formed until the 19th century.

7. Members of the Apprentice Boys of Derry must be of the Reformed Protestant religion, support the Throne of England, keep alive the memories of the Siege, and attend celebrations.

8. Two events – **the Shutting of the Gates** and **the Relief of the City** – are commemorated annually by the Apprentice Boys.

Organisation

9. The Apprentice Boys – which is a separate organisation from the Orange Order – are governed by a General Committee. This is representative of the eight Parent Clubs and of the Amalgamated Clubs.

10. The **Parent Clubs** are: the Apprentice Boys of Derry Club, named after the 'Brave 13' apprentices who closed the gates; the Walker Club; the Mitchelburne Club; the No Surrender Club; the Browning Club; the Campsie Club; and the Murray Club.

   - All the clubs are named after heroes of the siege, except the No Surrender Club, which is named after the battle cry of the Siege.

11. Each of the Parent Clubs has branch clubs in other parts of Northern Ireland, and in Canada, Scotland and Australia.

   - New members are initiated within the Derry city walls, usually on 12 August or 18 December.
   - Lord Brookeborough, Terence O'Neill, Brian Faulkner and Ian Paisley were all initiated as members.

12. The Apprentice Boys hold celebrations on 18 December to commemorate the Shutting of the Gates, and on 12 August to commemorate the Relief of Derry.

13. Trains and buses bring members to the main parades in Derry, but local parades are also held, spreading the aims and ideas of the Apprentice Boys.

14. **Ceremonies** include firing a cannon which is a replica of the siege cannon known as 'Roaring Meg', a visit to the four gates of the old city, a ceremony of initiation of new members into the Order, a church service in St Columb's Cathedral, and a colourful parade through the streets of Derry.

- In December, an effigy of **Lundy** (governor of the city who wanted to negotiate a surrender) is burned as a reminder of his 'treachery'.
- A crimson flag is flown and crimson collarettes are worn by the members to commemorate the crimson flag flown from the cathedral during the Siege. Derry was the 'Maiden City' that refused to be broken.

15. The Apprentice Boys look on the parades as a celebration of civil and religious liberty, because after the victory of William, Britain was on the road to parliamentary democracy.

16. They also celebrate their Protestant religion and culture, and commemorate the union with Britain.

17. The Siege represents unity in adversity, no compromise and no surrender. It is a reminder to them of the danger of the traitor inside – never trust the enemy and exclude them from power.

18. **Growth of parades**: There was a growth in the membership of the Apprentice Boys from the 1940s to the 1990s.
    - About 1,000 new members were initiated each year.
    - There were 178 branches in 1971, and this grew to over 200 in 1989. There was also an increase in numbers visiting the city for parades.

19. **Why did numbers grow?** The Siege of Derry was a powerful symbol for unionists and Protestants in Northern Ireland. During the spread of the Troubles, unionists and Protestants saw their political and cultural heritage under threat.
    - In more recent times, the Apprentice Boys made efforts to broaden the appeal of their tradition by holding the Maiden City Festival to involve all Derry people.
    - In 1989, the 300th anniversary of the Siege was celebrated with widespread festivities in the city in conjunction with the nationalist city council.

Tension and conflict

20. However, the Apprentice Boys celebrations were flashpoints for riots which brought conflict with nationalists and Catholics in the late 1960s when the civil rights campaign began.

21. **Catholic/nationalist view**: Catholics looked on the Siege as a defeat of Catholic King James leading to the Protestant Ascendancy and the defeat of Catholics in Ireland.
    - They looked on the walk on the Walls of the City overlooking the Catholic Bogside as an attempt to humiliate them.
    - This was seen as part of nationalists' status as second-class citizens.

22. **Parades**: The Apprentice Boys said they had a right to parade, that the parades were 'traditional' and central to Protestant identity; they gave them a sense of belonging.
    - The Apprentice Boys did not regard civil rights parades as traditional and therefore said they should be banned.

23. **Derry, October (1968)**: A civil rights march was planned for Derry; this became a source of conflict/tension. The Apprentice Boys planned a march on the same route at the same time. This gave William Craig, Minister for Home Affairs, the excuse to ban the civil rights march. However, the civil rights march went ahead and this resulted in a clash with police (RUC).

24. **August 1969**: The Apprentice Boys march in August 1969 was the spark which led to the **Battle of the Bogside**.

   ● There was tension in August 1969 in the build-up to the parade – should the parade be banned?

   ● Some civil rights leaders argued that there was a danger of a breakdown of law and order. John Hume went to London and Dublin to try to get the parades banned; he failed.

   ● Prayers were said in churches that there would be no trouble.

   ● But there were warnings that the people of the Bogside would defend themselves. Barricades were built in the Bogside.

   ● Catholic youths were separated from the Apprentice Boys by the RUC. Bogside youths threw stones – they were attacked by the RUC.

   ● This led to the **Battle of the Bogside**, when the RUC tried to break past the nationalist barricades but failed. Instead, the British Army was brought in.

25. **Parades banned**: the Apprentice Boys parades were banned in 1970 and 1971 – church services were held instead. Parades were restricted to the (Protestant) Waterside for the next few years.

26. After that the Apprentice Boys were allowed into the walled city but not on to the walls because they overlooked the nationalist Bogside. Walking on the walls was banned until 1995, by which time significant efforts had been made to restore peace to Northern Ireland.

Key personalities

Terence O'Neill

1. Terence O'Neill was born in London in 1914. He was educated in England. He began to live in Northern Ireland in 1945 after serving in the Irish Guards in the Second World War.

2. O'Neill was elected **Unionist MP** for Bannside in 1946. He was appointed parliamentary secretary to the Minister of Health. He became **Minister of Home Affairs** in 1956 and **Minister of Finance** shortly after.

3. The North was going through a severe economic crisis in the late 1950s and early 1960s. For example, the Belfast shipyards lost 40 per cent of its jobs between 1961 and 1964. O'Neill sought help from Westminster to overcome the economic difficulties that faced the North.

4. O'Neill became Prime Minister of Northern Ireland after Brookeborough retired in 1963.
   - He favoured a **modernisation** programme for Northern Ireland.

5. O'Neill supported the proposals of the Matthew Report (1964) for road building and the development of new towns. He also backed the Wilson Plan (1965), which proposed to develop growth centres by attracting new industries to Northern Ireland.

6. O'Neill appointed the **Lockwood Committee** to enquire into university education in Northern Ireland. He backed the conclusion of the Committee in relation to locating a second university in Coleraine. But he did not close Magee College, Derry.

7. O'Neill had some success at the general election of 1965. His promise to modernise Northern Ireland and to attract new industries resulted in the Unionist Party winning back two seats from the Northern Ireland Labour Party.

8. O'Neill visited some Catholic schools to improve relations with Catholics.

9. He invited **Seán Lemass**, Taoiseach, to Northern Ireland in January 1965 to improve relations with the South. O'Neill did not inform his cabinet and this led to criticism of his action. Later, O'Neill visited Dublin.

10. The civil rights movement began to demand reforms for Catholics. O'Neill was under pressure from Ian Paisley, who criticised any moves that favoured Catholics. He also had critics in his own Unionist Party.

11. But O'Neill was pressurised by the events of the civil rights march in Derry in October 1968. O'Neill's Minister for Home Affairs, William Craig, banned the march and this led to the RUC batoning the protestors.
    - Wilson, Prime Minister of Britain, forced him to introduce some reforms: The Five Point Reform Programme.

12. **Reforms:** The reforms included a new points system for allocating houses and the abolition of the Special Powers Act. But the programme did not include one man, one vote, which was one of the major demands of the civil rights movement.

13. **Ulster at the crossroads:** The reforms did not satisfy nationalists, and they made unionists angry. O'Neill made a television address in which he said Ulster was at the crossroads and asked for time to allow his reforms to work. The nationalists agreed to suspend their marches for a month.

14. **People's Democracy march:** This march, organised by students from Queen's University in Belfast, was attacked by loyalists. This destroyed any hope O'Neill had of making his reforms work.

15. **General election**: O'Neill decided to hold a general election to defeat his critics in his party. He narrowly escaped being defeated in his own constituency by Ian Paisley. He failed to defeat his opponents.

16. **Resignation**: A series of bombs, including some aimed at Belfast's water supply, undermined O'Neill's position. He resigned in April 1969. One of his last actions was to grant one man, one vote.

17. O'Neill hoped to win over Catholics to a prosperous Ulster. But his reforms were too little for Catholics/nationalists and too much for Protestants/unionists.

Brian Faulkner

1. Brian Faulkner was the son of a successful businessman. He joined the Orange Order and the Unionist Party in 1946, and he was elected Unionist MP for East Down in 1949.

2. Faulkner was a champion of **'not-an-inch'** **Unionism** in the 1950s. He opposed the decision of the Minister for Home Affairs, Brian Maginnis, to ban an Orange march down the Catholic Longstone Road in 1952. When the ban was lifted in 1955, Faulkner led 15,000 Orangemen along the road, guarded by the RUC. Faulkner later opposed Catholic membership of the Unionist Party. He said Catholics would undermine the North.

3. He was appointed **Minister for Home Affairs** in 1959 during the IRA border campaign, which he opposed strongly. He gave permission for an Orange march through the mainly Catholic village of Dungiven, Co. Derry, in 1960 – this led to violent clashes with Catholics and a boycott of Protestant businesses in the village.

4. Faulkner was appointed **Minister for Commerce** by O'Neill. He succeeded in attracting major companies such as Ford, Rolls-Royce and Courtaulds. This increase in industry balanced the decline in traditional industries.

5. Faulkner did not get on well with O'Neill – he considered O'Neill aloof and distant, and out of touch with grass-roots unionism; O'Neill thought Faulkner was devious and attempting to undermine his position.

6. Faulkner criticised O'Neill for meeting Lemass without informing the cabinet. But he was later active in developing North–South tourist interests.

7. Faulkner did not take part in early moves to get rid of O'Neill. O'Neill made him Deputy Prime Minister, but he continued to disagree with O'Neill.

8. Faulkner was opposed to the demands of the Civil Rights movement – he supported the continuation of the ratepayer vote in local elections. He believed the demand for 'one man, one vote' was being used to discredit the Unionist government.

9. Faulkner resigned after O'Neill announced a commission of enquiry – the Cameron Commission – into the causes of the outbreak of violence at the civil rights march in Derry in August 1968.

10. Faulkner was narrowly defeated in the election for O'Neill's successor by James Chichester-Clark. But he was appointed **Minister for Development** in the government. He was responsible for the reform package in housing, creating the Housing Executive, and the overhaul of local government.

11. He defeated William Craig to become **Prime Minister** after Chichester-Clark resigned in March 1971.

12. As IRA and communal violence increased, Faulkner introduced **internment** of IRA suspects. This was disastrous, leading to increased violence and increasing the popularity of the IRA. After **Bloody Sunday**, February 1972, the British government suspended Stormont and introduced Direct Rule from Westminster.

13. Faulkner supported the **Northern Ireland constitutional proposals** introduced by Whitelaw. These proposed power sharing and an Irish Dimension (Council of Ireland).

    ● Faulkner's support led to divisions in the Unionist Party. In the 1973 Assembly elections, Faulkner's Pledged Unionists were opposed by Unpledged Unionists.

14. Faulkner negotiated a power-sharing agreement with the SDLP and the Alliance Party.

    ● This was not put into effect until after the Council of Ireland was agreed at the **Sunningdale Conference**. Here Faulkner was isolated and the Council of Ireland were given strong powers.

15. After Faulkner and the power-sharing Executive took over on 1 January 1974, the Ulster Unionist Council rejected the Sunningdale Agreement. Faulkner had to set up his own political party, the Unionist Party of Northern Ireland. His party was badly defeated in the Westminster general election in February 1974.

16. Faulkner's power-sharing government collapsed after the Ulster Workers' Strike in May 1974, and Direct Rule was re-imposed.

17. Faulkner's party only won five seats in the election for the Constitutional Convention in 1975.

18. Faulkner retired from politics in 1976. He was created a life peer and died in a hunting accident in 1977.

Ian Paisley

1. Ian Paisley was brought up in Ballymena, Co. Antrim. He followed his father and became a minister. In 1951 he founded the Free Presbyterian Church and remained its leader (Moderator) until 2008.

2. Paisley came to prominence in the late 1940s and early 1950s with his ability to **rouse a crowd**, and his appeal to the fears of Protestants.

   - He was bitterly opposed to Catholics. He attacked Popery and said the Education Act (1947) was 'subsidised Romanism'.

3. During the 1950s and 1960s, he attacked all attempts at **ecumenism** either between Protestant churches linked to the World Council of Churches or between Protestant churches and the Catholic Church.

4. His attacks on ecumenism forced the Prime Minister, Lord Brookeborough, to become more conservative.

5. Paisley became active in **Ulster Protestant Action** in the 1950s as Protestants organised against the threat of the IRA border campaign. The UPA also defended the interests of Protestants where jobs were being lost. This became the Protestant Unionist Party in 1966.

6. Paisley opposed O'Neill's efforts at improving relations between Catholics and Protestants, and between North and South.

   - Paisley protested against O'Neill's invitation to Seán Lemass to visit Belfast.
   - Paisley was opposed to any reforms by O'Neill which would give civil rights to Catholics. He organised counter demonstrations to civil rights marches. In 1969 he was jailed for organising an illegal demonstration against a civil rights march in Armagh.

7. He challenged O'Neill in the 1969 general election and was only beaten by him by a small margin. This contributed to O'Neill's downfall. Paisley benefited from growing fears among the unionist people, which he had stirred up.

8. Paisley was first elected to Stormont for **Bannside** (O'Neill's old constituency) in a by-election in 1970. This was followed soon afterwards with victory in North Antrim for the Westminster elections.

9. Paisley was influenced by Desmond Boal, a Unionist MP and lawyer. They founded the **Democratic Unionist Party** (DUP) in September 1971. Boal said 'it was right wing in being strong on the constitution but left on social issues'. Most of its members came from Paisley's Free Presbyterian Church.

10. After Stormont fell and Direct Rule was imposed from Westminster, Paisley wanted to restore Stormont.

- He was opposed to power sharing and the Council of Ireland as proposed in the Northern Ireland Constitutional Proposals and as agreed in the Sunningdale Agreement.

11. He became part of the **United Ulster Unionist Council** (UUUC), with Craig and West, to oppose Sunningdale.

12. Paisley was a member of the committee that organised the Ulster Workers' Strike in May 1974 which brought down the power-sharing Executive and ended the Sunningdale arrangement.

13. Paisley formed the **United Ulster Action Council** to protest against Direct Rule and to demand stronger security measures. They launched a general strike to force action from the British government but the strike collapsed in a few days (1977). This was a bad blow for Paisley. However, he was elected to the European Parliament two years later (1979).

14. Paisley was opposed to the Anglo-Irish relationship which Thatcher developed after she came to power in Britain. He organised the '**Carson Trail**' – a series of rallies around Ulster – because he feared a 'sell-out' by her.

15. Paisley was opposed to the **Anglo-Irish Agreement** (1985) because it represented interference in Northern Ireland by the Southern government. After this, Paisley and the DUP became associated with Ulster Resistance, a paramilitary organisation. The DUP lost some popularity because of this association.

16. Paisley was opposed to any concession to the nationalists. He was opposed to the **Downing Street Declaration** (1993) because it gave too much importance to North–South relationships.

17. It was after 1993 that Paisley began the rise to power which eventually took him to the position of First Minister in the new Northern Ireland government. He benefited from his opposition to the peace process. But the Ulster Unionist Party, led then by David Trimble, suffered from the long-drawn-out process of making peace. By 2005, Paisley's DUP had almost double the vote of the Unionist Party. In 2007, Paisley shared power with Sinn Féin in the Northern Ireland Executive.

John Hume

1. John Hume was born in Derry in 1937. He was the oldest child of a Catholic family living in the Bogside.

2. Hume benefited from the Education Act (1947). He was educated at St Columb's College, Derry, and at Maynooth College, Co. Kildare. He graduated in History and French and returned to teach in Derry.

3. Hume was a founder member of the **Derry Credit Union**. He was later President of the Credit Union League of Ireland from 1964 to 1968.

4. He also founded the **Derry Housing Association** with Father Anthony Mulvey to relieve the city's housing shortage.

5. Hume began his rise to prominence when he campaigned against the decision of the **Lockwood Committee** to favour Coleraine as the location of Northern Ireland's second university.

6. Hume founded the **University for Derry Committee** and acted as its chairman. Along with other leaders he met with Terence O'Neill, Prime Minister of Northern Ireland, to put forward Derry's case. He helped organise the huge motorcade to Stormont, but he did not take part in it.

7. He was disappointed that the government did not change the Lockwood decision.

8. Hume became a leader of the Civil Rights movement in the late 1960s. He was a member of the **Derry Citizens' Action Committee**, committed to ending discrimination against Catholics. He took part in the civil rights march in Derry in October 1968 which was baton-charged by the RUC.

9. He visited Dublin and London to ask to have the Apprentice Boys March of August 1969 banned because he believed there would be violence. When the march went ahead, he acted as a steward but could not prevent the clashes between Catholic youths from the Bogside and the RUC.

10. He escorted James Callaghan through the Bogside after the British Army replaced the RUC. By the end of 1969, he was the leader of moderate opinion in Derry.

11. Hume believed in **non-violent resistance**. He tried to prevent a conflict between youths and the British Army in 1968 and he was knocked down by a fire hose and arrested. He was fined £20 but refused to pay. He appealed his fine and won his case in the House of Lords in Westminster.

12. He favoured giving O'Neill a chance to bring in further reforms after O'Neill's famous Ulster at the Crossroads speech. But he declared an end to the truce on marching after the events of the People's Democracy march and rioting in Derry.

13. In 1969 Hume defeated the leader of the Nationalist Party, Eddie McAteer, in the Foyle constituency in Derry in the general election for the Stormont parliament.

14. By now he was committed to working for a new political movement based on social democratic principles, and having the future of Northern Ireland decided by its people.

15. He worked with former civil rights leaders and two Belfast MPs – Gerry Fitt and Paddy Devlin – to set up the **Social Democratic and Labour Party** (SDLP) in 1970. The Party believed in eventual unification of Ireland through consent.

16. In October 1971 he joined four Westminster MPs in a 48-hour hunger strike to protest at the internment without trial of hundreds of suspected Irish republicans.

17. After Bloody Sunday (January 1972), Hume moved towards a more traditional nationalist view. He said, 'It's a united Ireland or nothing.'

18. Hume was part of the SDLP team which agreed to a power-sharing executive with Brian Faulkner and the Unionist Party in 1973.

19. He played a major part in the **Sunningdale Agreement** (1973), which led to the foundation of the Council of Ireland and which granted a significant say in Northern Ireland to the Irish government.

20. He was Minister of Commerce in the power-sharing Executive which came into power on 1 January 1974.

21. He wanted to break the Ulster Workers' Council strike when it started in May 1974. He wanted to use the British army to take over some petrol stations. But the news was leaked and Hume had to back down. The power-sharing Executive collapsed.

22. In the later 1970s, Hume worked to influence **Irish-American opinion** to put pressure on the British government. This time saw the 'greening' of the SDLP. It led to the resignation of Paddy Devlin from the party because he thought too much pressure was being put on the Unionists.

23. In 1979, Hume succeeded Gerry Fitt as leader of the SDLP. He was also elected to the European Parliament. He looked to the model of European unity as an example by which Northern Ireland's problems could also be solved. He was elected to Westminster in 1984.

24. **Hunger strikes**: Hume was opposed to the British government's policy in relation to the hunger strikers; he was concerned that the popularity of the hunger strikers would increase the popularity of Sinn Féin and that the SDLP would lose out.

25. **New Ireland Forum**: This was Hume's idea – a gathering of constitutional nationalists with the aim of exploring ways of achieving nationalist aims by peaceful means.

26. **Anglo-Irish Agreement (1985)**: Hume supported this strongly – he believed it would lead along the road to peace, but he underestimated unionist opposition to it.

27. **Hume–Adams talks**: these did a great deal to bring Sinn Féin to the negotiating table.

28. **Downing Street Declaration (1993)**: Hume supported the ideas of the Declaration.

29. **Good Friday Agreement (1998)**: He played a major role in the negotiations which led to the Good Friday Agreement.

30. Hume was co-recipient, with David Trimble, of the 1998 Nobel Peace Prize. He is also a recipient of the Gandhi Peace Prize and the Martin Luther King Award. He is the only recipient of the three major peace awards.

31. Hume is credited with being the thinker behind many of the important political developments in Northern Ireland, from Sunningdale power sharing to the Anglo-Irish Agreement and the Belfast Agreement.

Jim Molyneaux

1. James Molyneaux was born in Co. Antrim in 1920. He was elected to Antrim County Council in the 1960s. In 1970, he was elected Unionist MP in Westminster for South Antrim.

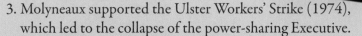

2. Molyneaux was opposed to Faulkner's policy of power sharing and the Council of Ireland.
   - He was an active member of the **United Ulster Unionist Council** (UUUC), which combined Unionist Party members, the DUP, Vanguard and the Orange Order in opposition to the Sunningdale Agreement (1973).

3. Molyneaux supported the Ulster Workers' Strike (1974), which led to the collapse of the power-sharing Executive.

4. After Direct Rule was imposed again, the Unionist Party was divided in its approach to the government of Northern Ireland. The leader, Harry West, favoured devolution (handing power back to Stormont).
   - But Molyneaux favoured integrating Northern Ireland fully with Britain.
   - He relied on **Enoch Powell**, a former Conservative MP, who was elected as a Unionist MP for South Down.

5. Molyneaux used the strength of the Unionist members in Westminster to get concessions from a weakened Labour government at the end of the 1970s. In particular, he won an increase in representation for Northern Ireland at Westminster, from 12 to 17 MPs.

6. Molyneaux replaced West as **leader of the Unionist Party** in 1979 after West's failure in the European elections. Molyneaux was faced with a growing challenge from Ian Paisley's Democratic Unionist Party (DUP).

7. Molyneaux took part in the Assembly elections as part of Jim Prior's proposal for 'rolling devolution'.

8. Molyneaux believed that Thatcher's Conservative government would not give anything away to the Southern Irish government. He was caught by surprise by the Anglo-Irish Agreement (1985), which gave a greater say in Northern Ireland to the Southern government.

9. Molyneaux and Paisley led the **'Ulster Says No'** campaign against the agreement, which included:
   - the resignation of Unionist MPs from Westminster, including Molyneaux
   - boycotting councils
   - a general strike in a 'Day of Action'.

10. During the various attempts at peace-making in Northern Ireland at the end of the 1980s and the beginning of the 1990s, Molyneaux still believed that he could protect the Unionist position at the highest levels in London. He was caught out again by the **Downing Street Declaration**. This undermined his leadership.

11. In 1995, he was challenged for the leadership by an unknown 21-year-old student. He resigned as leader after the Unionist Party lost an important Unionist seat in a by-election.

Margaret Thatcher

1. Margaret Thatcher was elected leader of the Conservative Party in 1975. For the next four years she was leader of the Opposition in the House of Commons under a Labour Government. She won the general election in 1979 and was Prime Minister of Britain for the next 11 years, until 1990.

2. When Margaret Thatcher became leader of the Opposition she **knew very little** about the problems of Northern Ireland.

3. Her spokesperson on Northern Ireland was Airey Neave. He supported tougher security measures, and he questioned the Conservatives' support for power sharing in the North.

   - He was assassinated by a car bomb as he was coming out of the House of Commons car park. This had a huge impact on Thatcher.

4. When Thatcher was elected Prime Minister, she visited Northern Ireland soon after a series of IRA bombings. She resisted bringing in tougher security measures. Instead she continued the policy of '**Ulsterisation**', handing over more responsibility for security to the RUC.

5. Thatcher's approach to Northern Ireland was influenced by Britain's 'special relationship' with the United States. The Irish-American lobby put pressure on the Thatcher government, which called a conference of the constitutional parties to begin a new process of devolved government.

6. When this process failed because the Northern parties would not agree on proposals, Thatcher began discussions with the Southern government of Charles Haughey. She agreed that they would consider 'the totality of relationships within these islands'.

7. **Hunger strikes**: Thatcher refused to grant special category status to IRA prisoners in the H-Blocks. The prisoners then decided that some would go on hunger strike. In spite of riots, ten deaths and widespread criticism, Thatcher refused to give in. The Provisional IRA called off the hunger strike without achieving political status, but the government gave concessions.

- Thatcher's actions on the hunger strike dealt a serious blow to British prestige abroad, and increased the popularity of Sinn Féin and the IRA in Ireland.

8. **Brighton bombing (1984):** Thatcher was lucky to escape when the Provisional IRA planted a bomb which destroyed the hotel in Brighton where the Conservative Party conference was being held.

9. **Out, Out, Out:** A week later, Thatcher gave a press conference where she rejected the three proposals of the New Ireland Forum (unitary state, federal government, joint authority) in her famous 'Out, Out, Out' speech. This worsened Anglo-Irish relations temporarily.

10. **Anglo-Irish Agreement (1985):** Thatcher was concerned that Sinn Féin would replace the SDLP as the majority nationalist party. She negotiated the Anglo-Irish Agreement with Garret FitzGerald. This gave a greater say in Northern Ireland to the Southern government. It also angered Unionists, who felt it was a sell-out. Unionist posters said, 'Mrs Thatcher is a Traitor'. She refused to give in to Unionist demands.

11. Over the next few years, Thatcher became disillusioned with the Anglo-Irish Agreement because it did not provide the improvements in security she had hoped for. She was critical of the Irish government's policy on the extradition of IRA suspects.

12. Thatcher resigned as Prime Minister in 1990.

Gerry Adams

1. Gerry Adams was born in West Belfast to a strongly republican family. After school, he became a bartender. In 1964, he joined Fianna Éireann (youth organisation) and Sinn Féin.

2. Adams was involved in the civil rights campaign. He joined the Northern Ireland Civil Rights Association (NICRA) in 1967 and took part in civil rights marches.

3. He was involved in defensive actions in his own community during 1969–70. After British soldiers were brought in to protect nationalists, he was horrified by Falls Road housewives giving them cups of tea.

4. Adams was **interned** in March 1972. He was opposed to the IRA ceasefire in 1972. He thought it would allow the British Army to regain control. But he was released to take part in secret talks between IRA leaders and the British government in London. Their demand for a British withdrawal in three years was turned down.

5. After the ceasefire ended, Adams was involved in planning the IRA bombing blitz in Belfast, known as Bloody Friday, in which 9 people were killed and over 130 injured.

6. Adams has always denied he was ever a member of the IRA. But historians believe he was by this time a senior member of the **Belfast IRA**, and that he was later a member of the **IRA Army Council**.

7. Adams was rearrested in July 1973 and spent the next four years in Long Kesh prison. He was opposed to the Southern leadership of Ruairí Ó Bradaigh and Daithí Ó Conaill. While in prison, he wrote under the pseudonym Brownie in the *Republican News*, calling for more political activity for republicans.

8. Adams argued for a change in republican tactics. He said they should be prepared for a **'long war'** because there would not be immediate British withdrawal from Northern Ireland.
   - He wanted the Long War to be fought politically as well as militarily.
   - Under his influence, Sinn Féin and the IRA moved towards electoral politics.
   - In 1978, Adams was elected Vice-President of Sinn Féin.

9. Adams also influenced the reorganisation of the IRA at this time, away from brigades and battalions to small active-service units.
   - A new Northern Command was set up, which allowed Adams and Martin McGuinness more control over the operations of the IRA.

10. Adams was initially opposed to the hunger strikes, believing that they might not succeed.
    - But he soon took advantage of the hunger strikers' propaganda success.
    - The victory of Bobby Sands in the Fermanagh–South Tyrone by-election showed that the republicans could succeed in elections.

11. Adams got Sinn Féin to adopt a **two-part strategy**, which was described by Danny Morrison at the 1981 Sinn Féin Ard Fheis as 'with a ballot paper in one hand and an Armalite in the other'. Sinn Féin wanted:
    - to show it had public support
    - to take over control of the nationalist community from the SDLP.

12. Adams was elected President of Sinn Féin in 1983, which meant that Sinn Féin was now dominated by Northern members.

13. Sinn Féin increased its electoral support in Northern Ireland, winning 10 per cent of the vote in 1982 Assembly elections and 13 per cent in the 1983 Westminster elections. Gerry Adams also defeated Gerry Fitt to become MP for West Belfast.

14. The British government lifted a ban on him travelling to Britain, but he refused to take his seat in the House of Commons in line with Sinn Féin's abstentionist policy.

15. Soon after this, Adams survived an assassination attempt by the Ulster Freedom Fighters (UFF), a branch of the Ulster Defence Association (UDA).

16. Sinn Féin changed its abstentionist policy in relation to Dáil elections at the 1986 Ard Fheis. This resulted in a split when some members set up Republican Sinn Féin and the Continuity IRA.

17. Adams began secret talks with John Hume in 1988. Hume wanted to persuade Adams that his view of the Northern problem was wrong.
   - Adams believed that if the British left Northern Ireland this would solve the problem.
   - Hume said that would still leave 1.5 million Protestants.

18. Sinn Féin lost support in the early 1990s and Gerry Adams lost his West Belfast seat to Joe Hendron of the SDLP. (He won it back at the next election in 1997.)

19. Albert Reynolds, the Taoiseach, wanted to bring Sinn Féin into politics, so he persuaded US President Clinton to grant a visa to Gerry Adams to visit the United States. This, along with the **Downing Street Declaration**, helped Adams to organise a 'complete cessation [end] of military operations' on 31 August 1994.

Conn and Patricia McCluskey

1. Conn and Patricia McCluskey lived in Dungannon, Co. Tyrone. Conn was a doctor and Patricia was a social worker.

2. In May 1963, Patricia McCluskey helped found the **Homeless Citizens' League** (HCL) in Dungannon, Co. Tyrone. This came about after a protest by local young women about the housing allocation in the town. They claimed that Dungannon Council was discriminating against them. Conn McCluskey joined later.

3. The actions of the protestors were inspired by civil rights protests in America at the same time.

4. The McCluskeys and the HCL took their case to the Stormont government and won concessions on housing.

5. The success of the Homeless Citizens' League encouraged Conn and Patricia McCluskey to set up the **Campaign for Social Justice** (CSJ). It was officially launched in Belfast in January 1964. They were critical of the existing leadership of the nationalist politicians.
   - Their members were educated Catholics who had been educated under the Education Act (1947).
   - They wanted to collect information on 'all injustices done against all creeds and political opinions including details of discrimination in jobs and houses'.
   - They wanted to publicise the information they would collect, mainly to influence British public opinion about the situation in Northern Ireland.
   - They published pamphlets on Northern Ireland's problems, including *Londonderry: One Man, No Vote* and *Northern Ireland: The Plain Truth*.
   - They were not concerned with the question of partition or unity.

6. In 1964, Patricia McCluskey wrote to Harold Wilson, the leader of the (British) Labour Party. He replied, criticising the religious discrimination and advocating a fairer system of allocating houses and jobs. The McCluskeys published his letters.

7. The McCluskeys created links between the CSJ and the Campaign for Democracy in Ulster (CDU), a British-based group which included many Labour MPs.

   • The McCluskeys wanted the British government to intervene in Northern Ireland and force the Unionist government to bring in reforms.

8. The McCluskeys were active in the **Northern Ireland Civil Rights Association** (NICRA).

   • Conn was a member of the executive.

9. In 1968, as a member of the NICRA executive, Conn McCluskey argued against going ahead with the civil rights march in Derry after Craig had banned the march from the walled city. The NICRA executive eventually agreed to go ahead with the march, which was attacked by the RUC.

10. In 1969, Conn McCluskey and others resigned from the executive of the Northern Ireland Civil Rights Association (NICRA) because they disagreed with links between NICRA and the People's Democracy, a radical student group based in Queen's University, Belfast.

11. The McCluskeys later moved to Australia and returned to live near Dublin.

Bernadette Devlin

1. Bernadette Devlin was born in Cookstown, Co. Tyrone. When she was a student at Queen's University, Belfast, she became actively involved in the civil rights campaign.

2. Devlin was a member of **People's Democracy**, a radical student group based at Queen's.

   • Devlin was influenced by socialist thinking, the student unrest in Europe in 1968 and the civil rights movement in the United States.

   • She participated in the main civil rights marches organised by the Northern Ireland Civil Rights Association (NICRA).

3. The People's Democracy (PD) decided to organise a **march** between Belfast and Derry, beginning on 1 January 1969. Devlin was one of the main organisers. She said the march was intended to provoke confrontation with loyalists. She said the march would re-launch the civil rights organisation as a mass movement with widespread working-class Catholic support. She also believed that O'Neill's reforms were shallow.

4. Devlin went on the march, which was attacked at several places by loyalist groups. The worst attack was at Burntollet Bridge, where the attackers included off-duty 'B-Specials'.

   • There were further attacks as the march entered Derry, and these led to rioting.

5. The march was responsible for heightening the tensions in Northern Ireland and opening the door to wider communal violence.

6. Bernadette Devlin was elected as a '**Unity**' candidate in a by-election for the Westminster parliament in the constituency of Mid-Ulster in April 1969. She was a committed socialist and at 21 the youngest woman to be elected to Westminster. But her support was a traditional Catholic/nationalist vote.

7. Devlin was involved in the defence of the **Bogside** (the Battle of the Bogside) after the Apprentice Boys march in August 1969. She carried a loudspeaker, encouraging others to build up the barricades. She featured often in news reports of the time.

   ● In 1970 she was sentenced to six months in jail for her involvement in the Bogside riots.

8. Bernadette Devlin was one of the leaders of the march in Derry on **Bloody Sunday** (30 January 1972). She pulled the hair of Reginald Maudling, Secretary of State for Northern Ireland, and slapped his face in the House of Commons the next day.

9. In February 1974 she lost her seat in Westminster.

10. In 1974–75, she was involved in the foundation of the Irish Republican Socialist Party (IRSP), which had split from Official Sinn Féin.

11. In 1979, she stood for election to the **European Parliament** to publicise the cause of republican prisoners who were looking for special category status. The prisoners did not want her publicity. She failed to get elected, but got a sizeable vote.

    ● Her limited success opened up the possibility of republican movement into politics.

12. She was later involved in organising support for the hunger strikers. But she was seriously injured in a failed loyalist assassination attack on her and her husband in February 1981.

13. Devlin continued her involvement in left-wing politics, but with little support. She was critical of Sinn Féin's involvement in the peace process.

Seamus Heaney

1. Seamus Heaney was born on a farm in Co. Derry in 1939. He was the eldest of nine children and was reared in a Catholic and nationalist family. He drew a great deal of inspiration for his writings from 'my local County Derry childhood experience'.

2. He was educated at St Columb's College, Derry, a Catholic boarding school. Here he did well at English, Irish and Latin.

   ● His Gaelic heritage was nurtured through playing underage Gaelic football and spending a summer studying Irish in the Donegal Gaeltacht.

3. He studied English language and literature at Queen's University, Belfast, where he published poems in a university magazine.

4. While lecturing in St Joseph's Training College he became involved with a poetry circle organised by Philip Hobsbaum, a lecturer in English at Queen's. Here Heaney came in contact with fellow Northern poets Derek Mahon and Michael Longley.

5. In 1966 he published his first full volume of poetry, *Death of a Naturalist*, which dealt with the experiences of his childhood and his growing into adulthood.

   ● His next two collections, *Door into the Dark* (1969) and *Wintering Out* (1972), drew on the locality of his childhood, including the area around Lough Neagh.

   ● He saw in the name of his home farm, Mossbawn, with its Scottish and Gaelic origins, a metaphor for the divided culture of Northern Ireland.

6. Between the publication of these two collections, the **Troubles** broke out in Northern Ireland (1968–69). The impact of the Troubles on Heaney is most clearly seen in his collection of poems, *North*, published in 1975.

   ● He commented on the political and social issues of the time while trying to avoid being a spokesman for either side.

   ● He did this largely through writing about these issues using mythology and Iron Age history. In 'Punishment', he uses images of a 2,000-year old bog body found in Denmark to comment on punishment beatings.

7. However, he was accused by fellow poets of glorifying the Troubles and using rites that were 'profoundly Catholic in character'.

8. In the mid-1960s during the O'Neill premiership, Heaney was optimistic about the future.

   ● He was hopeful that O'Neill's efforts to improve relations with Catholics signalled a brighter future. Not surprisingly, the Troubles had the effect of 'darkening the mood of Heaney's work in the 1970s'.

   ● Conor Cruise O'Brien, historian and Irish government minister during the Troubles, said, 'I have read many pessimistic analyses of "Northern Ireland", but none that has the bleak conclusiveness of these poems.'

9. The Troubles also forced Heaney to question the **role and responsibility of the poet** in society. In essays in *The Government of the Tongue* (1988) and *The Redress of Poetry* (1995), he is concerned about the pressures that come to bear on a poet in time of crisis.

10. *The Spirit Level* (1996) portrayed a more hopeful view of the North as the peace process was unfolding. The 1994 ceasefire in Northern Ireland was celebrated in 'Tollund': 'Ourselves again, free-willed again, not bad.'

11. In the 1980s, Heaney became involved in the **Field Day Theatre** and **Field Day Publishing** in Derry with Brian Friel, Stephen Rea and others. They hoped to explore 'the nature of the Irish problem' and as a result, more successfully confront it 'than it had been hitherto'.

    ● Field Day published *Sweeney Astray*, Heaney's translation of a medieval Irish poem.

    ● *The Cure at Troy*, a play based on Sophocles' *Philoctetes*, had parallels with Northern Ireland:

    > *Human beings suffer,*
    > *They torture one another,*
    > *They get hurt and get hard.*

12. At various times, Heaney lectured in Carysfort Teacher Training College, Dublin, was visiting professor at Harvard University, went on reading tours of Northern Ireland with other poets, and was appointed Professor of Poetry at Oxford University.

13. He was also presented with honorary degrees, won critical acclaim for his poetry and won the Whitbread Book of the Year Award. He won the Nobel Prize for Literature in 1995 for 'works of lyrical beauty and ethical depth, which exalt everyday miracles and the living past'.

14. Seamus Heaney died in 2013

Key concepts

Bigotry: Intolerance of other creeds or political beliefs.

Civil rights: The rights that people are entitled to, including free speech and movement, equality before the law and freedom to practise religion.

Cultural identity: The patterns, beliefs and activities of a group of people that mark them out from other groups.

Cultural traditions: The patterns, beliefs and activities that form part of the way of life of a people.

Ecumenism: A movement promoting understanding between religions, with the eventual aim of unity.

Gerrymandering: Rigging the boundaries of constituencies (electoral areas) to ensure a majority of seats at elections.

Power sharing: Sharing political power between different groups (e.g. unionists and nationalists in Northern Ireland).

Propaganda: Spreading information and ideas to support one's own side and undermine the other side with the aim of achieving political power.

Sectarianism: Adherence to a particular sect or group and hatred for an opposing group, usually based on religious differences.

Terrorism: The use of violence and threats to achieve political aims.

Tolerance: A fair and objective attitude to other people's views and opinions (intolerance – a refusal to accept other's views and opinions).

PART TWO

Modern Europe and the Wider World

4 Dictatorship and Democracy in Europe, 1920–45

1. Communism in Russia

aims In this section, you should understand:
- The role of Lenin (Key personality, p. 262)
- Why the Reds won the Civil War

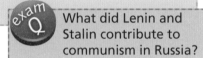
exam Q What did Lenin and Stalin contribute to communism in Russia?

The rule of Lenin

1. Lenin and the Bolsheviks took over Russia in a revolution in October 1917. They held on to power by setting up the Cheka (secret police) and making peace with Germany in the First World War (Treaty of Brest-Litovsk).

The Russian Civil War, 1918–21

2. The **Bolsheviks** (later called the Communists or the Reds) were jointly led by Lenin and Trotsky:
   - Lenin organised the economic and political areas.
   - Trotsky organised the military (the Red Army).

3. The Bolsheviks were opposed by the **Whites** in the Russian Civil War.
   - The Whites were composed of many different groups (former Tsarists, landlords, industrialists).
   - They were helped by the Allied powers (Britain, France and the United States) while the First World War was still on.

4. The Whites attacked the Reds from three sides:
   - General **Kolchak** attacked in the east. He was in danger of rescuing the former ruler of Russia, Tsar Nicholas, and his family, so they were executed by the Bolsheviks.
   - General **Deniken** attacked in the south.

Russian Civil War, 1918–21

- General **Yudenich** attacked in the west.

5. The Allies landed troops to help get Russia back into the First World War; but when the war finished, they withdrew from Russia.

6. All the groups were opposed by Trotsky's **Red Army**. The Red Army controlled the centre of Russia, used the trains to transport troops and defeated each attack in turn.

7. The Poles attacked from the west and took a good deal of land before peace was made.

8. Lenin organised **War Communism** – all industry and agriculture was geared solely to the war effort.

> **key point**
>
> COMMUNISM:
> Communists believed in government control of agriculture and industry.

   - **Industry**: forced mobilisation of workers.
     - Factories of more than ten workers were taken over by the government.
     - Strikes were banned.
   - **Agriculture**: Surplus crops were taken by government detachments sent to the countryside to take food from farmers.
     - Food was rationed in the cities.

9. The Reds also organised the **Red Terror**. Anybody accused of cooperating with the Whites was punished or executed by the Cheka.

10. **Why did Lenin and Trotsky win the Russian Civil War?**
    - Lenin and Trotsky provided **united leadership**.
    - Trotsky organised the Red Army: conscription was introduced; former Tsarist officers were used to train the soldiers; political commissars (loyal Communist Party workers) were used to watch the officers; there was harsh discipline.
    - The White Armies were divided: they attacked at different times; they were cruel to people in the countryside.
    - Lenin organised War Communism, which made sure that the Army and workers were kept supplied.

> **key point**
>
> DICTATORSHIP:
> Rule by one person or party, using propaganda and the secret police.

    - The Communists used **propaganda** – posters, leaflets. They instilled fear in the people about the return of the Tsar and the landlords.
    - The Communists used the Red Terror to put down opposition; Lenin set up a communist dictatorship.
    - The Allies withdrew from Russia and did not provide supplies for the Whites.

New Economic Policy (NEP)

1. The Soviet economy was in a bad state by 1921, owing to the First World War, the Civil War, and the policy of War Communism. There was serious discontent in both the countryside and the cities.

2. The sailors in the **Kronstadt** naval base, near Petrograd, revolted against the Communist Party and War Communism. Lenin and Trotsky ordered the Red Army across the ice and put down the rebellion.

3. Lenin decided to change economic policy. He introduced the **New Economic Policy** (NEP).

4. The main points of the NEP were:
   - the taking of food from the peasants was ended
   - there was a fixed tax in kind (grain)
   - peasants could sell their surplus produce
   - private enterprise was allowed in small industries
   - heavy industry (coal, iron, electricity) was controlled by the government.

5. The New Economic Policy was successful:
   - industrial and agricultural production rose
   - rich peasants (kulaks) benefited
   - Lenin and the Communists survived.

6. Lenin died in 1924 after a series of strokes. A **cult of Lenin** developed after his death.
   - He had a huge influence on the history of Russia.
   - He created the Communist Party.
   - He led a successful revolution when the Bolsheviks (Communists) took power in the October Revolution of 1917.
   - He ensured the survival of communism after the revolution by making peace with Germany in the First World War and by winning the Civil War.
   - He created a one-party communist dictatorship.

The rule of Stalin

 In this section, you should understand:
- The role of Stalin (Key personality, p. 263)
- Stalin's transformation of Soviet society and economy
- Stalin's purges and dictatorship
- Case study: Stalin's Show Trials (pp. 220–222)

How did Stalin become leader of the Soviet Union?

1. When Lenin died, there was a struggle for power between Stalin and Trotsky.

2. **Trotsky** had advantages:
   - He had commanded the Red Guards in the October Revolution of 1917.
   - He led the Red Army in the Civil War.
   - He was a good organiser and a good speaker.

   But he was arrogant.

3. **Stalin** was like a grey blur, so he was able to hide his ambitions.
   - He was general secretary of the Communist Party. He used this position to place loyal followers in important positions in the Party.

- How did Stalin achieve and maintain his power in the Soviet Union?
- To what extent did Stalin transform the society and economy of the Soviet Union?

- He was Commissar of Nationalities, which linked him to the various nationalities of Russia.
- He used clever political tactics – he joined with two of the Communist leaders, Zinoviev and Kamenev, in opposition to Trotsky, who seemed likely to succeed Lenin; Zinoviev and Kamenev agreed not to publish Lenin's Testament.

4. Trotsky and Stalin had **different policies:**
   - Trotsky favoured the policy of **permanent revolution**, in which workers in other countries would be encouraged to revolt and spread communism.
   - Stalin believed in '**Socialism in One Country**' – that the Soviet Union should be built into a modern, industrial state – rather than world revolution.
   - Stalin's policy was more popular with party members because Russia had suffered enough during the First World War, the Bolshevik Revolution and the Civil War.

5. Stalin turned against Zinoviev and Kamenev and they and Trotsky were expelled from the Politburo. Trotsky was exiled to Siberia before being banished from the Soviet Union. Stalin was now in complete control of the Communist Party.

The Stalinist state in peace

6. Stalin set about creating a **totalitarian dictatorship:**
   - The Communist Party controlled the press, radio and industry.
   - They used the secret police, the OGPU (later the NKVD), to put down the opposition, control Five-year Plans, and the labour camps (gulags).
   - The Party also controlled the Soviet Army.

TOTALITARIANISM:
Totalitarian governments control all aspects of life, from the people's actions to their thoughts.

7. A **cult of Stalin** was encouraged.
   - Stalin used **propaganda** to strengthen his control over Soviet Russia.
   - History was rewritten to make Stalin the hero of the October Revolution and the Civil War.
   - Posters, stamps and photographs of Stalin were produced; cities were named after him; he was treated almost like a god in poetry and song.

The Purges and Show Trials

8. **Why did Stalin begin the Purges?**
   - In the 1930s Stalin used purges to get rid of opposition to him in the Communist Party and elsewhere.
   - Forced industrialisation and collectivisation led to increased opposition in the Communist Party.

CULT OF PERSONALITY:
Worship of a leader. Propaganda is used to create an image of the leader as all-wise and all-powerful.

   - Criticisms by Trotsky in exile angered Stalin.
   - The assassination of Kirov (1934), leader of the Communist Party in Leningrad, was used as an excuse by Stalin to begin the purges. The assassin and his colleagues were shot.

Progress

9. Hundreds in the Communist Party were arrested. Ordinary Russians were arrested and disappeared. Many were sent to labour camps (gulags).

   - The cruelty and savagery of the Great Purge were imposed by Stalin; he was suspicious of everybody.

10. Stalin organised three **Show Trials** in Moscow as part of his Great Purge.

    - **First Show Trial** – Zinoviev and Kamenev and 14 other leaders.
    - **Second Show Trial** – Radek, Pyatakov and 15 others.
    - **Third Show Trial** – Bukharin, Rykov, Yagoda and 18 others.
    - All the old Communist leadership was wiped out.

11. Further purges:

    - **The Party**: Members were purged for plotting against Stalin.
    - **The Army**: 35,000 officers were either shot or jailed, including generals.
    - **The Secret Police**: Even the head of the secret police (Yagoda) was tried and executed.

12. As a result of the purges:

    - Stalin was now in complete control of the country.
    - The Red Army was weakened; this caused it to suffer in the early stages of the Second World War.
    - Many skilled workers and engineers were killed. This affected the industrialisation of the Soviet Union.

PROPAGANDA:

Spreading information to convince people of your point of view in order to achieve or retain power.

See Case study: Stalin's show trials.

Case study: Stalin's show trials

Why Show Trials?

1. Three show trials were held in Moscow. Stalin wanted to ensure greater power for himself and defeat the critics of collectivisation and industrialisation. He feared that **Trotsky** (who was outside of Russia) and others were plotting against him.

2. The Show Trials were an intensification of the **purges** already begun before this. They were public trials which Stalin used for propaganda purposes.

3. Stalin used the assassination of **Kirov**, leader of the Communist Party in Leningrad, as an excuse to begin the Show Trials. Zinoviev and Kamenev were

Ordinary level students should concentrate on the Case studies and the main Key personalities

What was the purpose of Stalin's show trials in the 1930s and what impact did they have on the Soviet Union?

already tried for complicity in the Kirov assassination. Now they were prepared for a show trial.

4. All the show trials followed a **similar pattern**:
   - accusations of treachery and plotting
   - written confessions
   - a bullying prosecutor
   - no rules of evidence
   - a judgement, usually, of execution.

5. **The First Show Trial, 1936**

   Zinoviev, **Kamenev** and fourteen other leaders were tried. Zinoviev and Kamenev were Old Bolsheviks who had helped Stalin in his struggle for power against Trotsky; then he turned against them.

6. They were accused of:
   - murdering Kirov, the leader of the Leningrad Communist Party
   - planning to kill Stalin
   - working with Trotskyites (supporters of Trotsky)
   - plotting with Nazi Germany.

7. The secret police (**NKVD**) forced confessions from Zinoviev and Kamenev by:
   - holding them in isolation
   - getting confessions against them from minor Party officials
   - threatening their families.

8. Once the confessions were obtained, Zinoviev and Kamenev and the others had to learn off their lines for the trial.

9. The trial was conducted by three judges, with an audience of workers and international journalists and diplomats. The prosecutor in all the trials was **Vyshinsky**.

10. The confessions were the only evidence. The defendants were cross-examined and pleaded guilty. They were found guilty and shot the next morning.

11. **The Second Show Trial, 1937**

    The defendants were **Radek**, **Pyatakov** and fifteen others; they were all former supporters of Trotsky.

    They were accused of:
    - conspiring with Germany and Japan against the Soviet Union;
    - wrecking and sabotage of the Five-year Plans.

12. Vyshinsky was the prosecutor. They confessed, were found guilty; thirteen were executed and four sent to labour camps.

13. **The Third Show Trial, 1938** (also called the **Great Show Trial**)

    The accused were **Bukharin**, **Rykov**, **Yagoda** and eighteen others.

- Bukharin and Rykov had been members of Lenin's Politburo; Yagoda was head of the secret police who carried out the purges.

14. They were accused of:
    - being members of the 'Anti-Soviet bloc of Rightists and Trotskyites'
    - wrecking and sabotage of the economy
    - attempting to assassinate Stalin
    - some doctors in the group were also accused of assisting in the murders of Party members.

15. They pleaded guilty. Bukharin pleaded guilty to save the lives of his wife and children.
    - They were all executed except for three minor officials.

16. **Reaction to the Trials**
    - Soviet newspapers carried full reports of the trials because Stalin had to ensure that people accepted them as legal.
    - Many international observers believed that the trials were legal.
    - Soviet people believed that there was a conspiracy against the Soviet Union.

17. **How the show trials were used by Stalin:**
    - Stalin directed the purges and show trials. He took a close and detailed interest in them.
    - Stalin used the show trials as **propaganda** because some of the problems of Soviet society could be blamed on the accused.
    - He was now in complete **charge of the Party**. He had gotten rid of the Old Bolsheviks in the Party and replaced them with younger more loyal followers.
      - The show trials were **characteristic** of Stalin's totalitarian state.
    - The show trials were used to intensify the purges so more people were sent to gulags (slave labour camps).

18. When Stalin died, Khrushchev condemned the purges and show trials at the 20th Party Congress in 1956.

The Soviet alternative: Transforming society and the economy

Industrialisation – The Five-year Plans

1. The Soviet economy was different from Western economies. It was **centrally planned**, with government control of industry and agriculture.

2. Stalin introduced **Five-year Plans** to:
   - give himself greater control of the Soviet Union

exam focus

In a question on the Soviet economy from 1920 to 1945 or the Soviet economy under Lenin and Stalin, you could include War Communism, the NEP, Stalin's Five-year Plans, collectivisation and the Soviet economy during WWII.

- improve food production for the cities
- modernise Russia so that it could catch up with the West.

3. **The First Five-year Plan (1928–32)** set targets for manufacturing industry, transport and raw materials. **Gosplan** (Central Planning Commission) set the targets. The plan concentrated on heavy industry – coal, iron, gas and electricity.

4. As a result of the First Five-year Plan:
   - production of machinery, oil and electricity all increased
   - new towns such as Magnitogorsk were built east of the Ural Mountains
   - some of the products were faulty.

5. In the **Second and Third Five-year Plans**:
   - there was still concentration on heavy industry
   - transport was developed, e.g. railways, including the building of the Moscow Underground
   - some consumer goods were produced – radios, washing machines
   - armaments were produced in the Third Five-year Plan, owing to the increased risk of war.

6. The Five-year Plans resulted in:
   - transformation of Russia from an agricultural to an industrial country, making it the second-largest economy in the world
   - the urban working class trebling in number
   - a better-educated workforce, as illiteracy was eliminated
   - Russia being now better prepared to face the danger of war from Nazi Germany.

7. The success of the Five-year Plans was due to:
   - hard working and living conditions for workers
   - wreckers were punished
   - a passport system prevented workers from moving jobs
   - punishment for absenteeism from work
   - an increase in the number of women workers
   - bonus payments for workers who exceeded their targets
   - the Stakhanovite movement encouraging workers to produce more
   - the use of slave labour in some projects.

> **Summary: Stalin's dictatorship**
> - Struggle for power
> - Totalitarian dictatorship
> - Cult of personality and the use of propaganda
> - Purges and show trials and the use of terror
> - Control of the economy

Collectivisation

8. Stalin also brought in collectivisation – the taking over by the government of individual farms and combining them into collective farms. Stalin began collectivisation because:

- he wanted to modernise agriculture and increase the output of grain
- he wanted to get rid of the New Economic Policy and bring in a more communist form of agriculture with greater state control.

9. Richer peasants (kulaks) and others resisted collectivisation. They slaughtered animals and burned crops.
   - This resulted in **famine**.

10. Stalin demanded the elimination of about 5 million kulaks. He also allowed small private plots of land.

11. Collectivisation was achieved by 1940:
    - but farming was still inefficient
    - labourers who were not needed in the countryside went to work in factories in the cities.

COLLECTIVISATION:
The policy of Stalin's government in the Soviet Union to force peasants (farmers) to give up their farms to the government and to form large collective farms.

2. Origins and growth of fascist regimes in Europe

In this section, you should understand:
- The origins and growth of fascist regimes
- The role of Mussolini – his rise to power and his rule in Italy (Key personality, p. 266)
- Church–State relations under Mussolini

The growth of dictatorships

1. Between the First and Second World Wars, many countries in Europe had dictatorships.

2. Some of these dictatorships were totalitarian dictatorships, whereby the government sought to control all aspects of the people's lives.

3. Some were fascist dictatorships.

4. These dictatorships **rose to power** because of:
   - the effects of the First World War
   - economic depression
   - unstable governments and weak democracy
   - fear of communism
   - strong leadership and the use of violence.

During the inter-war period, what conditions in Europe contributed to the growth of fascist regimes?

You can develop your notes for these headings from Mussolini's Italy and Hitler's Germany.

DICTATORSHIP:
Rule by one person or party, using propaganda and the secret police.

Mussolini and Fascist Italy

What caused Mussolini's rise to power in Italy?

1. Italian **nationalists** were disappointed at the end of the First World War because Italy did not gain all the land it wanted after the Paris Peace Conference. It failed to get the city of Fiume and the region of Dalmatia.

2. The Italian **economy** was in a depressed state. Soldiers were demobilised; 2 million were unemployed; there was over 500 per cent inflation between 1914 and 1920. All classes suffered.

3. There were **strikes and riots** in the cities. Labourers in the countryside took over landed estates.

4. **Industrialists and landed gentry** thought communists would take over Italy.

5. The Italian **governments** were weak and were not able to solve the economic and social problems of the country. Many blamed democracy for the changes of government.

6. Mussolini formed the Fascio di Combattimento, also known as the **Blackshirts**.

key point

FASCISM:

Fascists believed in nationalism, dictatorship, racism and the use of violence. They were opposed to democracy and communism.

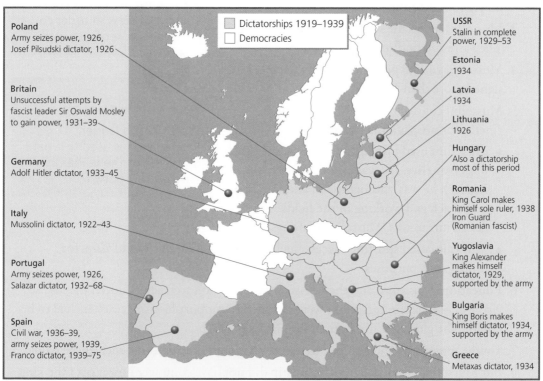

Poland
Army seizes power, 1926, Josef Pilsudski dictator, 1926

Britain
Unsuccessful attempts by fascist leader Sir Oswald Mosley to gain power, 1931–39

Germany
Adolf Hitler dictator, 1933–45

Italy
Mussolini dictator, 1922–43

Portugal
Army seizes power, 1926, Salazar dictator, 1932–68

Spain
Civil war, 1936–39, army seizes power, 1939, Franco dictator, 1939–75

Dictatorships 1919–1939
Democracies

USSR
Stalin in complete power, 1929–53

Estonia
1934

Latvia
1934

Lithuania
1926

Hungary
Also a dictatorship most of this period

Romania
King Carol makes himself sole ruler, 1938 Iron Guard (Romanian fascist)

Yugoslavia
King Alexander makes himself dictator, 1929, supported by the army

Bulgaria
King Boris makes himself dictator, 1934, supported by the army

Greece
Metaxas dictator, 1934

Dictatorships and democracies in Europe, 1918–39

- They attacked socialist and communist groups, and broke up strikes.
- They got support from industrialists and landowners.
- By 1922, they had 250,000 members – mostly soldiers and ex-officers.

7. Mussolini organised the **March on Rome** (October 1922).

- As fascist groups prepared to march, the prime minister, Facta, asked the king, Victor Emmanuel II, to declare a state of emergency and to bring out the army. He refused.
- When Facta resigned, the king appointed Mussolini as prime minister of Italy.

How did Mussolini establish dictatorship?

1. Mussolini wanted to establish a Fascist dictatorship. He passed the **Acerbo Law** (1923), which held that the party with the greatest number of votes in the next election would get two-thirds of the seats in Parliament. In the next election, Mussolini used violence to ensure that his party got the largest number of votes.

> **TOTALITARIANISM:**
> Totalitarian governments control all aspects of life, from the people's actions to their thoughts.

2. A socialist leader, Giacomo Matteoti, was murdered by fascists. In protest, the Socialist Party withdrew from Parliament (in what was called the Aventine Secession). This gave greater power to Mussolini.

3. Mussolini set up the secret police, the **OVRA**. They arrested political opponents.

> **PROPAGANDA:**
> Spreading information to convince people of your point of view in order to achieve or retain power.

4. Mussolini got the power to **rule by decree**. He signed more than 100,000 decrees.

5. Mussolini controlled the press, radio and cinema for **propaganda** purposes.

- Mussolini used propaganda to develop a **cult of personality**. He was called **Il Duce** (the Leader); he was photographed and filmed on horseback and working in the fields. The fascist motto was 'Mussolini is always right.'

> **CULT OF PERSONALITY:**
> Worship of a leader. Propaganda is used to create an image of the leader as all-wise and all-powerful.

- Mussolini used sporting success, such as Italy winning the World Cup, for propaganda purposes.

6. **Education:** Mussolini and the fascists used education to teach children the fascist virtue of obedience; textbooks were changed to support fascism; teachers had to be fascists; the glories of the Roman Empire were taught.

7. **Youth:** Young boys and girls had to join fascist youth organisations, such as the Balila.

8. But Mussolini's totalitarian dictatorship did not have complete power over the king or the Catholic Church.

Church–State relations under Mussolini

1. Relations between the Italian government and the Pope and the Catholic Church had been poor since Italy was united in 1870. When Mussolini came to power he improved relations by:
   - bringing back compulsory religious education in primary schools
   - allowing crucifixes in the classroom
   - marrying in a Catholic ceremony.

2. Mussolini and the Pope agreed the **Lateran Treaty and Concordat (1929)**.
   - The Pope recognised the Italian state and Italy recognised the Pope's control of the Vatican City.
   - Italy paid £30 million compensation for taking Rome from the Pope in 1870.
   - The Roman Catholic religion was recognised as the sole religion of the state.
   - The government paid the salaries of the bishops and priests.
   - Religious instruction was given in state schools.

3. This agreement increased Mussolini's popularity in Italy and abroad; some saw it as his greatest political success.

4. **Further Conflicts:** Mussolini was jealous of the power of Catholic Action, a lay Catholic organisation, which had nearly 700,000 members in 1930. Mussolini forced Catholic Action to limit itself to religious activities.

5. In the late 1930s, the Catholic Church became critical of Mussolini's new anti-Semitic policy and his more aggressive foreign policy. Pope Pius XII wanted to keep Italy out of World War II but Mussolini ignored his wishes.
   - The Catholic Church also tried to protect Italian Jews by hiding them in convents and monasteries.

6. The strength of the Catholic Church in Italy shows the limitations of Mussolini's Fascism. Fascism was not strong enough to bring the Church under the control of the state. (See also *Church–State relations under Hitler*, pp. 233–34)

Corporate state

1. Mussolini set up a Ministry of Corporations. The economy was divided into 22 corporations, e.g. industry, agriculture. Employers, workers and the Fascist government were represented on each corporation. The corporations decided on wages and working conditions.

2. The corporations resulted in more bureaucracy and more fascist control.

The economy

1. Mussolini's Minister of Finance, Alberto di Stefani, cut government spending and reduced unemployment.

2. Mussolini fired him, brought in protectionism (taxes on imports) and revalued the lira.

3. Mussolini and the Fascists followed a **policy of self-sufficiency**. They organised a series of 'battles', e.g.:
   - the Battle for Grain to increase grain production
   - the Battle for Land Reclamation, in which the Pontine Marshes near Rome were reclaimed for extra land and to eliminate a source of malaria.

4. The Fascists also increased electricity production, built new motorways (*autostrada*), and electrified the railways.

5. The workers were given a **Labour Charter** (1927). But Italy was hit by the Great Depression; unemployment rose and workers became worse off.

6. Mussolini set up the Dopolavoro (After Work) organisation to improve workers' leisure time by controlling sports clubs, choirs, day trips and tours.

INFLATION:
An increase in the prices of products, usually a large increase.

DEPRESSION:
When an economy is doing badly, factories close and unemployment increases.

Mussolini's foreign policy: The expansion of Fascist Italy

1. Mussolini's **aims** in foreign policy were:
   - 'I want to make Italy great, respected and feared.'
   - to expand the power of Italy around the Mediterranean Sea (Mare Nostrum – Our Sea)
   - to re-create the glories of the Roman Empire.

How successful was Mussolini as ruler of Italy?

2. Mussolini's initial successes:
   - He refused to return Corfu to Greece until he was given £50 million in compensation for the death of Italian soldiers on the Greek border;
   - He obtained Fiume after negotiations with Yugoslavia.

3. For the rest of the 1920s, Mussolini appeared to be a **man of peace**.
   - He signed the **Locarno Pact**, which guaranteed Germany's existing borders with France. He signed the Kellogg–Briand Pact, which outlawed war.

4. In the 1930s, after he had consolidated power at home, Mussolini began to expand his empire.

5. **Mussolini and Hitler** disagreed at first. Hitler attempted to unite Austria with Germany after the Austrian prime minister, Dollfuss, was assassinated. He was stopped by Mussolini, who was afraid Hitler would claim land that Italy had acquired from Austria after the First World War.

Know the significance of certain key dates so that you can understand what is being asked in questions.

6. Mussolini formed the **Stresa Front** with Britain and France against Hitler.

7. **Invasion of Abyssinia, 1936**: Mussolini invaded Abyssinia because he wanted to enlarge his empire and avenge the Battle of Adowa (1896), in which the Abyssinians defeated the Italians.

   - The Italians easily defeated the Abyssinians. The Abyssinian emperor, Haile Selassie, appealed to the League of Nations. The League imposed sanctions on Italy but excluded oil, so the sanctions had little impact.
   - As a result of the invasion of Abyssinia:
     - The Stresa Front was broken.
     - The League of Nations was shown to be weak.
     - Hitler and Mussolini drew closer together because Hitler supported Mussolini.
     - They also grew closer together because they helped Franco and the Nationalists in the Spanish Civil War.

8. Hitler and Mussolini agreed the **Rome–Berlin Axis (1936)**.

   - They also agreed the **Pact of Steel (1939)**, by which both countries agreed to help each other in time of war.

9. As a result of becoming closer to Hitler, Mussolini introduced the **Charter of Race** in Italy, which persecuted the Jews. They were deprived of Italian nationality, had to leave state jobs and could not marry non-Jewish Italians.

The road to the Second World War

1. Mussolini did not enter the Second World War when it broke out in September 1939 because he realised the Italian Army was too weak.

2. But when Hitler was successful in Poland, Norway and France, Mussolini invaded southern France. The war showed up the weaknesses of the Italian Army. Mussolini was commander-in-chief and he was held responsible for Italy's defeats.

Italy at war

   - Italy did badly in the war, and was defeated in North Africa and the Balkans.
   - Then Italy was invaded by the Allies. Mussolini was removed by King Victor Emmanuel and imprisoned. He was rescued by German commandos.
   - Mussolini set up the **Salo Republic** in Northern Italy, but he was captured by Italian guerrilla fighters and killed.

3. The Nazi state in peace – origins and growth

In this section, you should understand:
- The causes of Hitler's rise to power
- The characteristics (features) of the Nazi state/Hitler in power
- Propaganda and terror in Nazi Germany
- The role of Goebbels (Key personality, p. 268)
- The role of Riefenstahl (Key personality, p. 269)
- Case study: The Nuremberg Rallies
- Church–State relations under Hitler
- Anti-Semitism and the Holocaust

After the First World War, Germany was ruled by the **Weimar Republic**. It was a democracy and it faced many political, social and economic problems. The republic was succeeded by Adolf Hitler and the Nazi Party.

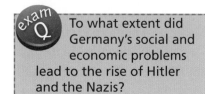

To what extent did Germany's social and economic problems lead to the rise of Hitler and the Nazis?

How did Hitler rise to power?

1. Adolf Hitler and the Nazi Party ruled Germany from 1933 onwards. Hitler owed his rise to power to a number of causes.

2. **The Great Depression**
   - In 1929 the value of shares in the New York Stock Exchange on Wall Street collapsed. This began the Great Depression.
   - Americans called in loans they had given to Germany and so German companies went bankrupt. Unemployment in Germany rose from 1.5 million in 1929 to 6 million in 1932. Middle- and working-class families were badly hit. Some joined the Nazi Party.

3. **Weaknesses of the Weimar government:**
   - The Weimar government was unpopular because it was associated with defeat in the First World War and the harsh Treaty of Versailles. The leaders of the Republic were called the 'November criminals'.

DEPRESSION:
When an economy is doing badly, factories close and unemployment increases.

   - The ruling classes (judges, generals) of the old German Empire undermined the Weimar Republic.
   - The government made the economic problems of the Great Depression worse by cutting back on government spending.
   - The Weimar government also used President Hindenburg's power to rule by decree. This undermined democracy.

4. **Hitler's leadership:** Hitler rose to power also because of his tactics and policies. He wanted to use democracy to destroy democracy.

- The Nazi Party had branches all over Germany. They also had the SA (Brownshirts – storm troopers) and SS (Blackshirts) to attack opponents.

5. Hitler's **policies** appealed to many different groups. He got support from nationalists, industrialists, farmers and the lower middle class. He outlined his ideas in *Mein Kampf* (*My Struggle*), his autobiography.
   - He attacked the Treaty of Versailles.
   - He promised to unite all the German-speaking peoples.
   - He was strongly anti-communist.
   - He promised to solve the economic problems.

6. Hitler and the Nazis used **propaganda** to get their message across:
   - He was an outstanding public speaker.
   - He used newspapers, aircraft, films and loudspeakers from trucks.
   - The Nazis used uniforms, salutes and mass rallies so as to appear strong.

7. Support for Hitler and the Nazi Party grew quickly. In 1928 they held 12 seats in the Reichstag; by 1930 they had over 100 seats, and in July 1932 they became the largest party, with 230 seats.

8. Hitler was helped by right-wing (conservative) Germans like von Papen. He persuaded President Hindenburg to appoint Hitler chancellor, because he said he would control him.
   - Hitler was appointed chancellor in January 1933.

How did Hitler establish dictatorship?

Hitler immediately set about creating a totalitarian dictatorship (which would control all aspects of life – political, social, economic and religious).

1. He called a **general election**. The Nazis used terror and propaganda against opponents; 400,000 SA were enlisted in the police. During the election campaign, a Dutch communist (van der Lubbe) set fire to the Reichstag. Hitler blamed the incident on the Communist threat. In the election, the Nazis increased their number of seats.

2. After the election Hitler passed the **Enabling Act**, which gave him power to rule by decree. The Weimar democracy was at an end.

3. He used a **policy of coordination** to destroy all opposition:
   - He outlawed the Communists and the Social Democratic Party.
   - The Nazis were the only political party allowed.

TOTALITARIANISM:
Totalitarian governments control all aspects of life, from the people's actions to their thoughts.

PROPAGANDA:
Spreading information to convince people of your point of view in order to achieve or retain power.

CULT OF PERSONALITY:
Worship of a leader. Propaganda is used to create an image of the leader as all-wise and all-powerful.

- He replaced trade unions with the German Labour Front.

4. In the **Night of the Long Knives**, Hitler used the SS to kill Ernst Röhm and other leaders of the SA who threatened his leadership. Röhm had planned a people's army to replace the German Army.

5. When President Hindenburg died, Hitler combined the offices of president and chancellor.

   - He became **der Führer** (the Leader). The German Army had to swear an oath to him.

6. Hitler appointed Joseph **Goebbels as Minister of Propaganda**. He used all the media – press, radio and cinema – to control public opinion.

   - Goebbels organised a public burning of anti-Nazi books.
   - Editors of newspapers followed the Nazi line.
   - Goebbels thought radio was very important for influencing people. Families bought the People's Radio to listen to Nazi broadcasts. Loudspeakers were used to broadcast in the streets.
   - Goebbels also used cinema and film to broadcast Nazi achievements.
   - Leni **Riefenstahl** produced the propaganda films *The Triumph of the Will*, on the Nuremberg rally of 1934, and *Olympia* on the 1936 Berlin Olympics.
   - The Nazis also used huge gatherings to influence people, such as the **Nuremberg rallies**, torchlight parades and marches.
   - Goebbels also developed the **cult of personality** around Hitler: posters of Hitler were everywhere; special feast days such as Hitler's birthday were held; 'Heil Hitler' was used as a form of salute; slogans such as *Ein Reich, Ein Volk, Ein Führer* (One Country, One People, One Leader) were introduced.

7. **Education** was used as a propaganda tool. School subjects were used to get across Nazi ideas; teachers had to belong to the Nazi Teachers' Association. Boys were geared towards military service and girls towards housekeeping.

8. **Youth**: Boys joined the Hitler Youth and girls joined the League of German Maidens.

9. Hitler and the Nazis created a **police state** through the use of terror.

   - The SS destroyed opposition to Hitler; the Gestapo (state secret police) arrested anybody on the slightest pretext and used torture to get 'confessions'.
   - The judges were Nazis, so nobody could get a fair trial.
   - Concentration camps such as Dachau were used to hold people who were given hard labour and punishments.

The Nazis and the economy

1. Hitler and the Nazis had two main aims for the economy:
   - to reduce unemployment
   - to develop self-sufficiency (autarky).

2. Hitler reduced unemployment from 6 million in 1933 to 200,000 in 1939 by:

- public works programmes – he had 7,000 miles of motorway (*autobahn*) built
- introducing conscription (compulsory military service)
- beginning rearmament, which led to the growth of the coal, iron and steel industries.

3. Hitler wanted to develop **self-sufficiency** in food and raw materials to prepare for war.
   - He failed to produce enough food.
   - He introduced synthetic products to develop raw materials.
   - But his policies on self-sufficiency were not successful, so Hitler intended to use *Lebensraum* (living space in Eastern Europe) to provide the food and raw materials needed.

Church–State relations under Hitler

Hitler and the Catholic Church

1. Hitler wanted to control the Catholic Church in Germany. He condemned Christianity for defending the weak. He hated the Jewish–Christian creed.

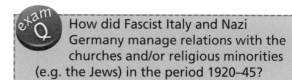

How did Fascist Italy and Nazi Germany manage relations with the churches and/or religious minorities (e.g. the Jews) in the period 1920–45?

   - Hitler saw the Catholic Church as a major obstacle to creating his totalitarian state and so he was determined to control it.

2. Hitler made a **Concordat** with the Catholic Church (1933). He promised to respect the rights of the Catholic Church if priests stayed out of politics. This Concordat helped Hitler gain international prestige.

3. Hitler soon broke his promises, as Catholic civil servants were fired and priests were arrested for sexual immorality and currency smuggling. These trials became part of a huge anti-

When the question asks for '**and/or**', you will not lose marks if you only answer one part, e.g. 'the churches' or 'religious minorities (e.g. the Jews)' in the question above. When the question says '**and**' or '**both**', you will lose marks if you do not refer to both parts.

Catholic **propaganda** campaign led by Goebbels to undermine the influence of the Church.
   - Hitler also tried to control Catholic youth organisations.
   - Even though the Catholic Church complained privately to the Nazis, publicly they declared their support for them in the hope of stopping the anti-Catholic attacks.

4. The Pope published an encyclical, *With Burning Anxiety*, which was read in Catholic churches and which criticised the Nazis. This led to further attacks on the Catholic Church. Many Catholics blamed the attacks on officials, and not on Hitler.

By 1939, the power and influence of the Catholic Church in Germany was severely limited.

5. The Catholic Church also criticised the Nazi programme of euthanasia during the Second World War. Bishop Galen protested against the killing of mentally ill people.

Hitler and the Protestant Churches

6. The Protestant population was divided into many different Protestant Churches. Hitler wanted to unite them in one national church. He wanted to abolish 28 regional Churches and create one National Reich Church (Reichskirche) under Nazi control. He used the **German Christians** to try to achieve this.

REICHSKIRCHE:
Hitler's plan to unite all Protestant churches in one German national church, called the Reichskirche.

7. The Nazis set up the **Reichskirche** (or National Church) to replace the Protestant Churches. A Nazi nominee, Ludwig Muller, was elected Reich Bishop.
   - The clergy had to be loyal Nazis.
   - Pastors wore SA or SS uniforms.
   - Hitler's autobiography, *Mein Kampf*, was placed on the altar of each church, and swastikas were hung in churches.

8. Opposition in the Protestant Churches to Hitler was led by **Pastor Martin Niemöller**. Members of the opposition to Hitler founded the Confessing Church.

9. Hitler set up the Ministry of Church Affairs in 1935, which used repressive measures against the Confessing Church.
   - Pastors were banned and Niemöller and about 700 other pastors were arrested. Niemöller was later sent to concentration camps until 1945.
   - But Hitler's actions failed to create a unified Protestant Church or to stop the opposition.

10. Hitler failed to crush the Christian Churches, but he weakened them. (See also *Church–State relations under Mussolini*, p. 227)

The Nazis and the Jews: Anti-Semitism and the Holocaust

1. Hitler said the Germans were the Master Race or *Herrenvolk*. He believed the Jews were inferior and said they were the source of all evil.

ANTI-SEMITISM:
Hatred and persecution of Jewish people. Nazis saw the Jews as an inferior race.

2. The Jews were portrayed as very rich and cunning.

3. When Hitler came to power, he banned Jews from the civil service, universities and newspapers. The Nazis also boycotted Jewish shops.

4. After a couple of years, Hitler began the systematic persecution of the Jews.

- In the **Nuremberg Laws**, Jews were forbidden to marry pure-blooded Germans.
- Jews were deprived of German citizenship.

HERRENVOLK:

The Nazi idea of the Germans as a master race, superior to all other races.

5. The Nazis attacked the Jews on *Kristallnacht* (the **Night of Broken Glass**) in November 1938. When a Polish Jew killed an official in the German Embassy in Paris, the SA burnt Jewish shops and synagogues; over 100 Jews were killed.

HOLOCAUST:

The slaughter of Jews by the Nazis in extermination camps during the Second World War.

6. Before the beginning of the Second World War, half of Germany's Jews emigrated, including the scientist Albert Einstein. During the war, Jews from all over Europe were sent to concentration camps in Germany and Poland.

7. The Nazis began the **Final Solution** (or extermination of the Jews). About 6 million Jews were killed during the Second World War.
   - Jews were killed in camps such as Auschwitz and Treblinka.
   - They were gassed in chambers designed like large shower rooms.
   - Many were used as slave labour until they died.

Case study: The Nuremberg Rallies

1. The Nazis held the **annual party rally** in Nuremberg in southern Germany in August or September. Nuremberg was a medieval city with links to the Holy Roman Empire – 'the most German of German cities' – and it had easy access by road and train. It was also a Nazi stronghold.

How did the Nuremberg Rallies and/or Leni Riefenstahl contribute to the Nazi regime?

2. The rallies were held in 1927 and 1929. The biggest rallies began in 1933, after Hitler became chancellor of Germany; then after that, they were were held each year until 1938. The rally in 1939 was cancelled because of the beginning of the Second World War.

PROPAGANDA:

Spreading information to convince people of your point of view in order to achieve or retain power.

   - Prior to Hitler's coming to power, the rallies were used to show the strength of the Nazi Party and to impress German public opinion. Hitler used the rallies to denounce the Weimar Republic and to criticise democracy as weak.

3. Albert **Speer**, an architect, was asked by Hitler to develop a plan for the Nuremberg Rally grounds outside Nuremberg. He used a large swastika, huge banners and searchlights in his design.
   - Hitler and Speer wanted to create buildings which would last 1,000 years.
   - Hitler was impressed with Speer's work because he believed that all that remained to remind men of the great epochs of history was their large public buildings.

4. The rallies were held in **large open spaces** such as the Zeppelin Field, the Luitpold Arena and the March field so that the thousands of Nazi supporters gathered together would look impressive.

5. The Nazis **planned** each rally very carefully. They had to cater for about 500,000 people for the week, with accommodation, food, washing and toilet facilities – the organisation of these events was also meant to impress.

6. During the 1930s, the Rallies were used for **many purposes**: to glorify Hitler and cement his relationship with the German people; spread Nazi ideology; celebrate Nazi achievements; mobilise the mass of the German people. They played a central role in propagandising Party members as well as a forum for further recruitment.

7. One way of spreading Nazi propaganda was that each rally had a different **theme**, usually celebrating recent Nazi achievements. Hitler and the Nazis used the Nuremberg Rallies to get across their **policies**.

   Examples:
   - 1933 Congress of Nations: Rally of Victory to celebrate coming to power
   - 1935 Rally of Freedom to celebrate breaking the Treaty of Versailles with the introduction of conscription.
     - At this Rally also, the Nuremberg Laws against the Jews were passed at a special meeting of the Reichstag in the city.
   - 1938 Rally of Greater Germany to celebrate the union with Austria (Anschluss).

8. Each rally was opened by the **Party Roll of Honour** of those who had died for the Party.
   - During the week, each part of the Nazi organisation presented themselves before Hitler: the Hitler Youth, the SA, the SS and the German Labour Front.
   - Hitler's speech was the highlight of each occasion.

9. **Leni Riefenstahl** filmed *Victory of Faith* at the 1933 Rally. Since it included Ernest Roehm, leader of the SA, almost all copies of it were destroyed after the Night of the Long Knives.

10. Hitler commissioned Riefenstahl to film the 1934 Rally.
    - The film was called *The Triumph of the Will* and was used for Nazi propaganda, especially to spread the cult of Hitler.
    - It shows Hitler's arrival, godlike, with processions, rallies and speeches.

11. Other aspects of Nazi propaganda associated with the Nuremberg Rallies included:

Religious experience and Ritual: Ritual reinforced Nazi ideas in the minds of the people and the use of 130 searchlights by Speer from 1934 onwards created the Cathedral of Light around the Zeppelin field at night.

Enemies: Speeches from the Nazi leaders highlighted the enemies they blamed for the problems of Germany – the Treaty of Versailles, the Bolsheviks (Communists) and the Jews.

German power and Unity: The architecture, the parades, the thousands marching and the scale of the organisation were deliberately done to emphasise both Nazi and German power.

12. Nuremberg became a **symbol of Nazism**. But it was only one element of Nazi propaganda. Goebbels made use of press, radio and cinema, and the use of parades all over Germany.

13. During the war, Nuremberg was bombed heavily. After the Second World War, the swastika was blown up. The trials of the Nazi war criminals were held in the town.

4. Economic and social problems of Germany in the inter-war years

 In this section, you should understand:
 ● The economic and social problems of Germany between the wars

1. After the First World War, the German economy was in a depressed state.
2. The Weimar government printed money to pay for war debts and reparations.
   ● This caused **inflation**.
3. When Germany failed to pay reparations, the French and Belgians invaded the Ruhr industrial region in Germany (January 1923). This caused a huge fall in the value of the German mark. Weimar Germany experienced very rapid inflation (hyperinflation).

INFLATION:
An increase in the prices of products, usually a large increase.

   ● The mark became worthless.
   ● The middle classes suffered; their savings and pensions were ruined.
   ● Workers became poorer.
   ● Unemployment rose.
   ● Industrialists and landowners gained because they owned property.
4. The German government created a new currency. It also obtained loans under the **Dawes Plan** (1924). This plan, by an American banker, cut reparations payments and gave American loans to Germany.

5. In the middle of the 1920s the German economy improved.
   - Industrial production increased, wages improved and unemployment fell to 8 per cent by 1928.

6. But Germany was hit badly by the **Wall Street Crash** (1929). This caused the **Great Depression**. America withdrew loans from Germany; companies went bankrupt; factories closed and unemployment rose rapidly. It rose from 1.5 million in 1929 to 6 million in 1932.

7. The economy was made worse by the actions of the Weimar government. The government cut spending on wages, pensions and unemployment benefit.

8. All Germans suffered.

9. **The economy under the Nazis:** When Hitler took power in January 1933 he promised to reduce unemployment and to create self-sufficiency (autarky).
   - To reduce unemployment, Hitler:
     - spent money on public works, such as building *autobahns* (motorways)
     - introduced conscription
     - rearmed, which led to the growth of heavy industry
     - developed a Four-year Plan, which led to huge increases in coal, iron and steel production.
   - German economic recovery depended heavily on government investment. As a result, German unemployment was reduced to 200,000 by 1939.

10. Hitler's plan for **self-sufficiency** was not so successful:
    - grain and potato production declined
    - some foodstuffs had to be imported
    - some synthetic products were developed for raw materials.

11. So Hitler had to wait for the Second World War to bring in his policy of *Lebensraum*, by which he planned to use the conquered Eastern European countries to provide self-sufficiency.

12. Workers' wages increased, but working hours became longer.

13. The Nazis set up:
    - 'Beauty Through Joy', to improve working conditions; and
    - 'Strength Through Joy' to improve leisure time. They organised cheaper holidays, coach tours and sports meetings for workers.
    - Hitler also encouraged the production of the *Volkswagen*, the 'people's car'.

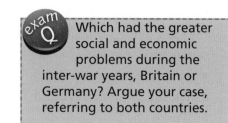

exam Q Which had the greater social and economic problems during the inter-war years, Britain or Germany? Argue your case, referring to both countries.

5. Economic and social problems of Britain in the inter-war years

 In this section, you should understand:
- The economic and social problems of Britain between the wars
- Case study: The Jarrow March, October 1936
- The role of J.M. Keynes (Key personality, p. 273)

1. The British economy was in depression during the inter-war years.

2. The economic depression was **caused** by:
   - the decline of older industries (coal, iron and steel, ships)
   - American competition
   - British wage costs
   - the decline of British trade.

- What were the main social and economic challenges facing Britain, 1920–45?
- How did the Jarrow March (October 1936) draw attention to the social and economic problems in Great Britain at that time?

3. British shipbuilding declined owing to:
   - the surplus of ships after the First World War
   - the United States and Japan producing their own ships.

4. British coal was more expensive to mine than American, German or Polish coal.

5. The **depressed areas** of Britain were mainly Clydeside (central Scotland), Tyneside (northeast England), Lancashire and South Wales.

6. These depressed areas had high unemployment, fewer women working and high infant mortality.

7. But London and the Midlands **prospered**, because they had newer industries such as electrical goods and motor cars.

8. Government policy did not help:
   - The government wanted to balance the budget, so it wasn't prepared to borrow money to help the depressed industries.
   - The government also set the value of the pound sterling too high against the gold standard. This made British exports too expensive.

9. Unemployed workers were given unemployment benefits, but this was too low to feed a family and they received the benefit for only 15 weeks a year. After that they had additional benefits – called the dole – for which they had to queue.

10. Clashes between mine owners and coal miners led to the **General Strike of 1926**. Mine owners wanted wage cuts, but the coal miners' leader said, 'Not a penny off the pay! Not a minute off the day!'

11. A government commission, the Samuel Commission, said there should be wage cuts and longer working hours. When negotiations between the Trades Union Congress (TUC) and the mine owners broke down, there was a general strike.

12. About 2 million other workers in transport, building and electricity went on strike in sympathy with the coal miners.

13. The government had plans to distribute food and transport people to work. The other workers went back to work when the government said it would not give in.

14. The miners gave up after six months and returned with lower pay and longer working hours.

15. The General Strike was a defeat for the trade union movement, and the government banned further general strikes.

16. Britain was hit by the **Great Depression** after the Wall Street Crash of 1929.
    - Unemployment rose from 1.5 million in 1929 to 3.5 million by 1932.
    - The older industries were the worst hit.

17. The government:
    - took Britain off the gold standard
    - cut unemployment benefits and introduced a means test
    - cut the wages of civil servants and teachers
    - introduced protectionism (taxes on imports) to safeguard British industry.

> **key point**
>
> PROTECTIONISM:
> Using tariffs (taxes) to protect home industry and employment from foreign competition.

18. The newer industries around London and the Midlands were not hit so badly.

19. Britain recovered quickly from the Depression, but the older industries still suffered.
    - Unemployment remained high in those areas with older industries.

20. Unemployment caused a great deal of poverty. This led to death and diseases amongst the poorer classes.

21. Hunger marches were organised to protest against unemployment.

Case study: The Jarrow March, October 1936

1. Jarrow, a town in north-eastern England, was in a **depressed state** in the 1920s and 1930s.
    - It suffered from poor housing, unemployment, poverty and high mortality.

2. Its main industries, shipbuilding and iron and steel, declined. The last shipyard, Palmers, was sold off in 1934.

> **exam Q**
> How did the Jarrow March reflect the social and economic problems of industrial England in the 1930s?

> **exam focus**
> Jarrow is an example of the depressed areas of Britain. Some areas such as the south and Midlands were more prosperous.

3. **Unemployment** in Jarrow varied between 41 per cent in 1922 to 72 per cent in 1932, compared to 15 per cent in the country. The unemployed depended on unemployment benefit, which was means tested. (The wages of all family members were taken into account when deciding whether or not relief should be paid.)

- The experience of Jarrow was more like other areas in the North of England suffering from declining industries after the First World War, and from the Great Depression.
- In contrast, the south of England around London had more modern industries and less unemployment.

The Jarrow March, 1936

4. In 1936, the Jarrow Borough Council decided to present a **petition** to Parliament in London.

- The petition asked the government to provide industry for the town.
- The Council was supported by **Ellen Wilkinson** (Red Ellen), Member of Parliament for Jarrow.
- Two hundred men were selected to march to London, 300 miles away.

5. The march was called a **crusade** to distinguish it from the 'hunger marches' organised by the National Unemployed Workers' Movement (NUWM), which had connections with the Communist Party.

6. The petition asked the government to provide work for the town. It was signed by over 11,000 Jarrow people, and it was carried in an oak box by the marchers.

7. The marchers carried a banner before them, 'Jarrow Crusade', and they were led by a mouth-organ band. A transport van carried food and sleeping equipment. At the end of each day's march, the men slept in town halls, schools or drill halls.

8. Speakers explained the case of Jarrow to the people of the towns they stopped in. The leaders emphasised the causes of Jarrow's unemployment problems; the impact of unemployment on the town; and a call on the government to provide jobs for the town.

9. Ellen Wilkinson presented the case of Jarrow to the **Labour Party Conference**, but the Conference criticised her because hunger marches were associated with Communist organisations.

10. The march took twenty-three days and two rest weekends. The marchers presented the petition through their MP, Ellen Wilkinson – but the government did not do anything for the town.

- When the men returned to Jarrow by train, their unemployment benefit was reduced because they had not been available for work.

11. The March failed in its main aim of getting the government to provide jobs for the area. But **Jarrow's economy** improved shortly after this, mainly because of the coming of the Second World War which gave a boost to rearmament, engineering and shipbuilding (elsewhere along the Tyne).

- The example of the march – and the effect of mass unemployment in the 1930s – contributed to the setting up of the Welfare State in Britain after the war.

6. Anglo-American popular culture in peace and war – radio and cinema

In this section, you should understand:
- The features of Anglo-American popular culture from 1920 to 1945
- The role of Charlie Chaplin (Key personality, p. 270)
- The role of Bing Crosby (Key personality, p. 272)

1. Popular culture of the 1920s and 1930s was associated with radio, cinema, jazz and sport. These expanded because of:
   - a shorter working week
   - more women working
   - people being better off.

2. Popular culture was a youthful culture, heavily influenced by American trends.

3. In Britain, **radio** was first broadcast in 1922. The BBC (British Broadcasting Corporation) was set up in 1926 to control radio broadcasting. By the late 1930s, 75 per cent of British houses had radios or 'wirelesses', as they were called.

4. BBC programmes were mainly news, information and entertainment.
   - They boosted popular music – artists such as Bing Crosby and Glenn Miller became more popular when their songs and music was played on the radio.
   - They kept people better informed – it was through radio announcements that people heard the main news events of the time, e.g. the death of George V and Chamberlain's news of war with Germany.

   > **exam focus**
   > Use information from *Key personalities – Charlie Chaplin* and *Bing Crosby* when writing about cinema and radio (pp. 270–73).

   - Politicians such as Stanley Baldwin, three times prime minister in the inter-war years, realised the propaganda value of radio.

5. Radio spread rapidly in **Weimar Germany**. The number of listeners rose from 10,000 in 1924 to over 4 million by 1932, second only to Britain in Europe. Programmes were largely for entertainment and education.

In **Nazi Germany**, 70 per cent of households had a radio by 1942. Goebbels believed in the use of radio for propaganda so he encouraged the sale of a cheap radio, the **People's Radio**. Hitler

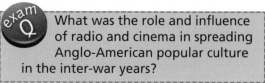

exam Q

What was the role and influence of radio and cinema in spreading Anglo-American popular culture in the inter-war years?

used the radio to broadcast directly to the people, and the Nazis got across their views on national pride and on anti-Semitism.

6. **Cinema** was popular in the 1920s, but expanded even further in the 1930s.
   - In the 1920s black-and-white silent movies were very popular.
   - Sound film was developed at the end of the 1920s and this led to another huge expansion of cinema in the 1930s. It started with Al Jolson in the film *The Jazz Singer*.

7. Many more cinemas were built in Britain. Some were super-cinemas which could hold 3,000 people. Cinema-going was the most popular form of entertainment in Britain in the 1930s. By 1939, 50 per cent of people went to the cinema once a week. It was open to all social classes. For some it was a form of escapism from a drab life.

8. In **Weimar Germany**, the number of cinemas increased from about 2,300 in 1918 to over 5,000 in 1930, with Germany having the most cinemas of any country in Europe. The German film industry produced some famous films such as *The Cabinet of Dr Caligari* (1920). But Charlie Chaplin was also popular, especially *The Gold Rush* (1926).

   Cinema attendance increased during the **Nazi years** from 250 million in 1933 to one billion by 1942 during the Second World War. The Nazis ensured that different genres of films such as love stories, comedies, historical adventures, military and crime thrillers were shown. Sometimes they included a political or social message. Very often the leadership role of Hitler was highlighted as in Leni Riefenstahl's *Triumph of the Will* on the Nuremberg Rally.

9. Charlie Chaplin, the London-born star of the silent era, developed the character of the tramp. His films such as *The Kid*, *The Gold Rush* and *The Circus* were very popular in Britain and the continent.

   Chaplin resisted the advent of sound. *City Lights* and *Modern Times* were largely silent. His first fully talking movie was *The Great Dictator*. (See Key personality: *Charlie Chaplin*, p. 270.)
   - Charlie Chaplin's *The Gold Rush* was banned in Germany in 1935 by Goebbels because Chaplin was labelled a Jew.

10. Cinema influenced culture in a number of ways:
    - The stars of cinema set trends in lifestyle – fashion, mannerisms and hairstyles.
    - They spread Anglo-American culture throughout Britain and Europe.
    - Sex symbols (e.g. Mary Pickford and Rudolf Valentino) spread the attraction of cinema.

- The advent of sound in cinema created new stars in the 1930s, but some silent stars, such as Charlie Chaplin, survived into the sound era.
- Musicals became a new film type (or genre), with stars like **Fred Astaire**, **Ginger Rodgers** and **Bing Crosby**. Astaire and Rodgers became famous as a singing and dancing duo in *Top Hat, Swing Time* and *Shall We Dance*. Crosby acted in the musical comedy *Road* movies with Bob Hope. (See Key personality: *Bing Crosby*, p. 272)

11. The lives of young women changed in the 1920s and 1930s.
    - The 'bright young things' cut their hair short, wore knee-length skirts and smoked.
    - They were in rebellion against the older generation, but they were mainly middle- and upper-class young women.
    - They featured mostly in the large cities of London, Paris and Berlin, where jazz and swing had become popular.

12. **Jazz** became popular – it was helped by records, radio and cinema. It spread from America to Britain and the Continent, especially to cities like London, Paris and Berlin. It brought new dances, such as the Charleston and the Foxtrot.
    - A change came in Germany when the Nazis rose to power in 1933. Jazz was regarded as 'nigger music', and jazz musicians were harassed and persecuted.

13. **Sport** also spread through the influence of radio and cinema. It was a time of mass spectator sport. Sport also had its heroes and stars such Jesse Owens, the American athlete, and Joe Louis, the boxer, as well as national soccer in various European countries.
    - Owens rose to fame during the 1936 Berlin Olympics.
    - Soccer became the national sport of Britain as millions attended football league matches. The World Cup finals held in the 1930s attracted a great deal of attention.
    - Boxing and athletics were also popular, but tennis and golf were largely confined to the middle classes.

14. **Radio and cinema in the Second World War:**
    - Radio and cinema played important roles in propaganda in the Second World War.
    - They reached mass audiences, created a sense of national unity and boosted morale.
    - Churchill in Britain and the Nazis in Germany made powerful use of radio to get their messages across.
    - Nazi propaganda was organised by Joseph Goebbels during the war.
    - The BBC beamed German language programmes into Germany while Goebbels used William Joyce, 'Lord Haw-Haw', who always started his broadcasts with 'Germany calling, Germany calling', to threaten Britain.
    - Radio and cinema provided the main news of the events of the war for people.

15. Cinema produced films with a war message. In Britain, films showed the Allies as good and the Nazis as evil. Cinemas stayed open during the war in Britain.

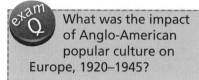

What was the impact of Anglo-American popular culture on Europe, 1920–1945?

- Charlie Chaplin produced, directed and acted in *The Great Dictator* in 1940. This was a satire on Hitler as dictator. Some Americans saw it as trying to encourage America to become involved in the war.
- Stars such as Bing Crosby and Bob Hope used radio broadcasts and visited troops to boost morale. The main British star was **Vera Lynn** whose song, 'We'll Meet Again', became a very popular wartime hit.
- Charlie Chaplin took a different line – he refused to perform for the troops. Instead he called for the opening of a second front to help the Soviet Union. This got him labeled as pro-Communist and led him into trouble after the war was over and the Cold War had begun.

7. Politics and administration in France – the Third Republic and the Vichy State

In this section, you should understand:
- The problems facing the Third Republic
- Why France was unstable between the wars
- The role of the Vichy state – collaboration and resistance

1. France was badly affected by the First World War: over 1 million people died; large areas of northern France were destroyed and the cost of reconstruction was estimated at over 100 million francs.

2. In the inter-war years (1920–39), there were many **changes of government** (political instability). Sometimes governments had to rule by decree to bring in laws.

3. The **Bloc National** – a coalition (group) of right-wing (conservative) parties – won the general election of 1919. They were faced with a general strike in May 1920 as trade unions became more militant in demanding increased wages. The government dealt ruthlessly with the general strike and brought it to an end.

4. The **Bloc National** began reconstruction.
- Roads and railways were repaired, and factories rebuilt.
- Two million immigrant workers were needed because of a shortage of manpower.
- The French government wanted to pay for reconstruction with German reparations (compensation).

5. French foreign policy demanded harsh measures for Germany to ensure the security and safety of France. Most of these were achieved through the Treaty of Versailles.

6. Government policy tried to ensure the security of France by isolating Germany and enforcing the Treaty of Versailles:

- France isolated Germany by making treaties with countries around Germany, such as Belgium, Poland and Czechoslovakia.
- French (and Belgian) troops invaded the Ruhr industrial region when Germany failed to pay reparations. The troops were withdrawn when Germany agreed to pay revised reparations under the Dawes Plan.

7. The **Cartel des Gauches** (Coalition of the Left) won the general election of 1924. But this government failed, because it was unable to solve the economic problems caused by the decline in the value of the franc.

8. The **Government of National Unity** (led by Raymond Poincaré) took action to save the value of the franc.

9. The Cartel des Gauches again took power in 1932.
   - They were faced with the economic problems brought about by the Great Depression.
   - They were also faced with the rise of right-wing leagues and the coming to power of Hitler in Germany.

10. The right-wing leagues or groups were anti-parliamentary, anti-communist, anti-Semitic and very nationalistic. They wore coloured shirts. They included Action Française, Solidarité Française and La Croix de Feu.

11. The **Stavisky Affair** caused a crisis in France. Stavisky was involved in a financial scandal, but when police sought him, he shot himself.

12. The right wing said Stavisky was murdered to hide his ties with politicians. There were nightly riots in Paris against the government.

13. When the government sacked the prefect of police, Chiappe, the right-wing groups organised a huge demonstration in Paris on the day Parliament opened. The rally turned into a riot and 14 rioters were killed. The prime minister, Daladier, resigned.

14. Some saw the riots as an attempt to overthrow the Third Republic; but the rioters had little chance of success because the groups were uncoordinated, and democracy had a strong tradition in France.

15. The riots led to the formation of the **Popular Front** government (of left-wing parties). Workers took over the factories, thinking they would be handed over to them. They organised sit-in strikes; but eventually employers and workers compromised with the Matignon Agreement:
    - an increase in wages
    - collective bargaining between trade unions and employers
    - nationalisation (government ownership) of some industries.

> exam Q
> What problems did the Third Republic encounter between 1920 and 1940?

16. But the French government faced further economic problems, such as inflation, unemployment and the devaluation of the franc. The government tried to bring in changes by decree; but eventually the Popular Front government collapsed.

17. It was replaced by the **Government of National Defence** (right-wing).

18. **French foreign policy** was directed by **Aristide Briand**.

- He wanted to bring Germany back into the political and economic life of Europe, to prevent future war.
- He worked well with Gustav Stresemann, German foreign minister. They signed the Locarno Pact (along with Britain and Italy), which recognised the borders of Germany.
- The Kellogg–Briand Pact was agreed to renounce war as an instrument of policy.

19. France also built the **Maginot Line** (a huge line of fortifications on the border with Germany).

20. French foreign policy was still governed by the insecurity of Germany. France concluded a system of alliances to protect the country.

21. **Pierre Laval**, foreign minister, formed the Stresa Front with Britain and Italy against Germany. But the Stresa Front collapsed with Mussolini's invasion of Abyssinia.

22. Hitler's actions showed up the weakness of France. He broke the Treaty of Versailles, but France did nothing.
- The French had a defeatist attitude towards Germany.
- They also followed Britain. But the British policy of appeasement conceded gains to Hitler in order to stop a war. The French people, too, wanted to avoid a European war.
- In the Spanish Civil War France followed a policy of non-intervention, even though a Popular Front government was attacked by a nationalist Army backed by Hitler and Mussolini.
- France agreed to the handing over of the Sudetenland to Germany at the Munich Conference.

23. France had to follow British policy. Britain changed its policy against Hitler, especially after he took over the remainder of Czechoslovakia. When Britain declared war on Hitler after he invaded Poland in September 1939, France did the same.

Collaboration and resistance in Vichy France

exam focus

Collaboration and resistance can be included in a question on Society during World War II. (See Society during the Second World War, pp. 259–261)

exam Q

What was the impact of World War II on the civilian population of Britain and/or France?
What did you learn about World War II from your study of collaboration/resistance?

1. Germany invaded Belgium, Holland and France in May 1940. France was very divided.
- The Communists were opposed to a French war against Germany.
- The right wing wanted a peace treaty with Germany.
- Germany's blitzkrieg tactics easily defeated France.

2. The Maginot Line was captured and the French government retreated to Bordeaux. The government signed an armistice with Germany.

3. France was divided between **Occupied France**, which was ruled directly by the Nazis, and **Vichy France**, which ruled through a French government.

4. The new French government was called the Vichy government. It was led by Marshal Pétain and Pierre Laval.

5. The Vichy government **collaborated** with Germany.
   - They rounded up Jews and deported them to Germany.
   - Hitler used Vichy France as a source of raw materials and food.
   - French workers were sent to work in German factories.
   - The Vichy government put down French resistance.
   - They had to pay the costs of German occupation.

RESISTANCE:
Resisting enemy troops when they have taken over a country. The Resistance was usually a secret organisation involved in surprise attacks on the occupying army.

6. Very soon Vichy France operated directly under German control.

7. The **French Resistance** movement worked against the Germans by collecting military intelligence, sabotaging railways and organising ambushes.
   - The Resistance was made up of different groups, such as Combat and the Franc-Tireurs.
   - The French Communists joined them after Hitler invaded the Soviet Union in June 1941.

COLLABORATION:
Co-operating with the enemy when they have taken over your own country.

8. The French Resistance was taken over by **General de Gaulle**, leader of the Free French in London. The Resistance increased their attacks on the run up to D-Day (Normandy landings) in June 1944 – but the Germans inflicted huge reprisals, e.g. at Oradour-sur-Glane.

9. After the war, the French Resistance took revenge on the collaborators: 9,000 were executed without trial. In order to control this, de Gaulle's government began the systematic punishment of collaborators. Laval was executed.

8. Hitler's foreign policy (1933–39) and the causes of the Second World War

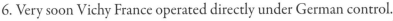

In this section, you should understand:
- How Hitler's foreign policy contributed to the causes of World War II

1. Hitler's **aims** in foreign policy were to:
   - destroy the Treaty of Versailles by re-arming the German army, navy and air force, uniting with Austria (*Anschluss*) and remilitarising the Rhineland

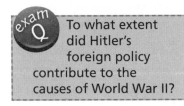

To what extent did Hitler's foreign policy contribute to the causes of World War II?

- create a Greater Germany (*Grossdeutschland*) by uniting all German-speaking people
- create **Lebensraum**, living space in Eastern Europe, to supply Germany with food and raw materials.

2. Hitler had early successes.

- He withdrew from the Disarmament Conference and the League of Nations because France refused to disarm as Germany had done.
- He formed a ten-year Non-Aggression Pact with Poland.
- In the Saar Plebiscite, the people of the Saar voted to become part of Germany. (The Saar had been given to France by the Treaty of Versailles (1919).)

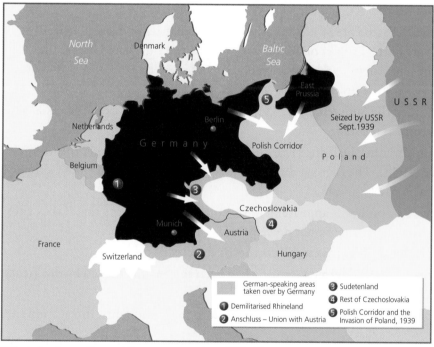

Hitler's foreign policy and German expansion, 1933–39

3. But Hitler failed to unite Germany with Austria when the chancellor, Dollfuss, was assassinated.

- Mussolini rushed troops to the Austrian border, and Hitler backed down.

4. Britain, France and Italy formed the **Stresa Front** (1935) because of fear of German expansion.

5. Hitler began **destroying** the Treaty of Versailles.

- He began rearmament (1935) – conscription was introduced and submarine construction begun.

- The Luftwaffe (air force) was secretly set up.
- He was helped by Britain, which signed the Anglo-German Naval Agreement (1935). This allowed Hitler to increase the German Navy up to 35 per cent of the size of the British Navy, but there were no restrictions on submarines.
- He remilitarised the Rhineland (1936).

6. The Italian invasion of **Abyssinia** brought Hitler and Mussolini closer together.
   - It also led to the ending of the Stresa Front.
   - It showed up the weakness of the League of Nations.

7. Hitler and Mussolini were also brought closer together by the **Spanish Civil War** (1936–39), in which they gave help to Franco and ensured his victory.

8. Hitler and Mussolini formed the **Rome–Berlin Axis** (November 1936).
   - Hitler gave up his claim to the German-speaking people of the South Tyrol. In return, Mussolini agreed to Hitler's takeover of Austria. They later agreed the **Anti-Comintern Pact** (against Russia) with Japan.

9. **Anschluss** with Austria (1938): When the Austrian chancellor decided to hold a plebiscite (vote of the people) on union with Germany, Hitler acted before the plebiscite; he sent troops to the Austrian border and the German Army was invited into Austria to 'restore order'. Austria was taken over.

10. Hitler demanded the **Sudetenland**, a German-speaking part of Czechoslovakia. The Czech government resisted.

11. Chamberlain (Britain), Daladier (France), Mussolini and Hitler met at the **Munich Conference** (1938). They agreed that the Sudetenland should be given to Germany; Czechoslovakia had to give in.

12. Britain followed a **policy of appeasement** towards Hitler, believing that if they gave in to Hitler's demands, this would prevent war.
    - Britain did not want to repeat the horrors of the First World War.
    - Many British people felt that Germany had been too harshly treated by the Treaty of Versailles.
    - Hitler and Nazi Germany were seen as a block to the Communist threat from the USSR.
    - The French government and people also supported appeasement.

13. Six months after getting the Sudetenland, Hitler took over the rest of Czechoslovakia in March 1939. This showed the futility of the policy of appeasement.

14. **The Polish Corridor**: Poland was now surrounded on three sides by Germany. Hitler next demanded the Polish Corridor, a strip of land that separated East Prussia from the rest of Germany.
    - Poland refused to give up the Corridor, and Britain and France supported Poland. Hitler did not believe they would do anything.

15. Hitler made the **Pact of Steel** with Mussolini, to help each other in war.

16. He also made the **Nazi–Soviet Pact** with Stalin, the Soviet leader.
   - In it, they agreed not to attack each other for 10 years and to divide Poland between them.
   - The Pact allowed Hitler to attack Poland without Russia intervening.

17. Hitler invaded **Poland** on 1 September 1939. Britain and France declared war on Germany two days later. The Second World War had begun.

Summary: Hitler's foreign policy and the causes of WWII
   - Hitler's foreign policy
   - Policy of appeasement
   - American isolationism
   - Failure of the League of Nations

exam focus

In answering a question such as, 'To what extent did Hitler's foreign policy contribute to the causes of World War II?' you can concentrate on Hitler's foreign policy and make short references to the other causes in assessing 'To what extent . . . ?'

9. The Second World War

aims In this section, you should understand:
   - The reasons for early German victories
   - The reasons for eventual German defeat
   - The part played by the Soviet Union in the war
   - The technology of war
   - Wartime alliances
   - The role of Winston Churchill (Key personality, p. 271)

The defeat and partition of Poland

exam Q
   - What developments took place in the technology of warfare during the period, 1920–45?
   - How significant was the role played by the Soviet Union in World War II?
   - What did you learn about World War II from your study of one or more of the following: wartime alliances; collaboration/resistance; technology of warfare?

1. Germany invaded Poland on 1 September 1939. Germany used **blitzkrieg** (lightning war) tactics.
   - The Luftwaffe got control of the air by knocking most of the Polish air force out of action on the ground.
   - German tanks (panzers) advanced rapidly, using a pincer movement to cut off supplies from the Polish Army.
   - German infantry units defeated the rest of the Polish Army.

2. The Soviet Army invaded Poland from the east as part of the Nazi–Soviet Pact. Germany and Russia divided Poland between them.

- The British and French declared war on Germany on 3 September, but could not give help to Poland.

3. During the winter of 1939–40, the **Russo-Finnish War** was fought. It took the Soviet Union three months to defeat the much smaller country.

4. In the west, this was the time of the **Phoney War**, when there was no fighting. Instead Britain, France and Germany built up their supplies. The French felt safe behind the Maginot Line.

The invasion of Norway and Denmark

1. Hitler's invasion of Norway and Denmark in April 1940 brought the Phoney War to an end. Hitler wanted to protect valuable Swedish ore supplies which came through the Norwegian port of Narvik in winter. The Germans easily captured the two countries, using ships to transport troops, and paratroopers to capture bridges and airfields in Norway. Hitler imposed Quisling, a Norwegian Nazi, as prime minister of Norway.

2. **Chamberlain**, the Prime Minister of Britain, resigned; **Churchill** became Prime Minister on 10 May 1940, the day Germany began its attack on France.

3. **The fall of France**: The German invasion of France again used blitzkrieg tactics. When the attack began, French and British troops moved into Belgium to face the German Army; but Hitler's panzers came through the wooded mountains of the Ardennes in Luxembourg.
   - They cut off the French and British armies, who were forced to retreat to Dunkirk.

4. The British organised **Operation Dynamo** to rescue 300,000 British and French troops from the beaches of Dunkirk. Churchill made it seem like a victory. The German Army easily took the rest of France. Mussolini joined the war when he saw Hitler's successes.

> **key point**
>
> BLITZKRIEG:
> The German lightning tactics during the Second World War, which used planes, tanks and fast-moving infantry to defeat the enemy.

5. The new French government, headed by Marshal Pétain, signed an armistice with Germany. Germany controlled most of France, while part, called **Vichy France**, remained under French government control.
   - France had to pay for the cost of German occupation.
   - General de Gaulle set up the Free French government in London.

6. **Hitler's success** in 1939–40 was due to:
   - a stronger Army and air force
   - the use of blitzkrieg
   - the weakness of France
   - the failure of France to attack Germany when it was attacking Poland.

7. **The Battle of Britain**: Hitler's plan for the invasion of Britain – Operation Sealion – was begun. The Luftwaffe attacked British radar stations and airfields to gain control of the air.

8. One of the biggest German attacks was on **Eagle Day** (13 August), when five waves of bombers and fighters attacked. The RAF Spitfires and Hurricanes were a match for the German Stukas and Messerschmitts – but the RAF pilots were exhausted.

9. Hitler switched his attack to bombing London. He wanted to break the morale of the population. This relieved pressure on the RAF at a crucial time.

10. Hitler called off the Battle of Britain. Churchill's tribute to the RAF was, 'Never in the field of human endeavour was so much owed, by so many, to so few.'

> **exam focus**
> When explaining German success, you should give an account of the campaigns.

11. But Hitler continued bombing British cities in the **Blitz**, which lasted over the winter of 1940–41. Cities such as London, Coventry and Birmingham were attacked at night. In London people hid in the Underground or left the city. The Blitz came to an end when Hitler prepared for the invasion of Russia.

12. **War at sea**: In the war at sea, German commerce-raiders such as the *Admiral Graf Spee* and the *Bismarck* posed a threat to British ships bringing supplies to the country. They were eventually sunk.

13. German **U-boats** were a more serious threat. They were based in Norway and France to advance into the Atlantic. Groups of U-boats (called wolf packs) attacked convoys of ships crossing the Atlantic. The British (and later the United States) won the Battle of the Atlantic by giving greater protection to convoys, employing long-range aircraft, depth charges and radar, and using Ultra to crack German naval codes.

14. In the Desert War, the German Army had to help the Italians in North Africa. Hitler sent Rommel with the Afrika Corps. However, Montgomery defeated them at the Battle of El Alamein. This was the first victorious Allied campaign; it was a **turning point in the war**.

Operation Barbarossa – the invasion of the Soviet Union

1. Hitler planned the invasion of the Soviet Union (**Operation Barbarossa**) to get oil, gas and living space (Lebensraum) for his 'master race', and to destroy Communism. He believed that he would easily crush the Russians because of their poor performance against Finland. Hitler said, 'We have only to kick in the door and the whole rotten structure will come crashing down.'

> **key point**
> LEBENSRAUM:
> Hitler wanted additional land or territory in Eastern Europe to make Germany self-sufficient in food and raw materials.

2. The Germans invaded using blitzkrieg tactics on 22 June 1941. It was a three-pronged attack towards Leningrad, Moscow and Kiev. They advanced rapidly.

Operation Barbarossa, 1941

3. The Russians retreated in an orderly fashion. They used scorched-earth policies to destroy crops, buildings and bridges. Stalin, the Soviet leader, encouraged the people to fight the Great Patriotic War.

4. The German Army could not cope with the Russian winter; lorries and tanks seized up and soldiers froze.

5. In 1942 Hitler attacked **Stalingrad**. The Russians defended it street by street. The Russian general, Zhukov, broke through weakened German lines north and south of Stalingrad and cut off the German Army under von Paulus. After three months von Paulus was forced to surrender. The Battle of Stalingrad was a major turning point in the war. The Russians followed this with a victory in a major tank battle at Kursk. From then on the Soviet Union advanced towards Germany.

6. The German Army **lost** in Russia because:
   - there was a delay in starting the campaign in 1941
   - Stalin relocated factories beyond the Ural Mountains, out of the range of German planes

Summary: The Soviet part in WWII
- Nazi-Soviet Pact
- The invasion of Poland
- The Russo-Finnish War
- Operation Barbarossa
- Battle of Stalingrad and advance to Germany
- Stalin's role in the war
- Wartime alliances

- Stalin used the call of nationalism to resist the Germans
- German use of terror made the Russians resist more.

7. In December 1941 Hitler declared war on the United States, after the Japanese attack on Pearl Harbor. Hitler now had to fight a long war against countries with greater resources of men and raw materials.

Wartime alliances

1. Hitler and Mussolini made the **Pact of Steel** before the Second World War, but Mussolini did not join the war until he saw Germany defeating France. Hitler's alliance with Italy contributed to his eventual defeat.

2. Hitler and Stalin divided Poland according to the **Nazi–Soviet Pact**; but Hitler broke the Pact when he invaded the Soviet Union in Operation Barbarossa.

3. The **Anti-Comintern Pact** was made by Germany, Italy and Japan before the war. But Germany and Italy could not help Japan, nor Japan help Germany and Italy, because of the distance between them. However, Hitler declared war on the United States after Japan bombed Pearl Harbor. This led to his defeat.

4. Roosevelt, President of the United States, and Churchill, Prime Minister of Britain, met in Newfoundland and issued the Atlantic Charter (1941):
   - All people have the right to decide their own form of government.
   - All people should live their life in freedom from fear and want.

5. **Churchill** realised that Britain could not defeat Germany on its own, so he worked very hard to ensure he got help from America through the Lend-Lease scheme and later he developed the alliance with the Soviet Union.

6. Roosevelt and Churchill met in **Casablanca** in North Africa (January 1942). (Stalin, the Soviet leader, could not attend.) They decided to:
   - organise a major anti-submarine campaign
   - organise the bombing of Germany
   - invade Italy
   - seek unconditional surrender from Germany.

7. Roosevelt, Churchill and Stalin (the 'Big Three') met together for the first time in **Teheran** (1943). They decided:
   - to plan the D-Day landings
   - to form a new organisation for peace after the war to replace the League of Nations
   - that Russia would take part of Poland after the war, and Poland would take part of Germany.

8. Roosevelt, Churchill and Stalin met again in **Yalta** (1945) in the Crimea. They decided:
   - the borders between Poland and Russia and Poland and Germany
   - that the United Nations would be formed
   - that Germany would be divided into four Occupation Zones
   - that Germany would pay reparations, mainly to the Soviet Union.

9. When the war in the East against Japan was over, Truman, the US president, Churchill (later replaced by Attlee) and Stalin met in **Potsdam** (1945), near Berlin. Tension was evident. They decided that:

- Nazi war criminals would be prosecuted
- German reparations would include machinery and equipment from factories.

The technology of war, 1920–45

1. The most important weapons of World War II – tanks, planes and submarines – were developed during World War I. In between the wars, military thinkers in Germany, France and Britain developed new ideas about how they should be used in war.

> **exam focus**
>
> When answering questions on the technology of warfare, you should use examples of battles and campaigns to show how the technology was used, e.g. blitzkrieg and the invasion of Poland with tanks and planes.

2. Tanks and aircraft played a large part in the Second World War. They were used by the Germans in blitzkrieg (lightning war) tactics. They gave speed and surprise by:

- the use of planes to gain control of the air
- the use of tanks to cut off enemy supplies.

3. New **tanks** were developed during the war. The Russians built the **T-34** to compete with the German panzers. So the Germans improved their tanks by building the **Tiger**, with stronger armour and more powerful guns.

4. Tanks featured in some of the main battles of the war: the Battle of El Alamein, the Battle of Kursk.

5. As well as being used for blitzkrieg, **aircraft** were also used in bombing cities, towns, industries and rail links. The Battle of Britain was a battle between two air forces: the RAF and the Luftwaffe. Britain developed radar as an early-warning system and this played a big part in winning the battle.

6. Larger bombers were built to carry greater loads of bombs further and faster. Long-range fighter aircraft (Mustangs) were developed to protect the bombers.

7. Air navigation systems were improved: the Knickebein (German) and Oboe (Allied) systems were used to improve bombing over enemy countries.

8. Jet aircraft were developed too late in the war to affect the outcome.

9. The Germans developed **V-1** flying bombs and **V-2** rockets. These caused panic in Britain towards the end of the war. They were stopped as the Allies advanced through Belgium and Germany to capture the launch sites.

10. Technology played a big role in the war at sea. The Germans built larger and more powerful submarines (U-boats) to attack convoys from the United States. The British used sonar to detect submarines. They also used Ultra to crack the secrets of the German Enigma machine for sending coded messages to U-boats and Army commanders.

German conquests by 1942

11. **Air war**: After the United States joined the war in December 1941, the Allies began the systematic bombing of Germany. They wanted to destroy the German industrial, military and economic systems. Their targets were oil refineries, railways, bridges and munitions factories in Hamburg and in the cities of the Ruhr.

12. The British used area bombing of German cities by night. The United States used precision bombing by daytime, using Flying Fortresses. They suffered huge losses, but by 1944 they had control of the air over Germany.

   - There was great destruction of German cities, especially when using incendiary bombs to create firestorms such as in Dresden, when 30,000 people were killed.

The end of the war

1. In **Operation Husky** the Allies invaded and captured Sicily. This led to the dismissal of Mussolini. The Germans defended Italy by building strong defensive lines, the Gustav Line and the Gothic Line.

2. The Allies agreed to invade France to open up a second front against Hitler. General Eisenhower was appointed commander-in-chief to plan **Operation Overlord**, the Allied landing in Normandy on D-Day (6 June 1944).

3. Troops from the United States, Britain and Canada landed on five beaches in Normandy. The Germans had been led to expect a landing at Calais, so the Allies were able to break through German resistance.

4. The Allies brought in reinforcements and supplies through Mulberry piers (floating artificial harbours). Oil was brought by PLUTO (an undersea pipeline).

5. The Allies soon captured Paris and advanced on Germany from all sides:
   - In the east, Russia took Poland and set up a communist satellite state.
   - In the west, the British captured the sites of the V-1 and V-2 bases in Belgium – but they lost the Battle of Arnhem. The US Army was halted at the Battle of the Bulge.
   - In the south, progress was slow in Italy.

6. As the Russians approached Berlin, Hitler and a loyal band of followers, including Goebbels, committed suicide in a bunker there. The German government surrendered to the Allies; the Allies had won Victory in Europe (V-E).

7. The Germans **lost the war** because:
   - Hitler's strategy failed – the war developed from a short war into a long one
   - the Allies had greater resources of population, soldiers and oil production
   - the United States was the arsenal of democracy
   - the Italian Army was too weak; Hitler was forced to go to Mussolini's aid.

8. Other factors were:
   - Allied bombing raids
   - the success of D-Day
   - victory in the war at sea.

> **exam focus**
>
> You should use historical information from the battles and campaigns of the war to support your reasons for Germany losing the war.

9. As a **result** of the Second World War:
   - Between 40 and 50 million soldiers and civilians were killed.
   - Cities, towns and countryside were destroyed.
   - There were about 20 million refugees, many of them Germans fleeing from eastern Europe.
   - Fascism and Nazism were defeated.
   - Germany was divided in two and remained that way for 45 years.
   - Two superpowers – the United States and the Soviet Union – were created; this led to the Cold War.
   - The United States suffered less than other countries. The country was prosperous compared to the poverty of Europe.
   - The United Nations and the movement towards European unity were established to create peace.
   - Improvements in aircraft led to an expansion of air travel.
   - The development of rockets led to the space programmes of the United States and the Soviet Union.
   - The development of the atomic bomb began the nuclear arms race.

10. Society during the Second World War

 In this section, you should understand:
- How the war affected life for civilians in Germany, France and Britain

The Home Front in Germany

1. Germany had to organise all its resources and the resources of its conquered lands to fight the war. The war became a total war. Civilians were as much part of the war as soldiers, as they worked in war industries.

2. These included many women and children, and the 7 million foreign workers who were used as forced labour. Two million prisoners of war were also used for war production.

3. Food shortages meant that food had to be rationed. Civilians suffered from Allied air raids by day and night.

4. Germany used its conquered lands:
   - the conquered people had to pay for the cost of the occupying troops
   - most exports, especially food, were sent to Germany
   - forced labour was used in local projects or sent to Germany.

5. The **Gestapo** and the **SS** were used to put down the people of Germany and the people in the occupied lands. They used shootings, torture and concentration camps.
   - There were also reprisals, such as at Lidice in Czechoslovakia and Oradour-sur-Glane in France, as revenge.

6. **The Jews**: The Nazis took over 3 million Jews in Poland and 4 million in other countries in Eastern Europe. The Jews were put in ghettoes, e.g. the Warsaw Ghetto. Special Action Groups carried out mass killings of Jews.

7. In 1942 at the **Wannsee Conference**, the extermination of Jews – the **Final Solution** – was planned.
   - Six main camps (e.g. Auschwitz) were used as extermination camps.
   - Jews from all over Europe were sent there.
   - Gas chambers were used to kill the Jews.
   - Their bodies were cremated or buried in mass graves.

8. **Resistance** to Hitler was based on national pride and the brutality of the Germans.

ANTI-SEMITISM:
Hatred and persecution of Jewish people. Nazis saw the Jews as an inferior race.

HOLOCAUST:
The slaughter of Jews by the Nazis in extermination camps during the Second World War.

RESISTANCE:
Resisting enemy troops when they have taken over a country. The Resistance was usually a secret organisation involved in surprise attacks on the occupying army.

- Communists joined the resistance after Hitler's invasion of Russia.

9. Resistance was successful in some countries, for example, Tito's partisans in Yugoslavia, and in Soviet Russia, where partisans (guerrilla fighters) cut communications and attacked German troops. But in the west, such as in France, they were mainly useful when working with the Allied troops.

10. In Germany some groups, for example the **White Rose**, offered passive resistance.
    - Some Army generals planned to kill Hitler. Count von Stauffenberg organised the **July Plot** (1944), which almost succeeded in killing Hitler. The leaders of the plot were brutally killed.

11. In the occupied countries, e.g. France, **collaborators** helped the Nazis. They helped because some French people:
    - admired the German Nazi order
    - traded with the Germans for a living
    - hated the English.

12. Hitler used collaborators for police work and recruiting.
    - Collaborators were treated severely after the war – they were killed or imprisoned; women had their heads shaved.

Collaboration and resistance in Vichy France

1. Germany invaded Belgium, Holland and France in May 1940. France was easily defeated because:
   - The Communists were opposed to a French war against Germany.
   - The right wing wanted a peace treaty with Germany.
   - Germany's blitzkrieg tactics easily defeated France and the Maginot Line was captured.

COLLABORATION:
Co-operating with the enemy when they have taken over your own country.

2. The French government retreated to Bordeaux.
   - The government signed an armistice with Germany.
   - France was divided between Occupied France, which was ruled directly by the Nazis, and Vichy France, which ruled through a French government.
   - The new French government was called the Vichy government. It was led by Marshal Pétain and Pierre Laval.

3. The Vichy government **collaborated** with Germany:
   - They rounded up Jews and deported them to Germany.
   - Hitler used Vichy France as a source of raw materials and food.
   - French workers were sent to work in German factories.
   - The Vichy government put down the French Resistance.

4. Very soon Vichy France operated directly under German control.

5. The **French Resistance movement** worked against the Germans by collecting military intelligence, sabotaging railways and organising ambushes.

   - The Resistance was made up of different groups such as Combat and the Franc-Tireurs. The French Communists joined them after Hitler invaded the Soviet Union in June 1941.

6. The French Resistance was taken over by **General de Gaulle**, leader of the Free French in London. The Resistance increased their attacks in the run-up to D-Day (Normandy landings) in June 1944 – but the Germans inflicted huge reprisals, e.g. at Oradour-sur-Glane.

7. After the war, the French Resistance took revenge on the collaborators; 9,000 were executed without trial. In order to control the situation, de Gaulle's government began the systematic punishment of collaborators. Laval was executed.

The Home Front in Britain

1. **Conscription** (compulsory enlistment in the Army) was used in Britain before the war; only those working in industries vital to the war effort were excused. Single women could be enlisted into the WRNS (navy) or the WAAF (air force).

2. Food was rationed. Ration books were given to the people; advice was given about eating healthy food, and people were encouraged to grow their own food.

3. To protect against invasion, air-raid shelters were built, road signs were removed, church bells could not be rung, windows were blacked out, and city children were evacuated to the countryside.

4. The **Home Guard** (Local Defence Volunteers) were organised for guard duty and to fight against an invasion.

5. Industry was geared to the war effort as people worked longer hours. Unemployment disappeared. Women joined the workforce to replace men at war.

6. German bombing of cities such as London, Coventry and Birmingham during the Blitz resulted in many civilian deaths. People sheltered in the Underground in London. Later in the war, London was hit by V-1s and V-2s (rockets).

7. The British government kept up morale by **propaganda**:

   - censorship controlled the bad news
   - German plane losses were exaggerated
   - **Churchill** was a good speaker on radio. He also kept up morale by meeting people in the streets and amidst the ruins of buildings.

8. Entertainment was still put on – radio and music was played and cinemas and some theatres stayed open to keep up spirits (morale).

key point

PROPAGANDA:
Spreading information to convince people of your point of view in order to achieve or retain power.

Key personalities

Vladimir Ilyich Lenin

1. **Background:** He was leader of the Bolsheviks and he planned and carried out the October Revolution (1917). Lenin made Russia the first Communist state.

2. Lenin and the Bolsheviks (Communists) held on to power through signing the Treaty of Brest-Litovsk to make peace with Germany in the First World War.

3. **The Russian Civil War**
   - Lenin led the Communists or Reds (along with Trotsky) against the Whites.
   - Lenin used the policy of **War Communism** to supply the Red Army. (Trotsky organised the Red Army.)
   - All industry and agriculture was geared to the war effort; the government controlled the larger factories. Surplus food was taken from the farmers.
   - Lenin and the Communists controlled the central area around Moscow and Petrograd.
   - They defeated various attacks by the Whites.

4. **The Red Terror**
   - Lenin organised the Red Terror to ensure Bolshevik control. He used the Cheka to put down all opposition to the Reds. The Cheka became more aggressive after the attempted assassination of Lenin by Dora Kaplan.

5. **Communist Party dictatorship**
   - Lenin established a Communist Party dictatorship during the Civil War.
   - Power was in the hands of party members, and all opposition was banned.
   - Lenin's contribution to Communist victory in the Civil War:
     – Lenin and Trotsky provided united leadership.
     – Lenin used propaganda to create fear of the return of the tsar and the landlords.
     – He also appealed to Russian nationalism against the Allied armies.

6. **The New Economic Policy (NEP)**
   - **Reasons:** Lenin brought in the New Economic Policy after the Civil War because of:
     – workers' discontent due to shortages of fuel and raw materials
     – the Kronstadt Rising – sailors revolted against the Communist Party and War Communism. Lenin and Trotsky put this down.

- **Conditions of the NEP**: Lenin put an end to food confiscation. Instead peasants (farmers) had to pay a fixed tax in kind. The peasants could sell surplus food.
- Small-scale private industry was allowed, but heavy industry was still controlled by the government.
- Lenin defended the policy as a temporary retreat from communism to ensure the survival of the Communist Party.
- **Results of NEP**: The NEP helped Lenin and the Communist Party to survive. The economy improved. The rich farmers (kulaks) and rich merchants (nepmen) prospered.

7. **Death** of Lenin:
   - Lenin suffered a series of strokes and died at 53.
   - His body lay in state for a week as thousands of mourners passed. Lenin's body was embalmed and put in a special mausoleum in Moscow.
   - Petrograd was renamed Leningrad.

8. **Cult of Lenin**: A cult of Lenin developed after his death. Stalin encouraged this to boost his own power. Lenin would not have favoured that; he led a simpler life.

9. **Assessment**
   - Lenin led the first Communist revolution and created the first Communist state.
   - He ensured the survival of Communist power in Russia after the Revolution (but Russia was still a peasant society and poor compared to the West).

10. Succession
   - Lenin was concerned about succession to the leadership of Russia after his death; in his Last Testament he was opposed to Stalin, but he failed to stop Stalin coming to power.

Joseph Stalin

1. **Background:** Stalin was a Bolshevik and a follower of Lenin. He took part in the October Revolution of 1917 which brought the Bolsheviks to power. He was involved in the Russian Civil War in defence of Tsaritsyn.

2. **Struggle for power:** There was a struggle for power between Stalin and Trotsky after Lenin's death.
   - Lenin warned against Stalin in his Last Testament.

3. **Stalin's advantages:**
   - He was General Secretary of the Communist Party, so he appointed supporters to key positions in the Communist Party.

- He used clever political tactics – he joined with two other Communist leaders, Zinoviev and Kamenev, in opposition to Trotsky, who seemed likely to succeed Lenin.
- Stalin favoured the policy of 'Socialism in One Country' – the policy of building up the Soviet Union to become a powerful modern state (against Trotsky's policy of 'permanent revolution', which favoured spreading Communism around Europe).
- Stalin turned against Zinoviev and Kamenev once Trotsky had been defeated.
- Stalin was in complete control by 1928.

4. **Stalin's dictatorship**: Stalin created a totalitarian state where the Communist Party controlled all the people and the state (press, radio and industry).

5. **Cult of Stalin**: This was an important part of his dictatorship.
   - Posters, photographs, statues of Stalin were everywhere; cities were named after him.

Five-year Plans

6. These were economic plans for the Soviet economy based on central planning.

7. **Why?** To give Stalin greater control of the Soviet Union; and to modernise Russia so that it could catch up with the West.

8. **Plans in Progress**
   - Stalin set targets for heavy industry – coal, iron, gas and electricity – in the First Five-year Plan (1928–33).
   - More consumer goods (radios, washing machines) were produced in the Second Plan (1933–38), and the railways were expanded (e.g. Moscow Underground built).
   - There was greater production of armaments in the Third Five-year Plan (1938–43) because of the possibility of war in Europe.

9. **Overall results of the Plans**
   - Stalin's Plans changed the Soviet Union from a backward, mainly agricultural country into the world's second-largest industrial power.
   - The Soviet Union was better prepared to face the German invasion in the Second World War.

10. **How did Stalin achieve his Plans?**
    - Workers faced hard work and reduced living standards.
    - The Stakhanovite movement encouraged workers to work for the state.
    - Stalin used slave labour in the labour camps (gulags).

Collectivisation

11. What was collectivisation?
    - Stalin brought in forced collectivisation. Individual farms were taken over by the government and combined into collective farms.

- Stalin wanted to increase the output of grain to feed the workers in the cities.
- There was huge resistance from the kulaks (rich peasants); food production fell and Russia experienced famine. Stalin eliminated the kulaks. He also gave small private plots to the farmers.

12. **Results of collectivisation**
    - Many people died.
    - The collectives were still inefficient.

The Purges and Show Trials

13. Why did Stalin begin the Purges?
    - In the 1930s Stalin used purges to get rid of opposition to him in the Communist Party and elsewhere. The purges began when Kirov, the leader of the Communist Party in Leningrad, was assassinated.

14. The Great Purge began with the arrest of Zinoviev and Kamenev.
    - They were tried in the first show trial in Moscow; there were two more show trials; all the old leadership was wiped out. (See *Case study: Stalin's Show Trials*, pp. 220–22.)
    - Stalin also purged the army and the secret police. Many ordinary Russians were arrested; they were put into gulags (labour camps).

15. **Results of the Purges**
    - There was no challenge to Stalin's leadership.
    - The Red Army was weakened; it suffered in the early stages of the Second World War.
    - Engineers and scientists were killed; this weakened the growth of industry.

Stalin and the Second World War

16. Stalin called the Second World War 'the Great Patriotic War'.

17. He encouraged resistance to Hitler by remaining in Moscow during the war.

18. Stalin met the Western leaders, Roosevelt and Churchill, at wartime conferences to plan their war against Hitler. He also met Truman and Attlee at the Potsdam Conference. (See *Wartime Alliances*, pp. 255–56.)

Benito Mussolini

1. Mussolini was Prime Minister of Italy from the 1920s to almost the end of the Second World War.

2. He was originally a socialist, but he became a nationalist during the First World War.

3. He founded *fascio di combattimento* (combat groups) after the First World War.

   - They opposed the growth of socialism and communism in Italy.
   - They used violence to attack socialists.

4. He formed the Fascist Party.

5. Mussolini planned the **March on Rome** to demand places in government for the Fascists.

6. He became prime minister when King Victor Emmanuel did not support the existing government.

7. After becoming prime minister, Mussolini established a **totalitarian dictatorship**.

   - He controlled the means of propaganda: press, radio and cinema.
   - He passed the Acerbo Law, which stated that the political party with the majority of votes in the next election would get two-thirds of the seats in Parliament. Mussolini ensured he won the next election.

8. **Matteoti Affair**: When the Socialist leader, Matteoti, was murdered by the Fascists, the Socialist Party left the parliament in protest; this gave Mussolini more power.

9. He developed a **cult of personality**; he became Il Duce (the Leader).

10. He set up the Corporate State to give the Fascists greater control of the economy.

11. He built *autostrada* (motorways) and drained marshes, especially the Pontine Marsh near Rome; this reduced unemployment and malaria.

12. He made the **Lateran Agreement** with the Pope, which ended a dispute of 50 years between the Italian government and the Vatican. Mussolini and the Pope agreed that:

    - The Pope recognised the Italian state and Italy recognised the Vatican state.
    - Italy paid compensation for taking Rome from the Pope in 1870.
    - The Catholic religion was recognised as the sole religion of the state.

13. In foreign policy, Mussolini had some early successes; he regained Fiume for Italy, and he held on to Corfu until Greece agreed to pay 50 million lira to settle a dispute.

14. But he wanted to be seen as a man of peace in the 1920s, so he signed the Locarno Pact and the Kellogg–Briand Pact.

15. In the 1930s he wanted to expand Italy:
  - He attacked and defeated Abyssinia.
  - He helped Franco in the Spanish Civil War.

16. **Relations with Hitler**: He stopped Hitler from gaining Austria at first; then, when Hitler supported him over Abyssinia and both helped Franco, he made the Rome–Berlin Axis.
  - Later he agreed the Pact of Steel, committing Italy to joining the war with Hitler.

17. **Second World War**: When the war started, Mussolini stayed out of it because he knew the Italian Army was weak. He joined only when Hitler had conquered France.
  - The Italian Army performed badly; it was defeated in North Africa; Italy was invaded by the American and British armies.

18. Mussolini was deposed as leader by King Victor Emmanuel and held in a mountain fortress; he was rescued by Hitler's commandos. He set up the Salo Republic in northern Italy. Italian partisans (guerrilla fighters) captured and shot him.

Adolf Hitler

1. Adolf Hitler was born in Austria. He developed a hatred of the Jews, communists and democracy while living in Vienna. He served in the German Army during the First World War.

2. After the war, he joined the German Workers' Party in Munich. He became leader and changed its name to the National Socialist German Workers' Party (Nazi Party). The party's Twenty-five Point programme emphasised anti-Semitism, extreme nationalism, racial superiority and leadership.

3. Hitler organised the **Munich Putsch** to take over the Weimar Republic. The Putsch failed miserably and Hitler was jailed. In jail, he dictated *Mein Kampf* (*My Struggle*). Here he outlined his ideas about Germany, propaganda, the Jews and the communists.

4. He reorganised the Nazi Party after coming out of jail. But the Party was still small until the Great Depression affected Germany. Unemployment rose to 6 million and the popularity of Hitler and the Nazi Party increased.

5. Hitler's Party became the largest in the Reichstag. Hitler was invited to become chancellor by President Hindenburg in January 1933.

6. Hitler established a **totalitarian state** which controlled all aspects of life in Germany by using the Enabling Act, controlling propaganda, developing a cult of personality (Der Führer) and controlling the economy. He also tried to control the churches – he had more success with the Protestant Churches than with the Catholic Church.

7. He put down opposition in his own organisation by using the SS to kill Röhm and the leadership of the SA in the **Night of the Long Knives.**

8. Hitler treated the Jews cruelly by bringing in the Nuremberg Laws and supporting *Kristallnacht* (the Night of Broken Glass). During the Second World War he organised the Final Solution to exterminate the Jews.

9. Hitler had an aggressive **foreign policy.** He broke the Treaty of Versailles through rearmament, remilitarising the Rhineland, joining with Austria (*Anschluss*) and taking over the Sudetenland after the Munich Conference. Then he took over the rest of Czechoslovakia and demanded the Polish Corridor. This caused the Second World War.

10. In the Second World War he conquered Poland, Norway and Denmark. He invaded Holland and Belgium and conquered France. He invaded Russia with Operation Barbarossa.

11. By 1941 he controlled most of the continent of Europe.

12. But Hitler experienced defeat in the Battle of Britain, in North Africa and in Russia at the Battle of Stalingrad.

13. The Russians advanced from the east and the Allies invaded the Normandy beaches on D-Day.

14. Hitler and his close associates, such as Goebbels, retreated to a bunker in Berlin. He committed suicide along with his wife, Eva Braun, rather than be captured and shown off in a cage by the Russians.

Joseph Goebbels

1. Joseph Goebbels had a crippled foot and a permanent limp. He was educated in philosophy, history and literature at various German universities.

2. He joined the Nazi Party in 1922. He **admired** Adolf Hitler; 'Adolf Hitler, I love you,' he wrote in his diary. Hitler appointed him district leader of the Nazi Party in Berlin.

3. Goebbels edited his own newspaper, *Der Angriff* (*The Attack*). He spread Nazi ideas about Jews and communists. He organised public meetings and demonstrations in Berlin.

4. He was elected to the Reichstag in 1928. He was appointed **Reich Propaganda** leader of the Nazi Party; he organised Hitler's presidential election campaigns and general elections.

5. His propaganda was very important in Hitler's rise to power.

6. He was a master of propaganda techniques; he studied American advertising methods.

7. When Hitler became chancellor in 1933, Goebbels was appointed minister of propaganda; he brought all elements of German life under Nazi control – press, radio, cinema, theatre and sports. (See *How did Hitler establish dictatorship?* pp. 231–232 and Case study, The Nuremburg Rallies pp. 235–237)

8. Goebbels directed propaganda against the Jews.

9. In the **Second World War**, he used propaganda to maintain morale and fighting spirit by creating fear of communism.

10. Goebbels stayed with Hitler to the end in the underground bunker in Berlin. His wife poisoned their six children, then Goebbels shot her, and finally Goebbels shot himself – 'to end a life that will have no further value to me if I cannot spend it in the service of the Führer, and by his side'.

Leni Riefenstahl

1. Leni Riefenstahl began as a dancer in the early 1920s. Then she became an actress, director and producer of films.

2. She founded her own film company in 1931 – she wrote, directed, produced and played a leading role in *The Blue Light*.

3. She was made director and producer of making films for the Nazi Party. She made a short film on the **1933 Nuremberg Rally** called *Victory of Faith*.

4. Hitler asked her to film the 1934 Nuremberg Rally. She directed and produced *The Triumph of the Will*, a documentary on the rally. She used many film techniques– travelling shots, panoramic views – to make a **masterpiece of Nazi propaganda**. The film won many prizes in Germany and abroad.

5. The film celebrated Hitler's leadership of the Nazi organisation and the German people.

6. It showed all sides of the Nazi organisation – Hitler Youth, the German Labour Front, speeches by Hess, parades by night and day, flags, music. Hitler's speeches were the highlight. The planning for the rally was linked to the filming.

7. Hitler did not ask Goebbels before he appointed Riefenstahl, so Goebbels tried to stop the film and made every effort to pose difficulties for her.

8. Riefenstahl also made *Olympia*, a two-part documentary on the **1936 Berlin Olympics** which highlighted the Nazi organisation of the event, the role of Hitler and the excitement of the Games. This also won awards.

9. Riefenstahl claimed she was not a Nazi and she did not understand Hitler's plans. She said she was only making documentaries.

10. Riefenstahl was jailed after the Second World War. She awaited trial for her role in the Nazi propaganda machine. She denied her role and was released.

Charlie Chaplin

1. Charlie Chaplin was the greatest actor of the silent movies. But he was also a director and producer.

2. Charlie Chaplin was born in London. He played in music halls and theatres in England before establishing himself as a film star in America. He became the first actor to sign a $1 million deal.

3. He developed the character that made him famous – the little tramp. He represented the underdog who appealed to everybody.

4. He made a series of successful silent films in the 1920s – *The Kid*, *The Gold Rush* and *The Circus* – which he wrote, directed, produced and acted in. These films were released by United Artists, the company which he founded in 1919 with leading figures in Hollywood.

5. He travelled to Europe to promote his films.

6. Chaplin was slow to change from silent movies to sound. He released *City Lights* (1931) as a silent movie; despite the success of talkies after 1928, his film was a hit.

7. His **political views** caused controversy. He had a strong hatred for authoritarian governments. *City Lights* and *Modern Times* showed Chaplin's sympathy with workers and the poor against the advance of technology. Some accused him of criticising capitalism.

8. Chaplin was opposed to anti-Semitism (especially the policies of the Nazis). He visited Germany to promote *City Lights* and Nazi propaganda was critical of him.

9. His first full sound picture was *The Great Dictator* (1940). This mocked Adolf Hitler and fascism. Chaplin wanted the United States to abandon its policy of isolationism during the Second World War. During the war, he favoured opening up a second front in Europe. When Chaplin played an active role in the American Committee for Russian War Relief, his critics said he was a Communist sympathiser.

Winston Churchill

1. Winston Churchill was a British political leader who became Prime Minister during the Second World War.

2. Churchill was elected a Conservative Member of Parliament in 1924. He was Chancellor of the Exchequer from 1924 to 1929. He was not happy dealing with economic affairs. He returned Britain to the gold standard, which had bad effects on the British economy. He wanted to smash the trade unions in the General Strike of 1926.

3. He was out of office until 1939. He warned against appeasing Hitler. He advocated British rearmament. He wanted a **Grand Alliance** to be formed between Britain, France and the Soviet Union against Hitler. When the Second World War broke out in 1939, Chamberlain appointed Churchill to be in charge of the Royal Navy.

4. After Hitler's success in Poland and Norway, Churchill was appointed Prime Minister in May 1940, on the day Germany invaded France. He formed a coalition government and included many Labour Party leaders as ministers. He provided strong leadership during the Battle of Britain when Britain was standing alone against Germany. 'I have nothing to offer but blood, toil, tears and sweat.'

5. He inspired the British people to resist by making important speeches on the radio or in Parliament. He showed his qualities of courage and determination.

6. He built up a **personal relationship** with President Roosevelt of America. He benefited from the Lend-Lease Act, under which the United States gave military goods to Britain without payment.

7. He met Roosevelt in 1941 and agreed the Atlantic Charter with him. He played a very active role in developing the alliance between the United States, the USSR and Britain during the war. He travelled 40,000 miles to coordinate the efforts to defeat Hitler.

8. He was involved in all the wartime conferences at Casablanca, Teheran, Yalta and Potsdam. These took important decisions about the running of the war, and the shape of Europe after the war. (See *Wartime alliances*, pp. 255–56.)

9. He took an active part in key decisions in the war; he sent British troops to defend Egypt; he ordered the destruction of the French fleet in Algeria to stop it being taken by Germany; he opposed the opening of the second front until the defeat of Nazi Germany was certain.

10. His relationship with Roosevelt weakened in the last year of the war. Churchill feared the growth of communism in post-war Europe. He felt Roosevelt did not support him in the conferences at Teheran and Yalta to contain Soviet expansion after the war.

11. After the defeat of Germany, Churchill's Conservative Party was defeated in the general election by the Labour Party. Churchill was very disappointed. He began the writing of his six-volume history of the Second World War, which ensured his part in the war was highlighted.

Bing Crosby

1. Born in Washington State, Crosby went to California to become a singer in the mid-1920s.

2. He was successful as a singer, a recording artist, and a radio and film star. He benefited from the invention of the microphone and the recording tape for radio shows.

3. He was the **most successful recording artist** of the twentieth century. His crooning style and his wide range of songs from ballads to jazz made him popular.

4. His hits included 'Brother Can You Spare a Dime?', 'Red Sails in the Sunset', 'Alexander's Ragtime Band' and dozens more.

5. His biggest hit was 'White Christmas' (1942).

6. He had a **radio show** which he used to promote his records. He sang live on sponsored radio programmes.

7. Crosby became popular in Britain in the 1930s through his recordings and broadcasts on the BBC.

8. In films, he was a top box-office attraction in the 1930s and 1940s, in comedies and musicals. These included *Pennies from Heaven*, *Paris Honeymoon* and *Holiday Inn*.

9. Crosby won an Oscar Award for Best Actor in 1944 for his portrayal of Father O'Malley in the film *Going My Way*.

10. He was successful in the *'Road'* movies with Bob Hope.

11. During the Second World War, he entertained at military camps and promoted US government war bonds. He also broadcast to troops. After the war, he was voted the person who had done the most for soldiers' morale.

J.M. Keynes

1. J.M. Keynes worked as a civil servant, taught economics in Cambridge University and wrote many books and articles.

2. Keynes is best known for his economic ideas.

3. He was economic adviser to David Lloyd George, British Prime Minister, at the Paris Peace Conference. He warned about the effects of the Treaty of Versailles on Germany in his book, *The Economic Consequences of the Peace*. His views about the impact of reparations on Germany were correct.

4. Keynes opposed Britain's return to the gold standard in the 1920s. He also believed that the British government should help depressed areas.

5. He was brought up in the economic thinking of the time, which said that governments should not intervene in the economy. Governments should also balance their budgets.

6. The influence of the Great Depression undermined this thinking, which could not explain what was happening.

7. Keynes wrote his book *The General Theory of Employment, Interest and Money* (1936) to explain what was happening in the economy. Keynes said governments should borrow money for public works. Also, governments should lower interest rates.

8. These ideas began the **Keynesian Revolution** in economics and influenced governments, especially after the Second World War.

9. His ideas and the Beveridge Report (1942) laid the foundations for the Welfare State in Britain after the war.

10. During the Second World War, Keynes wrote *How to Pay for the War*. In this, he promoted the idea of compulsory saving and rationing to prevent inflation. His ideas were adopted in 1941.

11. In 1944, Keynes led the British delegation to the international conference in Bretton Woods in the United States where the details of the post-war currency system were worked out. The American 'White Plan', rather than the Keynes Plan, was accepted.

Key concepts

Anti-Semitism: Hatred and persecution of Jewish people. Nazis saw the Jews as an inferior race.

Blitzkrieg: The German lightning tactics during the Second World War, which used planes, tanks and fast-moving infantry to defeat the enemy.

Collaboration: Co-operating with the enemy when they have taken over your own country.

Collectivisation: The policy of Stalin's government in the Soviet Union to force peasants (farmers) to give up their farms to the government and to form large collective farms.

Communism: Communists believed in government control of agriculture and industry.

Cult of personality: Worship of a leader. Propaganda is used to create an image of the leader as all-wise and all-powerful.

Depression: When an economy is doing badly, factories close and unemployment increases.

Dictatorship: Rule by one person or party, using propaganda and the secret police.

Fascism: Fascists believed in nationalism, dictatorship, racism and the use of violence. They were opposed to democracy and communism.

Herrenvolk: The Nazi idea of the Germans as a master race, superior to all other races.

Holocaust: The slaughter of Jews by the Nazis in extermination camps during the Second World War.

Inflation: An increase in the prices of products, usually a large increase.

Lebensraum: Hitler wanted additional land or territory in Eastern Europe to make Germany self-sufficient in food and raw materials.

Propaganda: Spreading information to convince people of your point of view in order to achieve or retain power.

Protectionism: Using tariffs (taxes) to protect home industry and employment from foreign competition.

Reichskirche: Hitler's plan to unite all Protestant Churches in one German national church, called the Reichskirche.

Resistance: Resisting enemy troops when they have taken over a country. The Resistance was usually a secret organisation involved in surprise attacks on the occupying army.

Totalitarianism: Totalitarian governments control all aspects of life, from the people's actions to their thoughts.

5 The United States and the World, 1945–89

1. US foreign policy

aims In this section, you should understand:

- The development of US foreign policy
- Berlin, Korea, Cuba, Vietnam
- The role of President Truman (See Key personality, p. 298)
- The role of President Johnson (See Key personality, p. 300)
- Case study: Lyndon Johnson and Vietnam, 1963–68

US foreign policy and the Cold War

> **exam Q**
> - How important was Truman's and Johnson's contribution to US foreign policy?
> - Which had the greater impact on the United States: involvement in Korea or involvement in Vietnam? Argue your case referring to both.

1. President Truman was in office for the last months of the Second World War. He met Stalin, the Soviet leader, at Potsdam, where he warned Japan to surrender. When Japan did not surrender, Truman gave orders to drop atomic bombs on Hiroshima and Nagasaki.
   - He wanted to put an end to the war, and to save American and Japanese lives that would be lost in an invasion.

2. The dropping of the atomic bomb and the development of the USSR's atomic bomb led to an arms race in the Cold War.
   - This was supported by a **policy of deterrence**, to maintain a strong nuclear force so that the Soviet Union would be deterred from attacking the US.

3. Truman did not trust the Soviet Union. He believed the US should not appease (give in to) Russia in the way that Hitler had been appeased before the Second World War. The growth of a Soviet-controlled Eastern Europe was seen as the spread of Communist domination.

4. **Development of the policy of containment.**
   - George **Kennan's Long Telegram** said the Soviet Union was going to expand, and the only way to stop it was by adopting a policy of containment.
   - Winston Churchill said in a speech that 'an iron curtain' was descending across Europe and he called for firmness against the Soviet Union.

5. Truman introduced the **Truman Doctrine** to help Greece and Turkey to resist the spread of Communism. He wanted the US to help 'free peoples' to resist

Communism. He also introduced the **Marshall Plan** (European Recovery Programme) to help the economic recovery of Western Europe and assist it to stand up against Communism.

Internationalism

6. Truman's new policies showed the US was not going to follow a policy of isolationism (cutting itself off from Europe). Instead it was prepared to follow a policy of **internationalism** – that the US would become involved with other countries. His policies heightened tension with the Soviet Union and worsened the Cold War.

US foreign policy	
1945	Beginning of the atomic age
Late 1940s	Development of US policy of containment
1946	Churchill's Iron Curtain speech
	Truman Doctrine
	Marshall Plan
1948–49	Berlin Blockade and Airlift
1950–53	Korean War
1960	Bay of Pigs invasion, Cuba
1961	Building of Berlin Wall
1962	Cuban Missile Crisis
1964	Gulf of Tonkin incident and Gulf of Tonkin resolution
1965	Operation Rolling Thunder and increased US involvement in Vietnam
1968	Tet Offensive
	Johnson began peace negotiations
	Johnson decided not to seek re-election
1972	Nixon's visit to China and the Soviet Union; development of a policy of détente; SALT I
1973	US withdrawal from Vietnam
1975	Helsinki Agreement
1979	SALT II
1983	Reagan announced Star Wars programme
1987	Intermediate-Range Nuclear Forces Treaty
1991	Downfall of Communism in the Soviet Union

7. **US policy and Berlin:** The US, USSR and Britain agreed to divide Germany into four zones after the Second World War. But the US and Britain believed that the economic recovery of Germany was necessary for the wider economic recovery of Europe. They also wanted a strong Germany to be a barrier against Communism. Stalin, the Soviet leader, feared that a prosperous West Germany would undermine Communism in East Germany.

8. When the US and Britain introduced a new currency, the Deutschmark, Stalin blockaded West Berlin. Truman did not want to be forced out of West Berlin; it would be a victory for Communism and a defeat for the policy of containment.

9. The US and its allies organised a huge airlift of food and supplies to West Berlin in **Operation Vittles**. When they refused to give in, Stalin lifted the blockade after ten months (May 1949).
   - The policy of containment had worked.
   - The US, Canada and ten Western European countries set up NATO (North Atlantic Treaty Organization) to strengthen themselves militarily; it was the first peacetime military alliance by the US.

10. **More conflict in Berlin**: In the 1950s, West Germany and West Berlin were prosperous. Almost 3 million immigrants left East Berlin to go to the West for jobs. This affected the East German economy, which lost skilled labour.
    - Khrushchev, the Soviet leader, met the young president of the US, Kennedy, in Vienna. He demanded that the US withdraw from Berlin. Kennedy called up US reserves.
    - The Soviet Union and East Germany built a high wall between East and West Berlin. The US protested, but did nothing.
    - The Berlin Wall eased tensions between the two sides because it stopped the flow of immigrants. But now the Wall could be used as propaganda against Soviet communism. President Kennedy visited West Berlin and made a famous speech there in support of the city.

11. **US policy and Korea:** After the Second World War, Korea was divided between a Communist-backed North Korea and a US-backed South Korea. Communist-controlled North Korea invaded South Korea.
    - Truman intervened to maintain his policy of containment, because South Korea had suffered an unprovoked attack.
    - He committed US troops in the name of the United Nations. US forces, led by General MacArthur, and troops from twelve other countries pushed back the North Koreans. But the Chinese then invaded to help them.
    - The fighting eventually stopped and peace was agreed between two new leaders – President Eisenhower of the US and Khrushchev of the Soviet Union.

12. The US signed treaties with Asian countries. The US formed **SEATO** (South East Asian Treaty Organization) to contain Communism.

- The US brought West Germany into NATO to strengthen the defence of Western Europe.

13. **Eisenhower** followed the policy of containment. He also believed in the **Domino Theory** – that if one country fell to Communism, other countries would do so also.

   - He also followed a policy of deterrence against the Soviet Union (having nuclear weapons would prevent the USSR from attacking).

   - Later he followed a policy of peaceful coexistence (both sides to get along peacefully) with the Soviet leader, Khrushchev.

14. **US policy and Cuba:** tension arose between the US and USSR in the early 1960s because:

   - An American U2 spy plane was shot down over the USSR.

   - The Berlin Wall was built.

   - John F. Kennedy, the new President of the US, said a missile gap had opened between the USSR and the US.

   - Fidel Castro led a Communist revolution in Cuba.

   - President Kennedy made some anti-Communist speeches.

   - Kennedy believed in being firm and decisive against Communism. He backed an invasion of the Bay of Pigs in Cuba, but it failed.

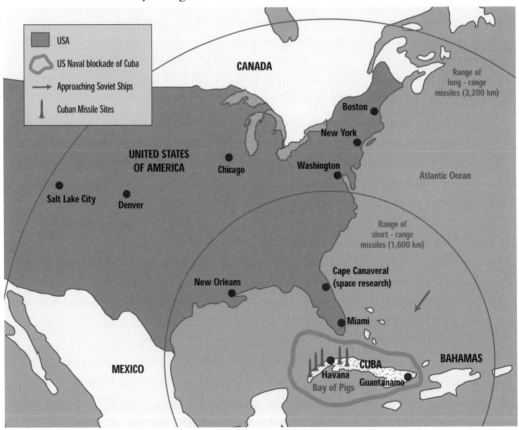

15. **The Cuban Missile Crisis:** The Soviet Union began building missile bases in Cuba that were within range of many US cities. U2 spy planes photographed these.
    - President Kennedy decided against an invasion of Cuba or air strikes. Instead, he blockaded Cuba to prevent future Soviet ships from reaching the island.
16. The US and USSR were on the brink of nuclear war.
    - Kennedy agreed not to invade Cuba and to call off the blockade.
    - Khrushchev and the USSR agreed to dismantle the missile bases.
17. This led to the setting up of a hotline (direct telephone link) between the US and USSR leaders to improve communications. They also agreed the Partial Test Ban Treaty (1963), which banned nuclear testing in the air, in space or under water.

> Why did the United States become involved in armed conflict in Vietnam and why did it eventually withdraw from that country?

18. **US policy and Vietnam:** The US became gradually involved in Vietnam.
    - Truman supported the French colonial empire in Indochina (Vietnam, Cambodia and Laos) against the Communist-backed Ho Chi Minh and the Viet Minh, a Vietnamese independence movement.
    - Eisenhower sent military advisors in support of the government of South Vietnam against the Vietcong (South Vietnamese communists).
19. The US increased their support following their policies of containment and their belief in the Domino Theory.
20. Kennedy provided a large increase in military advisors to train the South Vietnamese Army.

Case study: Lyndon Johnson and Vietnam, 1963–68

1. President Johnson followed the policies of his predecessors by increasing the number of military advisors in Vietnam.

> Why did Johnson increase US involvement in Vietnam and why did he begin the process of US withdrawal?

   - He believed US credibility was at stake.
   - His advisors believed in a military solution to the problem.
   - Johnson did not want to be 'the first president to lose a war'.

2. In the 1964 presidential election, he campaigned as a candidate of peace; but he soon realised that either he would have to withdraw from Vietnam or commit large numbers of troops to the war.

> **exam focus**
>
> Ordinary-level students should concentrate on the Case studies and the main Key personalities. Note also some important paragraphs which appeared in past exams.

3. Johnson used the clash between US Navy ships and North Vietnamese boats in the Gulf of Tonkin to increase US involvement in the war. Congress passed the Gulf of Tonkin Resolution, which gave Johnson almost unlimited power to wage war against the Vietcong and against North Vietnam.

4. Johnson authorised **Operation Rolling Thunder**. This operation launched massive air assaults on North Vietnam. He also built up US ground forces – there were half a million soldiers there by the end of 1967.

5. Johnson and the North Vietnamese government each rejected the other's proposals for negotiations.

6. The fighting continued and became more intense. The US used:
   - search-and-destroy missions
   - air bombardments using napalm (jellied explosives)
   - chemicals (defoliants)
   - free-fire zones

7. Johnson took a close interest in the operation of the war.

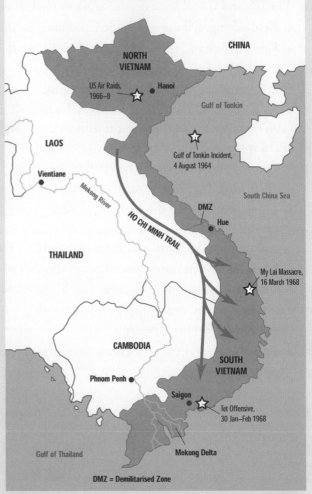

8. He claimed that the aerial bombings were aimed at military targets. He also claimed the US was winning the war. He had popular support for his handling of the war. (See *The anti-war movement and US foreign policy* pp. 283–84)

9. But the anti-war movement began in the US and gradually gained support as the **media** increased their reports from Vietnam.

10. The Vietcong and the North Vietnamese launched a surprise offensive in early 1968. This was called the **Tet Offensive**. It undermined Johnson's claim that the US was winning the war.

11. Johnson had to change his policy because:
    - it was taking away resources from his Great Society programme in the fight against poverty;

- the American people did not want to expand the war;
- the anti-war movement was growing.

12. Johnson's response was to:
- call a partial halt to the bombing of North Vietnam;
- withdraw from the presidential election race;
- begin talks in Paris with the North Vietnamese;
- put a halt to all bombing in North Vietnam just before he left office in January 1969.

13. Johnson's involvement in the war in Vietnam:
- illustrated the role of the US president in shaping US foreign policy;
- influenced Johnson's efforts to build a Great Society;
- caused great divisions in US society.

21. **Withdrawal from Vietnam**: President Nixon wanted to end US involvement in Vietnam because:
- opposition to the war was growing
- the costs of the war were increasing
- the US could not defeat the enemy
- he wanted to improve relations with Communist China.

22. Nixon began a policy of **Vietnamisation** to strengthen the South Vietnamese Army to take a greater part in the war.
- He also increased aerial bombing of North Vietnam.
- He secretly ordered the invasion of Cambodia to destroy Vietcong weapons dumps.

23. The US invasion of Cambodia led to a rebellion in Congress.
- Congress repealed the Gulf of Tonkin Resolution and passed the **War Powers Act** to control the president's use of troops.

24. The US and North Vietnam signed a **peace treaty** in Paris in January 1973. They agreed that:
- the US would withdraw from South Vietnam
- all prisoners of war would be released
- there would be further negotiations to decide the future of North and South Vietnam.

25. The US gave aid to South Vietnam after it withdrew in 1973. But North Vietnam attacked again and united North and South Vietnam under Communist leadership.

26. **Results of the Vietnam War**
- 58,000 US soldiers were killed and 180,000 injured.
- The war cost $150 billion, and it weakened the US economy.

- The policy of containment failed.
- America's image suffered because of incidents such as the My Lai massacre.
- There was great division in US society.
- The power of the US president was reduced.

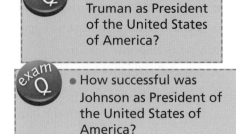

- How successful was Truman as President of the United States of America?

- How successful was Johnson as President of the United States of America?

For the **Truman presidency:** See Key personality: *Harry Truman*, pp. 298–99.

For the **Johnson presidency:** President Johnson took office after the assassination of President Kennedy. See Key personality: *Lyndon Johnson*, pp. 300–301

2. Domestic factors in US foreign policy

aims In this section, you should understand:
- How US foreign policy was influenced by McCarthyism, the anti-war movement and race relations
- The role of Joe McCarthy (See Key personality, pp. 301–2).

exam focus

When the question asks for **'and/or'**, you will not lose marks if you only answer one part, e.g. 'McCarthyism' or 'anti-war movement' in the question above. When the question says **'and'** or **'both'**, you will lose marks if you do not refer to both parts.

How did McCarthyism and/or the anti-war movement affect US foreign policy, 1945–72?

McCarthyism (and the Red Scare) and US foreign policy

1. McCarthyism was part of the **'Red Scare'**, which was a form of anti-Communist hysteria. McCarthyism was a witch hunt of federal and state government employees.

2. Senator Joe McCarthy said the US was in trouble in the Cold War because of traitors in the US government. He claimed to have a list of over 200 State Department employees who were Communists. He was chairman of the Committee on Government Operations. He began hearings on Communist infiltrations of the federal government.

3. McCarthyism heightened the **fear of Communism**.
   - It made the Cold War more extreme by leading Americans to believe that many events were part of a worldwide Communist conspiracy.
   - It reinforced the view that anti-Communism should be the main aim of US foreign policy.

- Many very able federal employees lost their jobs, especially in the State Department, which dealt with foreign affairs.
- McCarthyism damaged America's reputation (image) abroad, especially in Europe, because it was seen as undemocratic.
- McCarthy's reputation was destroyed when he held the Army-McCarthy hearings into his accusations that the US army was harbouring communists.

But '**McCarthyism**' – suspicion of communists everywhere – continued in the US.

The anti-war movement and US foreign policy

1. The anti-war movement began amongst university students. These were members of the **Students for a Democratic Society** (SDS).
2. They were opposed to the Vietnam War because:
   - They did not want the war to take away money from President Johnson's Great Society programme.
   - They saw the Vietnam War as a civil war.
   - Television pictures showed aspects of the war – such as saturation bombing – which they did not like.
   - They did not want to see the US defeated, but wanted a divided Vietnam with two governments.
3. They organised demonstrations and protest marches. One of the largest was when 300,000 people marched past the White House in 1969, each carrying the name of a dead soldier or a destroyed Vietnamese village.
4. Initially, the anti-war movement had little support. But gradually the huge cost of the war, and the greater number of soldiers fighting and dying, increased support for the anti-war movement.
5. The **Tet Offensive** in early 1968 undermined Americans' credibility in what their government was telling them about winning the war.
6. There was increasing violence and clashes at protests between demonstrators and police.
7. They were joined by senior politicians, such as Senators Eugene McCarthy and Robert Kennedy, who began campaigning for the presidency. The media also felt deceived, so many questioned the war.
8. The anti-war movement forced President Johnson to change his policies on Vietnam; he called a partial halt to the bombings of North Vietnam and began talks in Paris with the North Vietnamese.
9. President Nixon ordered a US invasion of Cambodia; this led to the deaths of four students in a protest at Kent State University.
   - The anti-war movement gained widespread public sympathy when news of the My Lai massacre was made public.

- The Pentagon Papers showed that the US government had deceived the people about the war.
- The anti-war movement undermined the US's will to fight; it contributed to the eventual peace.

Race relations and US foreign policy

1. US presidents were concerned about the image that bad race relations gave the US abroad.

> You can include reference to Muhammad Ali and Vietnam here.

- Truman and Eisenhower desegregated the US armed forces.
- Kennedy was worried that clashes in Alabama between black Americans and the police would undermine the US claim to lead the Free World against Communism.

2. Reaction of black Americans:

- As many black Americans enlisted in the **Vietnam War** as did white; but a higher proportion of black Americans were killed in the war. This turned some black Americans against the war.
- Black political leaders, including Martin Luther King, were against the Vietnam War because they feared it would take money needed for social and economic improvements for black Americans under President Johnson's 'Great Society' plan.
- Muhammad Ali was a member of the Black Muslims and he refused to be drafted into the US army on grounds of conscience.
- Black Americans were now more opposed to the war than white Americans. They were also less willing to serve in the war than before.

3. Decline of Cold War certainties

In this section, you should understand:
- How and why the US withdrew from Vietnam
- Cold War relations – détente, SALT and Star Wars

Nixon and Vietnam

> What were the significant developments in US foreign policy, 1973–89?

1. Nixon began a policy of **Vietnamisation** – to strengthen the South Vietnamese Army to enable it to take a greater part in the war.

- He also increased aerial bombing of North Vietnam.
- He secretly ordered the invasion of Cambodia in order to destroy Vietcong weapons dumps.

2. The invasion of Cambodia led to a rebellion in Congress.

- Congress repealed the Gulf of Tonkin Resolution and passed the War Powers Act to control the president's use of troops.

3. The US and North Vietnam signed a peace treaty in Paris in January 1973. They agreed that:
   - the US would withdraw from South Vietnam
   - all prisoners of war would be released
   - there would be further negotiations to decide the future of North and South Vietnam.

4. The US gave aid to South Vietnam after it withdrew in 1973; but North Vietnam attacked again and united North and South Vietnam under Communist leadership.

Nixon and détente

1. President Nixon developed his foreign policy with his adviser, Henry Kissinger, who later became Secretary of State.

2. Nixon believed in the policy of containment, but he also wanted to follow a policy of détente – developing friendly relations with the Soviet Union and Communist China. He hoped détente would ease relations so that he could cut military spending.

3. Nixon and Kissinger set up secret channels of communication. They organised Nixon's visit to China in 1972, which caught many people by surprise because Nixon had wanted to isolate Communist China since 1949.

4. Aims of Nixon's visit to China:
   - Nixon desired to:
     - improve relations with China
     - put pressure on the North Vietnamese in peace negotiations
     - play off Communist China against the USSR
     - gain popularity for the presidential election in the US.
   - Nixon achieved his aims.

5. Nixon then went to Moscow and met Brezhnev, the Soviet leader. They agreed on **SALT I** (Strategic Arms Limitation Treaty), which put a limit on the use of nuclear missiles. They also agreed to work together for peaceful coexistence.

6. The policy of détente was put under pressure by the Arab–Israeli War in 1973; but there was eventual agreement.
   - Also, Nixon behaved like a Cold War warrior by using the CIA to undermine the newly elected Socialist president of Chile, Allende. Allende was overthrown and assassinated.

7. Gerald Ford continued the policy of détente, advised by Henry Kissinger as Secretary of State. Ford met Brezhnev and, along with thirty-nine other countries, they reached the **Helsinki Agreement** of 1975:
   - to respect each other's borders, especially in Europe
   - to allow freedom of travel
   - to develop cultural links
   - to respect human rights.

8. Carter also followed a policy of détente, but it was to be based on moral principles of right and wrong. This put pressure on détente.

- Carter wanted to reduce arms, but was critical of the USSR over its treatment of dissidents (political protestors).
- He did not involve the Soviet Union in the peace agreement between Egypt and Israel.
- He refused to ratify SALT II (limiting missiles and bombs) when the USSR invaded Afghanistan.
- Carter suspended grain sales and boycotted the Olympic Games in Moscow (1980).
- This brought about the end of the policy of détente.

9. Tensions continued in the 1980s under President Reagan:

- He called the Soviet Union 'the evil empire' and began a huge build-up of arms.
- Mistrust between the two sides led to the failure of the Strategic Arms Reduction Talks (START).
- But Reagan wanted to use the arms race to force the Soviet Union to agree to arms reduction because they could not afford to compete.
- Reagan announced the Strategic Defence Initiative (SDI; popularly called 'Star Wars') – a defence shield to destroy incoming missiles.

10. Reagan and the new Soviet leader, Gorbachev, got on well together when they met in Geneva and then in Reykjavik.

- They agreed on the Intermediate-Range Nuclear Forces Treaty, which led to the dismantling of missiles in Europe.

11. Reagan visited Moscow in 1988, which led to a further improvement in relations.

12. Gorbachev's reforms in the Soviet Union led to the downfall of the Soviet Empire in Eastern Europe and the collapse of Communism in Russia in 1991.

- The US **policy of containment** contributed to the downfall, because the Soviet Union could not afford the huge amount of spending on arms required to keep up with the US.
- The policy also avoided war with the Soviet Union and discouraged a Soviet invasion of Western Europe.

13. **Critics of containment** said it led to unnecessary spending on arms. It also led to the development of a nuclear arsenal, which was now a danger to the environment.

4. Troubled affluence

In this section, you should understand:

- How racial conflict, urban poverty and drugs and crime affected US society and economy
- How Black Americans and other minorities won their civil rights
- The role of Marin Luther King (See Key personality, pp. 302–3)
- Case study: the Montgomery Bus Boycott, 1955–56

US Civil Rights	
1948	● Truman's Executive Order
1954	● *Brown v. Board of Education*
1955	● Emmett Till murdered
1955–56	● Montgomery Bus Boycott
1957	● Southern Christian Leadership Conference founded by Martin Luther King
	● Central High School, Little Rock, Arkansas
1960	● Lunch counter protests
1961	● Freedom Rides
1962	● James Meredith and the University of Mississippi
1963	● Protestors attacked by police in Birmingham, Alabama
	● Martin Luther King's 'I have a dream' speech
1964	● Civil Rights Act
1965	● Selma to Montgomery March
	● Voting Rights Act
	● Watts Riots
1968	● Martin Luther King assassinated

key point

Discrimination

exam Q

During the period, 1945–89, what was the impact of one or more of the following on American society: racial conflict; urban poverty; organised crime?

Racial conflict

1. The southern states of the US used '**Jim Crow**' laws to segregate blacks and whites.
   - Black Americans were also banned from voting.
   - The white supremacist organisation, the **Ku Klux Klan**, attacked blacks.
2. After the Second World War conditions for Black Americans changed.
3. **Factors** which brought about change for Black Americans included:
   - Black people migrated to cities and became easier to organise;
   - A new, educated black leadership emerged in the 1940s and 1950s;
   - Some of the leaders were Christian ministers, because Black Americans depended heavily on Christian churches.
   - Black Americans who returned from the Second World War had higher expectations for civil and political rights. Many had fought in the armed forces or worked in war industries for freedom and democracy.
   - Liberal whites wanted to give blacks more rights.
   - During the Cold War the US wanted to be seen as leader of the Free World, so it couldn't be seen to discriminate against black people.
   - The mass media (especially newspapers and television) showed how black people were being treated, especially in the southern states.

- How significant was the role of Martin Luther King in the civil rights movement?
- How successful was civil rights agitation in the United States during the period, 1945–68?

   - Black Americans organised themselves through the NAACP (National Association for the Advancement of Colored People) and CORE (the Congress of Racial Equality) to fight against discrimination.
4. **Desegregation**
   - **The Army**: President Truman desegregated the armed forces with an Executive Order in 1948.
   - **Education**: This battle was fought mainly through taking test cases to the Supreme Court. Chief Justice Earl Warren issued many decisions that opened up education to Black Americans.
   - *Brown v. Board of Education* (of Topeka, Kansas): The result declared that state laws that required public school segregation were unconstitutional.
   - In many southern states there was white resistance to integrated education (mixing people of different colours). White citizens' councils, state governors and the Ku Klux Klan led the resistance.
   - In **Central High School, Little Rock, Arkansas**, nine black students were prevented by National Guardsmen from entering the school. President Eisenhower had to send federal troops to protect the students from an angry mob.

- **Bussing**: Black and white students were bussed across cities to achieve racial balance in public schools. There was widespread resistance amongst white people, and even after many years of bussing there were many schools where desegregation did not work. This was caused by white, middle-class families sending their children to white private schools.
- **University of Mississippi**: James Meredith had to have federal marshals and troops to protect him from white mobs when he attended the previously all-white University of Mississippi.
- **Non-violent protest**: Non-violent protest became an important part of the methods used to challenge segregation.
- Black Americans boycotted the Montgomery, Alabama, bus system when Rosa Parks was arrested for refusing to give up her seat to a white man. (See Case study: The Montgomery Bus Boycott, 1955–56, pp. 291–9)
- Black students used it in the **lunch-counter protests** to end the existence of whites-only lunch counters.
- **Freedom Riders:** Black and white students took interstate buses to force the federal government to enforce desegregation in those buses.
- **Martin Luther King** led schoolchildren as demonstrators in Birmingham, Alabama. A white backlash led by police chief Eugene 'Bull' Connor and his men, when they used dogs and water cannon, was featured on television.
- Martin Luther King made his famous **'I have a dream' speech** in Washington, DC.
- State troopers attacked marchers from **Selma to Montgomery** who protested about their lack of voting rights. President Johnson sent federal troops to protect the marchers, now led by Martin Luther King. The success of the march led to the **Voting Rights Act (1965)** which banned literacy tests for voter registration and gave the federal government control of voting rights.

5. The civil rights movement was **weakened**:
   - Martin Luther King was assassinated in Memphis in 1968. This led to widespread rioting.
   - Malcolm X supported the use of violence and Black Nationalism. He advocated Black Power and the development of a separate black identity.
   - There were race riots in many cities, such as Los Angeles, Detroit and Newark.

6. **The federal government and civil rights**: The federal government played a vital role in bringing civil rights to Black Americans:
   - Truman and Eisenhower ended segregation in the armed forces.
   - The Civil Rights Act (1964) outlawed discrimination in public places, including restaurants, stadiums and cinemas.
   - The Voting Rights Act (1965) banned literacy tests for voter registration.
   - Affirmative Action – companies on federal contracts had to provide jobs for minorities.

7. **Impact on Black Americans:**
   - A new black leadership was created in sport, films, politics and music.
   - A new, black middle class was created.
   - More Black Americans were elected to the House of Representatives and the Senate.
   - But many black people still experienced poverty.
8. **Chicanos** (Mexican-Americans) were used illegally as farm labourers in California and Florida. Led by César Chávez, they used non-violent methods, e.g. boycotting, to get better conditions.
9. **Native Americans** suffered from bad education, poor housing, illness and high death rates. The American Indian Movement (AIM) got the Indian Self-Determination Act passed, which gave Indians control of their reservations.

Urban poverty

1. Michael Harrington's book *The Other America* showed how about 40 million (25 per cent) people were below the poverty line. Much of this was urban poverty.
2. The **causes** of urban poverty were:
   - the movement of Black Americans from the South to northern cities for work; when manufacturing industry declined, they lost their jobs;
   - the movement of White Americans to the suburbs; the city centres became black ghettos – places of high unemployment, poverty, bad housing and poor educational levels;
   - the cities lost tax revenue, so they were in financial trouble and unable to maintain streets and schools;
   - public-housing projects in cities consisted of high-rise apartments and were mainly occupied by poorer people;
3. **Government policies** tried to combat poverty:
   - Presidents Truman and Eisenhower set a minimum wage.
   - President Kennedy provided money for school and job-based training.
   - President Johnson began a war on poverty as part of his 'Great Society' programme. He set up:
     - Head Start (where children went to pre-school classes)
     - the Job Corps (to provide skills for inner-city youth)
     - Medicare for the elderly and Medicaid for poorer welfare recipients
   - The number of people below the poverty line fell from 40 million to 25 million.
4. **Watts Riots and other urban riots** – these began in the Watts district of Los Angeles and spread to other cities, such as Chicago, Cleveland, San Francisco, Detroit and Newark (New Jersey) between 1965 and 1968.
5. These **riots** were caused by:
   - the concentration of poverty and unemployment in these areas;

- the remaining barriers to improvement – rising expectations of a better life now that civil and political rights were largely won;
- the message of radical leaders such as Malcolm X, who preached Black Power with violence;
- tension between black youths and police (who were often white);
- the influence of television, which spread a general discontent.

Drugs and crime

1. The causes of crime in the US were:
   - poverty, unemployment and slum conditions
   - the wide availability of guns
   - drug addiction and the cost of drugs
   - a shortage of police.
2. Crime levels jumped rapidly in the 1960s.
   - The US had the highest rates of murders, rapes and robberies in the world.
3. Crime was mostly in **cities**. 30 per cent of all reported crimes in America took place in the six largest cities.
   - Criminals were mostly young, male, poor and black.
   - Criminals had become younger by the 1980s.
   - Most crime was committed by a small percentage of people.
4. Much crime became drug-related in the 1970s. Drug trafficking was operated by organised crime. Various gangs operated, whether Mafia, Jamaican, Puerto Rican or Mexican.
   - Drugs were linked to other problems – drug addicts stole to pay for their drugs; half of US murders were drug-related; AIDS spread partly owing to dirty needles used to take drugs.
5. The spread of crime caused fear; it also led to racial tensions between blacks and whites.
6. Crime became an issue in presidential elections; government policies were directed at the causes of crime by concentrating on job training, education and better housing. But also there was a crackdown on criminals.

Case study: The Montgomery Bus Boycott, 1955–56

1. Montgomery was the capital of Alabama in the American South. It enforced Jim Crow laws by having segregated schools and buses. Most Black Americans were poor and in low-paid jobs.

2. The bus company employed no black people as drivers. It put black passengers at the back of the bus and white passengers at the front.

> *exam Q*
>
> In what ways did the Montgomery Bus Boycott, 1955–56, advance the cause of the civil rights movement?

3. Rosa Parks, a seamstress, was a 42–year-old black woman. On 1 December 1955 she sat in the black section of the bus and refused to get up to give her seat to a white man on the orders of the driver. She was arrested and charged.

4. The Montgomery NAACP (National Association for the Advancement of Colored People) and the Women's Political Council of Montgomery got Parks' permission to use her case to fight for desegregation. They also organised black people to boycott buses the day Parks was being tried. Black ministers supported them.

5. Their leader was Reverend **Martin Luther King**, a Baptist minister. He became president of the Montgomery Improvement Association (MIA), which organised the boycott. King advocated non-violent means of protest.

6. Parks was fined $10. The bus boycott continued.
   - The MIA demanded black drivers be employed and that seats on the buses be filled on a first-come, first-served basis.
   - They also set up a taxi service and formed car pools.
   - The black churches raised money for the campaign.

7. City authorities, the Ku Klux Klan and the police all acted against the boycott. King's home was bombed. He was also arrested.

8. The boycott held out during 1956 until the Supreme Court ruled, on 13 November, that the Montgomery city laws were illegal. The boycott was victorious. It had lasted 381 days.

9. The Montgomery Bus Boycott:
   - proved that a well-organised and peaceful protest could succeed;
   - showed that Black Americans could use new methods to win their rights;
   - marked the rise to prominence of Martin Luther King;
   - demonstrated the influence of press and television, which broadcast the protest all over the US.

5. Advances in technology

In this section, you should understand:
- the influence of advances in military, space and information technology;
- how each of them impacted on the Moon Landing in 1969;
- Case study: The first Moon Landing (1969).

Advances in military technology

How did advances in military, space and information technology make possible the Moon Landing in 1969?

1. The US led advances in military technology because:
   - Involvement in wars provided the reason for weapons development;

TECHNOLOGICAL DEVELOPMENT: See p.304

- The powerful economy could afford the research;
- Superpower status needed to be maintained in competition with the USSR;
- Developments in military technology were backed by US public opinion.

2. **Nuclear weapons**: The US developed the atomic bomb in the Manhattan Project during the Second World War. They later developed the H-bomb.

- These bombs were delivered by the B-29 Superfortress bomber and later by the B-52 Stratofortress (which was also used in conventional bombing in Vietnam).
- Rocket development was boosted by former German scientists and captured German V-2 rockets.
- The US developed short- and medium-range missiles. The Pershing, with a range of 400 miles, was based in Western Europe.
- The development of the H-bomb improved rocket-guidance systems and new rocket fuels led to the development of the intercontinental ballistic missile (ICBM).
- The first ICBMs developed were the Atlas, Titan and Minuteman.
- These later had multiple warheads and could be launched from underground silos.
- The navy developed the Polaris and Poseidon to fire nuclear missiles from submarines.

3. **Early-warning systems** were developed to detect an attack.

- The US and Canada built the DEW (Distant Early Warning) Line – a series of radar stations in Alaska and northern Canada. They also used AWACS (Airborne early Warning and Control System) and reconnaissance satellites (SAMOS).
- In the 1980s Reagan announced the development of the Strategic Defence Initiative (SDI), popularly called 'Star Wars', to destroy Soviet missiles in space.
- But the huge costs and the end of the Cold War meant this project was not completed.

4. **Conventional technology** was needed for wars in Korea and Vietnam.

- **Air war**: Jet planes increased the speed and range of aircraft. They were equipped by missiles to attack other aircraft (air-to-air), tanks and airfields. Some of the air-to-air missiles were supersonic.
  - Bomber aircraft had greater range and accuracy. They carpet-bombed areas of the Vietnamese jungle, but only with computer-controlled bombs did they become more accurate.
  - Reconnaissance aircraft (such as the U2) played a key part over the USSR and in the Cuban Missile Crisis.
  - Helicopters were used for carrying troops and conducting search-and-rescue missions. Helicopter gunships were developed for the Vietnam War.
  - Surface-to-air missiles were developed to cope with faster aircraft (the Hercules, Sea Sparrow or Redeye).
  - Aircraft carriers provided mobility and rapid response; catapults were used to cater for larger and faster planes.

- **Land War**: Tanks were improved and given better engines and firepower, such as gun launchers to fire missiles (on the M60 and MBT-70). Soldiers had more accurate and powerful weapons to fight tanks and aircraft.

5. **Permanent war economy**: The US spent 10 per cent of its national income on military technology. The military-industrial complex developed when companies such as General Dynamics, Lockheed and Boeing formed close links with government (US Department of Defense).

Advances in space technology

1. The USSR sent *Sputnik 1* into space. The Soviet Union was ahead in the Space Race.

TECHNOLOGICAL DEVELOPMENT: See p.304

   - The US was shocked by later Soviet successes, e.g. the first man in space – Yuri Gagarin.
   - These events were a blow to US morale; they also increased the danger to national security during the Cold War.

2. The US set up NASA (National Aeronautics and Space Administration) to organise its space programme.
   - They launched their first satellite, *Explorer 1*, in 1958.
   - President Kennedy said the US would have a man on the Moon before the end of the 1960s.

3. **Preparing for the Moon – advances in technology**
   - The Mercury Project sent Americans into space, beginning with Alan Shepard in 1961; in *Freedom 7*, John Glenn orbited the Earth three times.
   - The Gemini Project involved two-man flights to test rendezvous and docking techniques and space walks.
   - They also photographed potential landing sites on the Moon.
   - With the Apollo Mission, the US developed a three-man spacecraft.

4. **Further advances in technology**
   - NASA had to overcome many more technological problems in order to send astronauts to the Moon and bring them back.
   - To select a suitable landing site, they developed special photography which became Computer-Aided Tomography (CAT) and Magnetic Resonance Imaging (MRI), now used in hospitals.
   - To feed astronauts on an extended voyage to the Moon, NASA developed freeze-dried food.
   - Cool suits were used to keep astronauts at a comfortable temperature while they were on the Moon.
   - They also developed boots for better shock absorption and stability on the Moon's surface.

- To help gather Moon rock, cordless power tools were developed.
- They also developed a heart conditioner to maintain the heart on long space voyages, insulation barriers of aluminium foil to protect instruments and astronauts from radiation, and water-purification technology to maintain a fresh water supply.
- Without these advances in technology, the United States would not have been able to put men on the Moon and return them safely.

5. *Apollo 11*, with Neil Armstrong, Buzz Aldrin and Michael Collins, voyaged to the Moon. Armstrong and Aldrin landed and walked on the Moon. (See Case study: The first Moon Landing, 1969, pp. 295–96)
   - Later Apollo missions made further landings and undertook scientific investigation of the Moon.

6. Much of the later advances in space technology involved sending unmanned spacecraft to planets such as Jupiter, Mars and Venus. There was also the development of space stations and space shuttles.
   - NASA developed the **Skylab space stations** to carry out experiments in space.
   - The US developed the **space shuttle** – a reusable space vehicle. The first was *Columbia* in 1981. But an explosion on a later shuttle, *Challenger*, declining public support and budget cutbacks led to fewer space flights.

7. Advances in space technology also helped weather forecasting, communications by radio, television and phones. Satellites were also put into space as 'spies in the sky'.

Case study: The first Moon Landing, 1969

1. The Russian (Soviet) space successes surprised the US. The US set up NASA (the National Aeronautics and Space Administration) in 1958 to organise US space exploration.

To what extent can the Moon Landing (1969) be seen as both a major advance in technology and as a statement of American foreign policy?

   - The Space Race was another aspect of Cold War rivalry.

2. President Kennedy committed the US to landing a man on the Moon by the end of the 1960s.

3. The **Apollo programme** was developed to land a man on the Moon. The Apollo missions tested the **Saturn** rocket, docking the command ship and the lunar module.

4. *Apollo 11* had three modules (parts):
   - the command module (*Columbia*) to carry the astronauts
   - the service module to hold the rockets and fuel
   - the lunar module (*Eagle*) to land on the Moon.

5. The astronauts practiced in simulators and experienced weightlessness in underwater tanks. The three astronauts were:

- Neil Armstrong, the commander
- Eugene 'Buzz' Aldrin, the pilot of the lunar module
- Michael Collins, the pilot of the command module.

6. The three astronauts took off from Kennedy Space Center in Florida on 16 July 1969.
   - Millions watched on television.

7. On the journey, each of the rocket stages was dropped off (jettisoned) once its fuel was used up. Then Collins guided the command module and the attached lunar module on the journey to the Moon. It took three days to reach the Moon.

8. On 20 July, Armstrong and Aldrin took the lunar module (*Eagle*) to the Moon, landing on the Sea of Tranquillity. Armstrong was the first man to step on the Moon.
   - He said: 'That's one small step for man, one giant leap for mankind.'

9. They walked on the Moon for over twenty hours, setting up scientific experiments and collecting rock samples. They also planted a US flag and a metal plaque, commemorating the landing.

10. The *Eagle* took off from the Moon and docked with the command module. They returned to earth, protected by a heat shield during their passage through the Earth's atmosphere. They splashed down in the Pacific Ocean. They were quarantined for twenty-one days.

11. The **significance** of the first Moon Landing:
    - There were over 400,000 employed in the Apollo project.
    - The US now led the space race against the USSR. It was a significant victory in the Cold War.
    - The US fulfilled President Kennedy's commitment.
    - The USSR concentrated on space stations, instead of the Moon race.
    - Budget cutbacks introduced a few years later meant nobody has landed on the Moon since 1972.
    - New information was collected on the formation of the Moon.
    - There was a debate about the cost of space exploration and whether the money should have been spent on economic and social problems.

Advances in information technology

1. The computer was developed to handle more and more information.
2. The US government and military were behind much of the development of the computer. They linked up with companies (such as IBM) and universities.
3. Mark 1 and ENIAC were two of the early computers; both were very large and needed a team of operators to work them.

4. IBM used the work of John Von Neumann, a mathematician, to build mainframe computers such as EDVAC and UNIVAC. The latter was used to count the census of 1951 and the presidential election of 1952.

5. The invention of the transistor by William Shockley led to the production of smaller computers. Seymour Cray designed the first fully transistorised computer in 1958.
   - There were only about 2,000 computers in the US by 1960.

6. The production of **integrated circuits and the microchip** was the next major step.
   - Smaller, personal computers became available by the 1970s. The computer industry expanded considerably.
   - Steve Jobs and Steve Wozniak developed Apple.
   - IBM made its own PC (personal computer).
   - The Apple operating system and the development of Microsoft made computers more user-friendly.
   - By 1991 there were over 65 million computers in the US alone.

7. The computer industry grew from $1 billion in 1958 to $17 billion by 1978.
   - The US had the largest computer industry, employing 1 million by 1990.
   - The US also had the greatest number of computers – half of the world's, compared to Japan (11 per cent) and Europe (25 per cent).
   - Research continued in Silicon Valley, California, around Boston and in the Research Triangle in North Carolina. Much production shifted abroad.

8. The **Internet** was first developed to combat fear of a nuclear war, so that military scientists could communicate after a nuclear explosion. Later it was developed so that businesses and individuals could use it.

9. The **effects** of advances in computer technology:
   - Computers influenced all aspects of life, from home to shopping to work.
   - They caused a rise in productivity.
   - There was a debate about the danger of technological unemployment.
   - Computers made some people very wealthy, e.g. Bill Gates, founder of Microsoft.
   - Computers continued the globalisation of industry, finance and culture – they helped the spread of American culture.
   - There was the danger of the invasion of privacy and the danger to democracy.

Key personalities

Harry Truman

1. Harry Truman was US president from 1945 to 1953. He was vice president under President Roosevelt, so when Roosevelt died Truman became president while the Second World War was still in progress.

2. Truman believed in the role of strong and honourable leadership. His motto was, 'The buck stops here.'

3. **Foreign Policy:** After Germany had been defeated Truman met Stalin, the Soviet leader, at Potsdam, along with the British Prime Ministers Churchill and Attlee (who replaced Churchill). They made plans for Germany after the war.

4. When Japan did not surrender, Truman gave orders to drop atomic bombs on Hiroshima and Nagasaki.
   - He wanted to put an end to the war, and to save American and Japanese lives in an invasion.

5. **The Cold War:** Truman did not trust the Soviet Union. He believed the US should not appease (give in to) Russia in the way that Hitler had been appeased before the Second World War.
   - He developed the **policy of containment** – that Communism must not be allowed to expand any further.
   - He backed this with a policy of deterrence, to maintain a strong nuclear force so that the Soviet Union would be deterred from attacking the US.

6. Truman introduced the **Truman Doctrine** to help Greece and Turkey to resist the spread of Communism. He wanted the US to help 'free peoples' to resist Communism. He also introduced the Marshall Plan (European Recovery Programme) to help the economic recovery of Western Europe and to enable it to stand up against Communism.

7. Truman's new policies showed that the US was prepared to follow a policy of internationalism – that the US would become involved with other countries. His policies heightened tension with the Soviet Union and worsened the Cold War.

8. **Berlin:** After the Second World War, Truman and the US and Britain believed that the economic recovery of Germany was necessary for the economic recovery of Europe. They also wanted a strong Germany to be a barrier to Communism.
   - When the US and Britain introduced a new currency, the Deutschmark, Stalin

blockaded West Berlin. Truman did not want to be forced out of West Berlin; it would be a victory for Communism and a defeat for the policy of containment.

- The US and its allies organised a huge airlift of food and supplies to West Berlin. When they refused to give in, Stalin lifted the blockade after ten months (May 1949).

9. Truman formed NATO (North Atlantic Treaty Organization) with Canada and ten Western European countries for the defence of Western Europe.

10. He fought the **Korean War** to oppose Communism in South Korea. (See *US foreign policy*, pp. 275–282)

11. **Domestic Policy: Congress**: Truman had difficulties with Congress. When he became president, Southern Democrats (Dixiecrats) disagreed with his **21-point programme** for social reform, so he failed to get it passed in Congress.

12. **1948 Presidential election**: The Republican candidate, Thomas Dewey, was favoured to win this election because the Democrats were divided between Truman, Strom Thurmond (a Dixiecrat candidate) and Henry Wallace (the Progressive Party candidate). But Truman won because he travelled 22,000 miles on his **'whistle-stop'** tour to meet people all over the country. His style pleased ordinary people. 'Give 'em Hell, Harry,' they said.

13. **Fair Deal:** After his re-election, Truman wanted to build on Roosevelt's New Deal. He proposed a **Fair Deal** – to increase minimum wage, improve healthcare, set up public works schemes and expand social security. He had some success – there was better social security, more public housing and slum clearance. But other proposals were rejected by Congress.

14. **Economy**: Truman passed the **Employment Act**, which showed that the US accepted more government involvement in the economy. Truman also passed the **'GI Bill'**, which gave loans for education, housing and business to veterans – 8 million veterans were helped by 1955. There was major economic growth in the US by 1950 and this continued after Truman.

15. **Civil rights**: Truman issued Executive Orders which ended racial discrimination in federal employment and he desegregated (ended racial segregation) the US armed forces.

16. **McCarthyism and the Red Scare:** There was a growth of anti-Communist hysteria in the US after the Second World War due to the Cold War.

- The House Un-American Activities Committee (HUAC) and Senator Joe McCarthy (McCarthyism) looked for Communists in the US, which heightened tensions.

- Even though Truman disliked McCarthy, his own actions played on the fear of Communism, e.g. in order to pass the Truman Doctrine and the Marshall Plan. He also set up **Federal Loyalty Boards** to remove people believed to be disloyal to US government.

Lyndon Johnson

1. Lyndon Johnson (LBJ) was president of the US from 1963 to 1969. He was vice president under President Kennedy and when Kennedy was assassinated, Johnson became president.

2. **Domestic Policy:** Johnson wanted to create a better and fairer society. He used the goodwill after the assassination of Kennedy to get the **Civil Rights Act (1964)** and the Voting Rights Act (1965) passed.
   - These outlawed racial discrimination in jobs, education and voting.

3. He had an overwhelming victory over Barry Goldwater, a Republican, in the 1964 presidential election. He also saw more liberal Democrats elected to Congress. These helped to overcome the resistance of conservative Southern Democrats and Republicans.

4. Johnson believed that the power of the presidency and federal government should be used to improve the lives of the people.
   - President Johnson began a war on poverty as part of his **'Great Society'** programme. He set up Head Start (where children went to pre-school classes) and the Job Corps (to provide skills for inner-city youth).

5. He was able to bring in many other laws as part of his Great Society programme. These included:
   - Medicare for older people
   - Medicaid for poorer people

6. **The Johnson treatment**: Johnson showed his ability as a negotiator in his dealings with Congress. He had a strong personality and usually got his way.

7. **Foreign Policy: Vietnam War**: Johnson's presidency from 1964 onwards was dominated by the Vietnam War. (See Case study: Lyndon Johnson and Vietnam, 1963–68, pp. 279–281)
   - He believed in the **Domino Theory** – that if Vietnam fell to Communism, other countries in Asia would follow. He did not want to be the first president to lose a war.

8. Johnson expanded US involvement in Vietnam after the Gulf of Tonkin Incident. He falsely claimed that the North Vietnamese Navy had attacked US Navy ships on a number of occasions.

9. When Congress passed the Gulf of Tonkin Resolution, Johnson had the power to send in more US troops.

- Johnson increased the number of US troops to half a million.
- He authorised Operation Rolling Thunder. This operation launched massive air assaults on North Vietnam.

10. Most Americans supported President Johnson in the war. But the Tet Offensive in early 1968 showed the US people that the North Vietnamese and Vietcong were not beaten.
    - Many people now said the US should withdraw from Vietnam.
11. Johnson was able to speak only at friendly meetings because of vocal opposition. He barely won the New Hampshire primary election in 1968 against the anti-war Democrat, Eugene McCarthy.
    - Johnson decided to cut back the bombing of North Vietnam and to organise peace talks with the North Vietnamese in Paris.
    - He declared he was not standing for re-election for president.
12. He began the process which reduced US involvement in Vietnam and eventually led to peace under the next president, Richard Nixon.

Joe McCarthy

1. Joe McCarthy was elected as senator for Wisconsin in 1946.
2. McCarthy had a poor record as a senator – he liked playing poker and drinking. He seemed likely to be defeated in the next election. He decided that the issue which would get him re-elected would be to go after subversives.
3. In February 1950 he claimed that the State Department had 200 employees who were Communists. He believed the State Department was partly responsible for the loss of China to the Communists.
4. He was chairman of the Committee on Government Operations. He began hearings on Communist infiltrations of the federal government. He questioned many witnesses about their suspected Communist affiliations.
5. His campaign led to the banning of over 400 writers by the State Department.
6. McCarthy's accusations were part of the Red Scare – the growing fear of Communism which spread across the US.
7. These accusations brought him fame – he was on the cover of *Time* and *Newsweek* – and also got him re-elected.
8. McCarthy was a strong and dramatic speaker.

- He attacked individuals and groups, accusing them of helping Communists. He attacked the Protestant clergy, the civil service, writers and scientists.
- He attacked the Eastern Establishment – the well-educated, often wealthy, mainly Protestant young men who ran government and much of industry at the time.

9. He linked liberalism and the New Deal (brought in by Roosevelt) with socialism and Communism.

10. McCarthy was supported by the Republicans, who encouraged his attacks on President Truman and the Democrats. He accused them of being soft on Communism.

11. After President Eisenhower was elected, McCarthy continued his attacks on the Democrats.

12. President Eisenhower seemed to be afraid of him, because he dropped a section of a speech defending George Marshall, a friend, when he was attacked by McCarthy.

13. McCarthy became chairman of a Senate committee investigating subversion.

14. He accused the US Army of harbouring Communists. This led to an investigation called the Army–McCarthy hearings. These were televised. They showed his bullying personality and led to his downfall. The Senate censored him for his unbecoming conduct. He died two years later from liver disease caused by his drinking.

15. McCarthyism heightened the fear of Communism.
- It made the Cold War more extreme. It led Americans to believe that all events were part of a worldwide Communist conspiracy.
- Many very able federal employees lost their jobs, especially in the State Department, which dealt with foreign affairs.
- McCarthyism damaged America's reputation (image) abroad, especially in Europe, because it was seen as undemocratic.

Martin Luther King

1. Martin Luther King was born in Atlanta, Georgia, the son of a Baptist minister. He also became a Baptist minister.

2. King was appointed pastor of a Baptist church in Montgomery, Alabama. He became leader of the Montgomery Improvement Association, which organised the

Montgomery Bus Boycott in 1955–56 (See pp. 291–92).

3. Martin Luther King was inspired by the teachings of Mahatma Gandhi, the Indian leader, on the use of non-violent protest.

4. The Bus Boycott was eventually successful when the Supreme Court ruled that the buses should not be segregated. This brought Martin Luther King to national prominence.

5. King founded the **Southern Christian Leadership Conference** (SCLC), which was prominent in fighting for civil rights for Black Americans.

   - He was involved in many non-violent demonstrations against segregation and was arrested several times.
   - He led demonstrations in **Birmingham**, Alabama, against segregated hotels and restaurants.
   - He deliberately provoked the Birmingham police to use violent methods, which were then publicised by press, radio and TV.
   - In 1963 he led 200,000 people in a civil rights protest in Washington, at which he made his famous 'I have a dream' speech.

6. In 1964, he was awarded the Nobel Peace Prize.

7. He saw the passing of the **Civil Rights Act (1964)**, which outlawed discrimination on the basis of race or sex.

8. He was involved in the **Selma to Montgomery March**, which led to the passing of the Voting Rights Act (1965) giving authority to the federal government over voter registration.

9. King's leadership of Black America was challenged by younger, more extreme black leaders such as Malcolm X, who were more prepared to use violence.

10. King became critical of other social and economic problems faced by Black Americans.

    - He was concerned that the Vietnam War was using up money which could be better spent on Johnson's Great Society programme.

11. King was under investigation by the FBI, who wanted to uncover any dirt to try to smear him.

12. King was planning a Poor People's March on Washington, DC, when he was assassinated in Memphis, Tennessee, in 1968 by a hired assassin, James Earl Ray.

13. King's death gave rise to widespread riots in black areas of many American cities.

Key concepts

Consumerism: This is when a great deal of goods and products are bought and sold, as part of the consumer society, and where the pursuit of happiness is based on the possession of goods.

Corporate capitalism: When capitalism (the economic system based on private property) is dominated by large companies or corporations.

Discrimination: This occurs when a group of people are treated unfairly because of their colour, religion, sex or age.

Feminism: The belief that women should be treated equally to men and have the same rights and opportunities as men.

Fundamentalism: The conservative religious movement among Protestants in the United States, which emphasised the literal truth of the Bible.

Globalisation: The spread of goods, services and culture worldwide (or globally), usually associated with US companies.

Imperialism: When one country has a great deal of power and influence over other countries.

Internationalism: A policy of co-operating with other countries.

Liberalism: The political belief concerned with personal freedom and social progress. American liberals wanted the government to intervene to help individuals.

Mass media: A medium of communication (newspapers, radio, television, cinema) that reaches a large audience or the mass of the people.

Military-industrial complex: The combination of the armed forces, the politicians who supported them and the industries who supplied them.

Moral majority: Those who support the application of strict or severe Christian standards of behaviour to society.

Presidential bureaucracy: The growth of the president's bureaucracy (civil service) used to implement his policies.

Public opinion: The views and attitudes of the people, measured in elections and by opinion polls.

Technological development: This is the application or use of scientific discoveries in industry.

For further notes on The USA & the World, 1945–89,
see online at www.moresuccess.ie